in six days

► why fifty ⑤⓪
scientists choose to
believe in creation

edited by john ashton

Master
Books

First printing: January 2001
Fourth printing: September 2003

ISBN: 0-89051-341-4
Library of Congress Catalog Card Number: 00-110204

Printed in the United States of America.

Please visit our website for other great titles:
www.masterbooks.net

For information regarding author interviews,
please contact the publicity department at (870) 438-5288.

Contents

Preface 5

science and origins

religion and origins

Preface

At a university lecture several years ago, I heard a research scientist state that he did not believe that any scientist with a Ph.D. would advocate a literal interpretation of the six days of creation. His comment was quite similar to statements made over the years by world-renowned scientists like Stephen Jay Gould and Ernst Mayr, both of Harvard. In reply to the lecturer's doubt about credentialed scientists agreeing with the Genesis account of origins, the meeting chairman offered the names of two well-known scientists who, he said, espoused belief in the biblical account. This incident stimulated me to research this book.

Why would educated scientists still believe in creation? Why wouldn't they prefer to believe in Darwinian evolution or even theistic evolution, where an all-powerful intelligence is seen as directing the evolutionary processes? Could scientists believe that life on earth is probably less than 10,000 years old? How would they deal with the evidence from the fossil record and the ages suggested by the radioactive dating of rocks as millions and billions of years old? The essays in this book raise issues which are hotly debated among scientists and educators and they offer a different perspective on our approach to scientific education.

During the past century, the biblical story of Genesis was relegated to the status of a religious myth and it was widely held that only those uneducated in science or scientific methods would seriously believe such a myth. However, my experience in organizing this book is that there are a growing number of highly educated critically thinking scientists who have serious doubts about evidence for Darwinian evolution and who have chosen to believe in the biblical version of creation.

In this book, 50 scientists explain their reasons for this choice. All the contributors have an earned doctorate from a state-recognized university in Australia, the United States, the United Kingdom, Canada, South Africa, or Germany. They include university professors and researchers, geologists, zoologists, biologists, botanists, physicists, chemists, mathematicians, medical researchers, and engineers.

The articles in this book are not exhaustive. Space and publishing deadlines did not permit me to include contributions from many other scientists. The 50 scientists who contributed to this effort gave their personal response to the question, "Why do you believe in a literal six-day biblical creation as the origin of life on earth?" No other requirements were specified. No one was asked to write on a particular topic or from a particular perspective. However, I have arranged the final papers in two sections that allow for a developing discussion from two key perspectives. The first, Science and Origins, is a selection of articles that deals with the scientific critique of evolution as well as the scientific basis for creation. The second, Religion and Origins, presents a more philosophical approach to the question of evolution and creation. Having reviewed the discussions posed by these scientists, in the light of my own education and experience, I am convinced that a literal understanding of the Genesis account of creation is the most reasonable explanation out of all the current theories of how we came to be here.

John F. Ashton

science and origins

jeremy l. walter

Mechanical Engineering

Dr. Walter is head of the Engineering Analysis and Design Department within the Energy Science and Power Systems Division at the Applied Research Laboratory (ARL) at Pennsylvania State University. He holds a B.S. in mechanical engineering with highest distinction, an M.S. in mechanical engineering, and a Ph.D. in mechanical engineering, all from Pennsylvania State University. He was a 1975 recipient of a prestigious National Science Foundation Fellowship, funding graduate study at the institution of his choice. At ARL, Dr. Walter has been the leader for a number of undersea propulsion development projects for the U.S. Navy. His research involves multi-disciplinary development and testing of advanced air-independent engines and thermal power systems for various autonomous undersea vehicles.

They Can't Be Wrong, Can They?

In 1961, President John Kennedy set a national goal for the United States to land a man on the moon before the decade was over, and in the summer of 1969 Neil Armstrong made his famous "giant leap for mankind" onto the lunar soil. In the midst of severe social unrest, science and technology seemed to provide an island of stability to a nation caught in internal tension, an unpopular war in Vietnam, and the deep freeze of the Cold War. "New and improved" became the harbinger of what was expected in technology, and harnessing the secrets of nature for man's benefit was the engine to propel us into a hopeful future.

This milieu was the incubator for many careers in science and engineering, and so it was for that of the author. Public education introduced the sciences of the space program, but also proclaimed as fact the 4½ billion-year age of the earth and that life had gradually evolved over millions of years from a single-cell organism, supposedly formed by chance in a primeval ocean. Students were compelled to accept the evolutionary model of earth history, as is the case for most people educated in this century. The ancient writings of Genesis were relegated as outdated and allegorical, and most Christian students reconciled an immature faith in God and the Bible with a casually contrived version of the "day-age" interpretation of the creation account. The days of Genesis were assumed to somehow represent the ages or stages of cosmic development that the scientists were now beginning to understand and describe more fully in our modern world.

For multitudes today, the story is the same. The implicit authority of the classroom combines with modern technological achievements to validate the "scientific" models of origins and the great antiquity of the universe. Genesis is viewed as myth, if not fairy tale, and our concept of truth is limited to the empirically derived and subjectively interpreted. But we need to ask the fundamental question mouthed by Pilate, "What is truth?" and determine the role that science plays in the overall development of truth.

The discussion in the following paragraphs takes a look at the nature of science, and how true science does not contradict God's inscription on stone that "in six days the LORD made the heavens and the earth, the sea, and all that is in them" (Exod. 20:11).

What Is Science?

Many intelligent people are thoroughly convinced that science has proven the earth to be billions of years old. How can they be wrong? The misconception builds on a neglect of the basic nature of "science" and a natural desire for moral autonomy. Actually, the age of the earth can be neither proved nor disproved by science. Scientific evidence can be compiled to support one model of earth history as compared to another, but such work amounts to a feasibility study, not proof.

Science is the human enterprise of seeking to describe accurately and quantitatively the nature and processes of our universe through observation, hypothesis, and experimental validation. Certain axiomatic principles must be accepted by faith for this method to be valid, the first of which is the expectation of order in the universe. A specific corollary of the order principle is the law of causality, or "cause and effect" relationships. This law states that one cause can have many effects, but no effect can be quantitatively greater or qualitatively superior to its cause.[1] Observed effects are assumed to have causes because of this law, and are not treated as purely random or chance occurrences. The inquisitive mind will speculate on the cause of an observed effect and then seek to recreate and test the cause experimentally. That is the essence of the so-called scientific method.

Note, however, that an observation is always an action of the present, not of the past. Additionally, the observer must recognize that observations are to varying degrees indirect, through an instrument of some sort that may distort his perception. For instance, our eyes are optical instruments that receive incident light, optically focus that light on the retina, which in turn converts the image to a complex system of electrical impulses, transmitted to the brain by the optic nerve. If the transmission of the image from an object to our brain is distorted at any point along the way, our visual perception will be incorrect. Some optical illusions are actually misinterpreted in the brain because of preconceptions, without any optical or electrical distortion. All observations must be similarly analyzed and scrutinized to develop accurate perceptions. The farther removed in time or distance an indirect observation is, the greater the opportunity for distorted perception.

Applying the foregoing discussion to the age of the earth, we recognize that we have no *human* record of observed events from great antiquity, but rather interpretations of recent observations of present realities. Often the establishment of a great age is built on observations from a very great distance or developed through tedious indirect means. Evidence contradictory to the hypothesis is either suppressed or ignored because of preconceived assumptions. Even the light arriving from distant stars is a present reality, not a direct observation of the past. These observations are of effects for which various hypothetical causes have been proposed. Those causes are sometimes gradual processes that would require very long times to produce the present state.

By way of illustration, consider geologic formations in the Great Basin of the western United States. The vast horizontal layers of hydraulically deposited sedimentary rock are said to take long periods of time to accumulate, based on the assumption that the rate of deposition was always similar to that observed today in a typical river delta. This concept of uniformity may seem like a reasonable starting point when considered abstractly, but no steady-state river flow could possibly cover such a vast area; neither would it produce the violently buried and mangled bodies found fossilized in many rocks of the region. The present–day erosion conditions applied uniformly in the past could not account for the unusual formations of the Grand Canyon, mesas, badlands, and other canyons. By contrast, the catastrophic processes observed during and following the eruption of Mount St. Helens in the Cascades of Washington state produced a scale model of the Grand Canyon in a very brief period of time. Sediments were rapidly deposited and then suddenly eroded by pyroclastic steam, water, and mud flows in the area northwest of the summit. Now the canyon walls resemble others that are assumed to be of great age, even though they are known to be less than 20 years old.[2]

The point to be recognized is that science deals with observations of present states and processes, and can only discuss the prehistoric past. In the example of geologic formations of the Great Basin, the assumption of uniformity can be contrasted with a model of catastrophic tectonic, volcanic, and hydraulic activity that would accompany a global cataclysm such as the great flood of Genesis. The observed eruption of Mount St. Helens demonstrated that rapid processes can produce effects commonly believed to require long periods of time, and thus gives credence, if not preference, to the concept that the earth's geology did not require long periods of time to develop. Many puzzling formations can only be explained through cataclysmic forces. Similarly, other methods of estimating the age of the earth or of the universe apply assumptions about processes and rates that extend into the distant past. Regardless of how apparently compelling such dating methods may appear to be, the fact remains that they are built on assumptions that must be critically questioned and evaluated.

All events of the past (even the recent past) are best reconstructed from the testimony of witnesses and the accumulation of corroborating evidence. That is the basis of the system of jurisprudence.

Science can contribute by determining what is possible, but cannot infallibly reconstruct the past. There are definite implications about prodigious age, however, that can be gleaned from applying known principles from the laws of science. We will now consider some of the corroborating evidence for the Creator's testimony.

Thermodynamics, Demons, and Evolution

The law of causality logically leads to the conclusion that human beings (an effect that has the qualities of life, intellect, emotion, and volition) should have a cause which is greater in quantity and qualitatively superior in life, intelligence, emotion, and will. In spite of such basic arguments, naturalistic evolution claims that the forces of nature and the passing of time are sufficient to produce the order and complexity of life without such a cause. Do the observed laws of nature support that claim? What is known about the general effects of the passing of time? The implications of the science of thermodynamics were instrumental in convincing this author that long periods of time are not only unnecessary, but also lethal to the theories of gradual and natural development of intelligent design.

Applying the laws of thermodynamics, especially as they relate to fluid flows and the conversion of energy into useful work in heat engines, is an important part of mechanical engineering. However, the laws of thermodynamics (usually numbered zero through three) have broader and more philosophical implications that are relevant to the study of origins and the development of order and complexity. The four classic laws can be logically derived from fewer general principles,[3] but the discussion in this context will be limited to the classical first and second laws.

The first law is one of conservation, and implies that the substance of the universe (matter and energy) is a constant. The second law additionally constrains the possible states that a given system can attain by a defined process, precluding perpetual motion machines and the spontaneous creation of the "availability" of energy. All real processes are shown to be "irreversible" by the implications of the second law, resulting in a decrease in energy available to effect further processes. Alternatively stated, real processes result in a net increase in the "entropy" of the universe, a property defined in thermodynamics as movement toward a final stable equilibrium where all processes cease.

The implications of these two laws are profound. The first law states clearly that no matter or energy is currently being added to our universe, and the second law states that, given infinite time, the universe will come to final equilibrium, where no processes can occur. That final state has been described as a heat-death of the universe. Since that condition has not yet been reached, the universe must have a beginning. These conclusions are perfectly compatible with the biblical declaration that all things were created *in six days*, and then God ceased doing the labor of physical creation (first law) (Gen. 2:1–2).

Furthermore, the fall of Satan and man brought about "the curse" which is the cause for the earth and the heavens to "wear out like a garment" (Ps. 102:26) and now "the whole creation groans and suffers" (Rom. 8:22) (second law). The second law of thermodynamics essentially precludes the spontaneous development of the earth's ecosystem or life itself. In engineering, we know that heat engines do not develop spontaneously, and without a heat engine, no efficient useful work is produced by the flow of heat. In addition, without both a source of work and a refrigeration machine, no heat will flow from a cold place to a warm place. Likewise, without the engine of reproduction (the genetic blueprint and the miracle of the womb), not even the material aspects of man could be built by raw power.

The problem is worse for the immaterial, since man's conscious and spiritual aspects defy strict scientific definition, much less a natural process of development.

The required patterns and engines of reproduction cannot be accounted for by spontaneous generation, and the passing of long periods of time cannot constitute or facilitate an independent cause for the development of human bodies, aptitude, or ability. The rule of history is not one of continual creation, but one of extinction, as specific creatures become unable to survive the decay of the earth's ecosystem and are eliminated from the planet forever.

In spite of the implications of the classical second law, many evolutionists believe the solution to the threat of the second law is to be found in statistical thermodynamics. Evolution is believed to take advantage of the statistical variation in molecular and genetic properties, and can selectively favor only those which promote the development of greater order. Enter the Maxwell demon. Although not a literal demon as found in the Bible, this troublesome imaginary character was conceived by James Clerk Maxwell in about 1891. In his classic mental experiment, the demon is theoretically able to defeat the second law by intelligently controlling the passage of individual molecules of gas through a partition that divides a sealed and insulated vessel. By strategically opening and closing a tiny door, he could measure and select only high-energy molecules for passage in one direction while simultaneously allowing low-energy molecules to pass in the opposite direction. The demon could then produce a final state where high-energy gas has been collected in one part of the vessel and low-energy gas is in the remainder, without having added any energy to the system. The potential for doing useful work has been intelligently created, or the net entropy decreased, solely by harnessing the statistical variation in the individual molecules.

The apparent contradiction to the second law was resolved in 1929 by Szilard in a paper in which he showed that the process of detecting the energy level and operating the door would consume at least as much energy as that gained by the passage of a molecule.[4] The statistical distribution of energy among the molecules could not be used, even by a precocious demon, to create order and potential energy. The second law stands, and the Maxwell demon fails.

In naturalistic evolution, life is believed to have originated as high fluxes of energy passed through a chemical soup of fortuitous composition. The problem here is much more difficult than that faced by the Maxwell demon, because life requires structures of incredible complexity, not just high energy levels. The most basic processes of living things are accomplished by molecular engines as complex as man's greatest inventions. Protein synthesis and DNA replication are marvelous examples of life's inner workings, and a being much more capable than the Maxwell demon is required to assemble the necessary components and start the first cell functioning. The presumed high-energy fluxes do not provide structure or intelligence any more than the proverbial explosion in a print shop will produce a novel.

At this point, it is instructive to consider that Nobel Prize winner Francis Crick both recognized this difficulty and then contradicted it as he contemplated *Life Itself*.[5] He stated that the complexities of life could not "have arisen by pure chance," but required a replication mechanism to preserve beneficial mutations as they occurred. However, the origin of the replication mechanism is never identified as anything other than chance. The combination of replication and mutation effectively becomes the Crick demon that produces "the marvelous capacity of such a system to improve itself." Aware of modern life's nearly infinite complexity, Crick then concluded that the earth was not old enough at 4½ billion years to have had life gradually evolve completely on this planet. Instead of turning to the great First Cause of the Bible, he preferred the "directed panspermia" concept, which placed the origin of life long, long ago and far, far away on some other planet in some other galaxy.

Interestingly, in this theory, intelligent life had successfully evolved there, even though such an outcome was considered too difficult to achieve on this planet. This foreign civilization then sent the seeds of life in the form of DNA replicators into the universe aboard sophisticated rocket ships looking for a good place to restart the evolutionary process. One such rocket apparently found earth, and here we are!

Notice the progression in Crick's reasoning: it starts from the impossibly improbable and ends with a fantastic imaginary world far away and long ago. Sufficient time and distance implicitly legitimize what otherwise would be impossibility. Ironically, the passage of time is shown by the second law to be neither an ally nor an engine of creation, but rather an ogre of destruction and death. In tenacious commitment to atheism, naturalistic evolution fashions the marriage of the false modern gods of Mother Earth and Father Time as an inferior substitute for the great and awesome Creator of the Scriptures. We would all do well to carefully consider these basic implications of ascribing great age to the universe and realize that our faith commitments greatly influence the development of scientific concepts. The authors of one thermodynamics text give lucid testimony of their conclusion on this subject:

Quite obviously it is impossible to give conclusive answers to these questions on the basis of the second law of thermodynamics alone. However, the authors see the second law of thermodynamics as man's description of the past and continuing work of a creator, who also holds the answer to the future destiny of man and the universe.[6]

Truth Adrift on the Post-Modern Sea

The discussion so far establishes from basic principles that science cannot prove the universe to be of great age, and that prodigious age would in fact be detrimental rather than beneficial to the development of complexity and order. The fact remains, however, that in published books and journals today, many detailed and sophisticated discussions of factual data exist for both sides of the age issue. Some seek to establish great age, whereas others show the earth, comets, and moon to be less than 10,000 years in age. The interpretation of these observed data hinges solidly on the concepts of truth held by the investigators, not the facts themselves. Faith commitments to either human reason or biblical revelation influence what hypotheses are considered and how data is accepted or rejected. This author sees the evidence for a young earth as overwhelmingly compelling, but many have such faith in particular arguments for great age that young-earth evidence is dismissed as erroneous.

Our world suffers from the false notion established during the modern era that reality and truth are limited to the empirical, and that man's knowledge and reasoning are our supreme guide. The concept of a living, volitional, personal, and loving First Cause is willfully rejected, even though it is completely compatible with both science and the Bible. The need for a supernatural beginning of the universe is implied by the laws of thermodynamics, and clearly declared in the Scriptures. However, the Bible also states that it is "by faith we understand that the worlds were prepared by the word of God, so that what is seen was not made out of things which are visible" (Heb. 11:3). Biblical faith cannot be a matter of formal proof, but neither is it a blind leap. Biblical faith is a confident and convinced trust in the testimony of the One who is both Creator and Redeemer. As His creatures, we need to exercise our faculties in humble submission to His revelation to see Him as our standard for truth.

The standard of truth that grew to dominance in the middle of the 20th century was built on a naturalistic objectivism that displaced theism. Academic institutions adopted the idea that open, objective debate in refereed publications would refine and build our understanding of truth, and the open debate does work well as long as concepts are observable and testable, and "referees" remain open-minded. However, if the mainstream academic community accepts an unproven concept as fact and excludes alternative thinking by decree, then the potential for error to be systematically preserved and promoted is institutionalized. In the opinion of the author, such unfortunate error has taken firm footing in the popular cosmogonies of geology, astronomy, and biology, as illustrated in our discussion about the nature of science and the laws of thermodynamics.

During the last decades of the 20th century, the modern world view of truth based on objective empiricism in science has slid into a sea of churning subjectivity. The atheism of the naturalistic world view disallowed the existence of a supreme, omniscient being, and quite logically led to the conclusion that no human can know absolute truth. The only remaining absolute is that there are no absolutes, and we are admonished to accept all views as valid concepts of truth. This new perspective is the so-called post-modern world view, and the progenitor of the popular pluralism and tolerance advocated today. Pilate's cynical question "What is truth?" now echoes around the world, since people have no anchor to tell them what truth is.

However, if an Almighty Creator God exists, His creation has value and purpose based purely on His own counsel and will, and His creatures would be of special value and interest to Him. His omniscience guarantees perfect design and knowledge, and He could provide a standard for all that is true. As a loving and personal being, it is reasonable that He would desire our fellowship and choose to reveal His purposes to us. The Bible claims to be His special revelation, and teaches exactly those truths about God. Many have found the Scriptures to be the marvelous work of One who could predict the future, transform the heart, and who lovingly revealed His two great works of creation and redemption. The revelation given by the loving One who knows all things would logically be both truthful and clearly communicated.

It is here that the watershed is found. What do the Scriptures say? Taking the most obvious meaning of the language, the Scriptures teach in Genesis that our universe was created fully functioning in six 24-hour days. Taken by faith, these words represent the testimony of the Creator himself, who made all things perfectly according to His own choosing. The principles and observations of true science do not contradict a literal interpretation of Genesis 1, but in fact offer support for the creation of all things *in six days!*

Notes

1 Henry M. Morris, *The Biblical Basis for Modern Science* (Grand Rapids, MI: Baker Book House, 1984), p. 36–37.

2 Steven A. Austin, "Mount St. Helens and Catastrophism," *Impact*, Article No. 157, Institute for Creation Research, El Cajon, CA, July 1986.
Steven A. Austin, *Mount St. Helens, Explosive Evidence for Catastrophe*, documentary video, Institute for Creation Research, El Cajon, CA, 1989.

3 George N. Hatsopoulos and Joseph H. Keenan, *Principles of General Thermodynamics* (New York: John Wiley and Sons, Inc., 1965), p. 368.

4 Ibid., p. xxxviii.

5 Francis Crick, *Life Itself, Its Origin and Nature* (New York: Simon and Schuster, 1981), p. 52–55.

6 Gordon J. Van Wylen and Richard E Sonntag, *Fundamentals of Classical Thermodynamics,* 2nd edition, SI Version (New York: John Wiley and Sons, Inc., 1978), p. 243.

jerry r. bergman

Biology

Dr. Bergman is instructor of science at Northwest State College, Archbold, Ohio. He holds a B.S. in psychology from Wayne State University, an M.S. in psychology from Wayne State University, a Ph.D. in evaluation and research from Wayne State University, an M.A. in sociology from Bowling Green State University, and a second Ph.D. in human biology from Columbia Pacific University. At Northwest State College Dr. Bergman has served as chairman of the academic affairs committee and as faculty advisor for degree programs. He has been a consultant for more than 20 science text books.

Almost every person at one time or another asks the question, "Where did life come from?" Bound up with the answer is the additional question, "What is the purpose of life on earth?" Essentially two viewpoints exist on this question: (1) the *atheist* position, which concludes that life came about through change, time, and a large number of fortuitous events; and (2) the *creationist* position, which teaches that every living organism type was created by a creator which most people call God. Christianity has, since its inception, taught that life was created by God for a specific purpose. "You (God) created all things, and because of your will they existed and were created" (Rev. 4:11). Likewise, Judaism and Islam have historically taught this creation doctrine (see Gen. 1:1–8).

Evolutionary naturalism, often called atheism, teaches that life began by the random collision of enough atoms to form complex molecules that produced accurate copies of themselves. These hypothetical molecules eventually evolved into cells and, in billions of years, evolved into all life extant today. The key to this molecule-to-human evolution was mutations (genetic copy errors) and natural selection (the selection of favorable mutations that alter the animal or plant so that they are more apt to survive).

The Requirements for Life

The thesis of this chapter is that the origin of life could not have occurred by a gradual process but must have been instantaneous. The reason this must be true is simple. Every machine must have a certain minimum number of parts for it to function, and if one part below this minimum is removed, the machine will cease to function. The example Behe uses is a common spring mousetrap which requires ten parts to function. The trap will no longer function if just *one* part is removed. No one has been able to show this concept to be erroneous — only that under certain conditions a certain machine can operate with *one fewer part*.

Many of these "one fewer part" examples, though, are misleading. Ruse (1993, p. 28) notes that a mousetrap can be fastened to the floor, thereby eliminating the base, he claims. In fact, it only uses a *different* base (the floor); a base is still necessary. Further, the mousetrap parts are useless without the intelligence to assemble them into a functioning unit. A trap is also useless without the bait, the knowledge and ability necessary to use the trap, and the existence of a mouse with enough intelligence to seek the bait but lacking in the experience and intelligence to avoid the trap. A simple mousetrap system is much more complex than it first appears.

The irreducible complexity argument can be extended to the creation process which produced life. The concept argues that both an organism and its parts, including organs, organelles, cells, or even its protein, cannot function below a certain minimum number of parts. In biological organisms the smallest unit of life is the cell, and the number of parts it contains at the subatomic level is usually much larger than a trillion. As Hickman notes:

> Cells are the fabric of life. Even the most primitive cells are enormously complex structures that form the basic units of all living matter. All tissues and organs are composed of cells. In a human an estimated 60 trillion cells interact, each performing its specialized role in an organized community. In single-celled organisms all the functions of life are performed within the confines of one microscopic package. There is no life without cells (Hickman, 1997, p. 43).

Even most bacteria require several thousand genes to carry out the functions necessary for life. *E. coli* has about 4,639,221 nucleotide base pairs, which code for 4,288 genes, each one of which produces an enormously complex protein machine. The simplest species of bacteria, Chlamydia and Rickettsia, are the smallest living things known. Only a few hundred atoms across, they are smaller than the largest virus and have about half as much DNA as do other species of bacteria. Although they are about as small as it is possible to be and still be living, these two forms of life still require millions of atomic parts (Trefil, 1992, p. 28). Many of the smaller bacteria, such as *M. genitalum*, which has 256 genes, are parasite-like viruses and can only live with the help of more complex organisms. For this reason, when researching the minimum requirements for life, the example of *E. coli* is more realistic.

If the simplest form of life requires millions of parts at the atomic level, higher life forms require trillions. All of the many macromolecules necessary for life are constructed of atoms, which are composed of even smaller parts. That life requires a certain minimum number of parts is well documented, and the only debate is *how many* millions of functionally integrated parts are necessary — not the fact that a minimum number must exist for life to live. All viruses are *below* the complexity level needed for life, and for this reason they must live as parasites that require complex cells in order to reproduce. Trefil noted that the question of where the viruses come from is an "enduring mystery" in evolution. They consist primarily of only a DNA molecule and a protein coat and

> ... don't reproduce in the normal way, [therefore] it's hard to see how they could have gotten started. One theory: they are parasites who, over a long period of time, have lost the ability to reproduce independently. ... Viruses are among the smallest of "living" things. A typical virus, like the one that causes ordinary influenza, may be no more than a thousand atoms across. This is in comparison with cells which may be hundreds or even thousands of times that size. Its small size is one reason that it is so easy for a virus to spread from one host to another — it's hard to filter out anything that small (Trefil, 1992, p. 9).

Oversimplified, life depends on a complex arrangement of three classes of molecules: *DNA*, which stores the cell's master plans; *RNA*, which transports a copy of the needed information contained in the DNA to the protein assembly station; and *proteins*, which make up everything from the ribosomes to the enzymes. Further, chaperons and many other assembly tools are needed to ensure that the protein is properly assembled. All of these parts are necessary and must exist as a properly assembled and integrated unit. DNA is useless without both RNA and proteins, although some types of bacteria can combine the functions of the basic required parts.

The problem for evolution caused by the enormous complexity required for life is quite well recognized, and none of the proposals to overcome it are even remotely satisfactory (Spetner, 1997). These proposals include the theory of panspermia advanced by Nobel Laureate Francis Crick. Panspermia is the hypothesis that the earth was seeded by life from other planets (Crick, 1981). This solution, though, only moves the problem elsewhere. Naturalism must account for both the parts necessary for life and their proper assembly. For life to persist, living creatures must have a means of taking in and biochemically processing food. Life also requires oxygen, which must be distributed to all tissues, or for single-celled life, oxygen must effectively and safely be moved around inside the cell membrane to where it is needed, without damaging the cell. Without complex mechanisms to achieve these tasks, life cannot exist. The parts could not evolve separately and could not even exist independently for very long, because they would break down in the environment without protection (Overman, 1997).

Even if they existed, the many parts needed for life could not sit idle waiting for the other parts to evolve, because the existing ones would usually deteriorate very quickly from the effects of dehydration, oxidation, and the action of bacteria or other pathogens. For this reason, only an instantaneous creation of all the necessary parts as a functioning unit can produce life. No compelling evidence has ever been presented to disprove this conclusion, and much evidence exists for the instantaneous creation requirement, such as the discovery that most nucleotides degrade rather fast at the temperatures scientists conclude existed on the early earth (Irion, 1998).

The problem is that the half-lives of many of the basic building blocks of life "are too short to allow for the adequate accumulation of these compounds. . . . Therefore, unless the origin of life took place extremely rapidly (<100 years) . . . a high temperature origin of life . . . cannot involve adenine, uracil, guanine, or cytosine" (Levy and Miller, 1998, p. 7,933). This finding is a major setback for abiogenesis, because high temperature (80°–100°C) origin of life is the only feasible model left (Levy and Miller, 1998). Creationists have only begun to exploit this huge stumbling block to Darwinism.

The simplest eukaryote life form is yeast. Most eukaryotes are much more complex than yeast, and a fertilized egg, called a zygote, is the minimum complexity possible for all multi-cell life forms. Further, the development of an organism from a zygote does not provide evidence of evolution, because a zygote cannot exist as an independent unit, but is dependent on a complex designed support system, such as a womb or an egg. A complex life system designed to produce the gametes first exists, and the zygote is only part of a series of stages designed to allow it to fulfill its potential.

An organ or an organism cannot function, nor will it be selected, until it is minimally functional. At this level it must be both enormously complex and dependent on many other parts of the system (Behe, 1996). A gamete contains all the information needed to develop into a complete organism. When the organism is first developing, all its cells are totipotent, meaning that each cell can develop into any one of the over 200 cell types needed for an adult human to live, including epithelial, muscle, blood and other cell types.

Evolutionists once argued that all life could develop from some hypothetical first cell, because even today all new life develops from a single cell, but we now realize that a cell can develop into a complex organism only because all of the parts and instructions are in the original cell produced from conception. The human mother passes not only 23 chromosomes but also an entire cell to her offspring, which includes all the organelles needed for life. A cell can come only from a functioning cell and cannot be built up piecemeal, because all the major organelles must have been created and assembled instantaneously for the cell to exist (Overman, 1997).

Cells require all their millions of necessary parts to remain alive, just as a mammal must have lung, liver, heart, and other organs to live. All of the millions of cell parts are required to carry out the complex biochemical business necessary for life. This business requires manufacturing and processing of proteins, and storing of genetic information to be passed on to the next generation. Trefil called the evolution of prokaryotes (cells without organelles) into eukaryotes (cells with organelles and other structures lacking in prokaryotes) an "enduring mystery of evolution" because of the lack of evidence of the evolution of organelles, and the total lack of plausible links between eukaryotes and prokaryotes.

> The differences between prokaryotic and eukaryotic cells are striking, to say the least. But if the latter evolved from the former, why are there no intermediate stages between the two? Why, for example, are there no cells with loose DNA and organelles? If the evolutionary line really went from prokaryotes to eukaryotes, and we have many living samples of each, why did none of the intermediate stages survive? (Trefil, 1992, p. 104).

This view is also reflected in the observation that the universe appears to be designed specifically to contain human life, and functions as a unit to allow and support life (Overman, 1997).

Creation of Humans

The problems of an instantaneous creation are best illustrated by the first man, Adam. If created as a mature adult, Adam would appear to be about, say, 30 years of age when he was only one day old. If Adam were examined medically, much scientific evidence in support of a 30-year age estimate would be found. Most medical tests completed on such a man would conclude he was and would have to be treated medically as if he, in fact, were at the prime of his life, even though only a day old.

This does not imply that God is deceptive, but only that to exist as a living organism, the human body *had* to be created fully formed. If his blood was not already circulating when Adam was created, the few minutes that it would take to prime the system and for blood to circulate to the brain could cause major cell death or damage. All of Adam's organs, including his heart, lungs, kidneys, and brain, must have been functioning simultaneously as a unit the second he was created. In other words, God created Adam as a mature man.

Although the physician who completed a physical on Adam a day after he was created would have had to conclude from development measures, such as bone-to-cartilage ratios, that Adam was 30 years old, some evidence for youth might have been found — in a one-day-old Adam, we might not have found certain effects of ageing, such as brain cell changes, which exist in the average 30 year old today. This, though, might have been because he was perfect, but this does not rule out the fact that some evidence, such as tissue culture examination of his cells, might have existed to prove he was in fact one week old.

Likewise, because the universe is enormously interrelated, the Creator could not have created the earth alone, but must have created the entire heavens and earth as a functioning unit. And as God likewise created the universe for a reason (such as a support system for the earth), and must have created Adam with blood *moving* in his veins, it is likewise a logical inference that the stars were created moving in their orbits and with their light in transit. Although this belief may not currently be provable, it may nonetheless be the most reasonable of the few possibilities that now exist.

This view is more viable than it may first appear. Nobel Laureate George Wald even stated that he believed that the universe was designed for life. In a recent interview he stated that he has concluded that the evidence is clearly obvious, because the elements carbon, hydrogen, oxygen, and nitrogen "have unique properties that fit the job and are not shared by any element in the periodic system" (interview in Levy, 1998, p. 12).

Creating the universe in parts would not be unlike creating a liver and waiting a *few* days before creating a brain, then several more weeks before creating a femur bone — until the body was eventually complete. No other method appears to exist to produce life other than creating instantaneously a fully functioning complete organism. This does not preclude that changes may have occurred since that time, only that a certain level of complexity must have existed for both an organism and a universe to exist.

Genetic drift, mutations, and the shuffling of the gene pool can bring about only minor changes in life, changes creationists label variations within the genesis kinds. Some creationists believe that these changes have historically been relatively significant, such as a pair of cat-kind animals producing by genetic recombination all cats existing today, including lions, tigers, and cheetahs. Anatomical comparisons support this and relatively minute differences exist, for example, between tigers and lions, at least compared with other animal kinds. Also hybrids of animals (such as tigons and ligers) have been produced to show the closeness of many animals.

The comparing of the creation of a human body with the creation of the universe has been supported by recent findings. Research has revealed that the universe is extraordinarily organized: our earth is organized into a solar system, which is part of a highly organized group of stars called a *galaxy*, that is part of a highly organized family of galaxies called *clusters* which, in turn, are organized into an enormous group of clusters called *superclusters*.

Life and Information

One of the most compelling evidences in support of the instantaneous creation world view is the daily observation that information does not come about by chance and, if left to itself, *disorder* usually soon results. Archeologists are normally easily able to discern if an object found in their field research digs was produced by humans or by natural events such as wind or rain. The criteria they use to do this is the *degree of information* the object contains (Yockey, 1992). Complexity and information are compelling evidence that some outside intelligent agency (which in the case of an archeologist's findings was another human) has applied design skills and intelligence to the natural world, adding a higher level of information and order on top of that which naturally exists in the non-living world such as rocks.

Both plant and animal kingdoms manifest enormous complexity and information in their genetic codes, but this order and information *pre-exists* in the animal or plant and was inherited and passed on through reproduction. Except for the living world and the "world" made by humans, *the natural world operates according to pre-existing physical laws and previous events.* The living world, which scientists are only now beginning to understand, represents a level of design complexity based on information existing in the genetic code which is not found anywhere in the non-living world except that created by humans. Hence the rationale for the belief that the living world could not come from the non-living world. As Nobel laureate research molecular biologist Komfield stated in a now-famous interview that occurred over 36 years ago:

> While laboring among the intricacies and definitely minute particles in a laboratory, I frequently have been overwhelmed by a sense of the infinite wisdom of God ... one is rather amazed that a mechanism of such intricacy could ever function properly at all ... the simplest man-made mechanism requires a planner and a maker; how a mechanism ten times more involved and intricate can be conceived as self-constructed and self-developed is completely beyond me (Komfield, 1962, p. 16).

In other words, the enormous amount of genetic information that is translated into the complexity that is evident everywhere in the living world is far beyond that found in both the non-living and human-manufactured world. Products produced by the non-living world (such as smooth stones polished by moving water) could never produce either plant or animal life because all life is based on information, and the parts produced by that information must be assembled according to a designed plan in an environment such as a certain ecosystem that supports life.

Mathematical Proof for the Designer Requirement

That a complex structure such as a living organism could be formed by chance without intelligent input has never been demonstrated in the lab or anywhere else. Given enough time, the naturalistic world view reasons, anything is at least possible. The problem with this view is that the degree of information and complexity required for living organisms to be able to "live" is such that, aside from deliberate intelligent design, from what we know now, no matter what the conditions, time alone will not allow for the naturalistic construction of life. Evolutionist Stephen Jay Gould stated that even if evolutionary history on earth repeated itself a *million times*, he doubts whether anything like *Homo sapiens* would ever develop again (Gould, 1989; also see Kayzer, 1997, p. 86).

Many researchers have concluded that the probability of life arising by chance is so remote that we have to label it an impossibility. For example, Hoyle (1983) notes that the probability of drawing either ten white or ten black balls out of a large box full of balls that contains equal numbers of black and white balls is five times out of one million! If we increase the number to 100 and draw sets of 100 balls, the probability of drawing 100 black or 100 white balls in succession is now so low as to be for all practical purposes impossible.

To illustrate this concept as applied in biology, an ordered structure of just 206 parts will be examined. This is not a large number — the adult human skeleton, for example, contains on the average 206 separate bones, all assembled together in a perfectly integrated functioning whole. And all body systems — even our cells' organelles — are far more complex than this.

To determine the possible number of different ways 206 parts could be connected, consider a system of one part which can be lined up in only one way (1 x 1); or a system of two parts in two ways (1 x 2) or 1, 2 and 2, 1; a system of three parts, which can be aligned in six ways (1 x 2 x 3), or 1, 2, 3; 2, 3, 1; 2, 1, 3; 1, 3, 2; 3, 1, 2; 3, 2, 1; one of four parts in 24 ways (1 x 2 x 3 x 4), and so on. Thus, a system of 206 parts could be aligned in 1 x 2 x 3 ... 206 different ways, equal to 1 x 2 x 3 . . . x 206. This number is called "206 factorial" and is written "206!".

The value 206! is an enormously large number, approximately 10^{388}, which is a "1" followed by 388 zeros, or:

10,000,000,000,000,000,000,000,000,000,000,000,000,
000,000,000,000,000,000,000,000,000,000,000,000,000,
000,000,000,000,000,000,000,000,000,000,000,000,000,
000,000,000,000,000,000,000,000,000,000,000,000,000,
000,000,000,000,000,000,000,000,000,000,000,000,000,
000,000,000,000,000,000,000,000,000,000,000,000,000,
000,000,000,000,000,000,000,000,000,000,000,000,000,
000,000,000,000,000,000,000,000,000,000,000,000,000,
000,000,000,000,000,000,000,000,000,000,000,000,000,
000,000,000,000

Achievement of *only* the correct general *position* required (ignoring for now where the bones came from, their upside-down or right-side-up placement, their alignment, the origin of the tendons, ligaments, and other supporting structures) for all 206 parts will occur only once out of 10^{388} random assortments. This means one chance out of 10^{388} exists of the correct order being selected on the first trial, and each and every other trial afterward, given all the bones as they presently exist in our body.

If one new trial could be completed each second for every single second available in all of the estimated evolutionary view of astronomic time (about 10 to 20 billion years), using the most conservative estimate gives us 10^{18} seconds; the chances that the correct general position will be obtained by random is *less than once in 10 billion years*. This will produce a probability of only one out of $10^{(388-18)}$ or one in 10^{370}.

If each part is only the size of an electron, one of the smallest known particles in the universe, and the entire known universe were solidly packed with sets of bones, this area conservatively estimated at 100 billion cubic light years could contain only about 10^{130} sets of 206 parts each. What is the possibility that *just one* of these 10^{130} sets, each arranging their members by chance, will achieve the correct alignment just *once* in ten billion years? Suppose also that we invent a machine capable of making not one trial per second, but a billion-billion different trials each second on every single one of the 10^{130} sets. The maximum number of possible trials that anyone could possibly conceive being made with this type of situation would permit a total of 10^{166} trials (10^{130} x 10^{18} x 10^{18}). Even given these odds, the chance that one of these 10^{166} trials would produce the correct result is only one out of 10^{388}, or only one in 10^{222} trials for all sets.

Further, all the parts must both first exist and be instantaneously assembled properly in order for the organism to function. For all practical purposes, a zero possibility exists that the correct general position of only 206 parts could be obtained simultaneously by chance — and the average human has about 75 trillion cells! The human cerebral cortex alone contains over 10 billion cells, all arranged in the proper order, and each of these cells is itself *infinitely complex* from a human standpoint. Each of the cells in the human body consists of multi-thousands of basic parts such as organelles and multi-millions of complex proteins and other parts, all of which must be assembled both correctly and instantaneously as a unit in order to function. This required balance and assembly must be maintained even during cell division.

This illustration indicates that the argument commonly used by evolutionists — "given enough time, anything is possible" — is wanting. Evolutionary naturalism claims that the bone system happened as a result of time, luck, and "natural" forces, the last element actually holding the status of a god. Time, the chief escape that naturalism must rely on to support its theory, is thus a false god. Complex ordered structures of any kind (of which billions must exist in the body for it to work) cannot happen except by design and intelligence, and they must have occurred simultaneously for the unit to function. Scientists recognize this problem, and this is why Stephen Jay Gould concluded that humans are a glorious evolutionary accident which required 60 trillion contingent events (Gould, 1989, see also Kayzer, 1997, p. 92).

Of course, the naturalistic evolution assumption does not propose that the parts of life resulted from an assembly of bones, but instead proposes that an extended series of step-wise coincidences gave rise to life and the world as we know it. In other words, the first coincidence led to a second coincidence, which led to a third coincidence, which eventually led to coincidence "i," which eventually led up to the present situation, "N." Evolutionists have not even been able to posit a mechanistic "first" coincidence, only the assumption that each step must have had a survival advantage and only by this means could evolution from simple to complex have occurred. Each coincidence "i" is assumed to be dependent upon prior steps and to have an associated dependent probability "Pi." The resultant probability estimate for the occurrence of evolutionary naturalism is calculated as the product series, given the following:

N the number of step-wise coincidences in the evolutionary process

i = the index for each coincidence: i = 1,2,3 . . .

Pi the evaluated dependent probability for the i'th coincidence

PE = the product probability that everything evolved by naturalism.

Innumerable steps are postulated to exist in the evolutionary sequence, therefore N is very large (i.e., N . . .). All values of Pi are less than or equal to one, with most of them much smaller than 1. The greater the proposed leap in step i, the smaller the associated probability Pi 1, and a property of product series where N is very large and most terms are significantly less than one quickly converges very close to zero.

The conclusion of this calculation is that the probability of naturalistic evolution is essentially zero. Sir Fred Hoyle (1982) calculated "the chance of a random shuffling of amino acids producing a workable set of enzymes" to be less than $10^{40,000}$, and the famous unrealistically optimistic Green Band equation gives the chance of finding life on another planet in the order of only one in 10^{30}.

These probabilities argue that the chance distribution of molecules could never lead to the conditions favorable for the spontaneous development of life. The reasoning that leads us to this conclusion is that living molecules contain a large number of elements which must be instantly assembled in a certain order for life. The probability of the required order in a single basic protein molecule arising purely from chance is estimated at 10^{43} (Overman, 1997). Since thousands of complex protein molecules are required to build a simple cell, probability moves chance arrangements of these molecules outside the realm of possibility. The smallest proteins have an atomic mass of 100,000 or more atomic mass units (AMU), which is equal to 100,000 hydrogen atoms (Branden and Tooze, 1991). And this calculation evaluates only the necessary *order* of parts, *not a functional* arrangement, i.e., one that works. Even if the gears of a clock are arranged in the correct *order*, the clock will not function properly until the gears are properly meshed, spaced, adjusted, the tolerances are correct, and the system is properly secured.

A problem with understanding the concept "life" is that although we now have identified many of the chemicals which are necessary, researchers do not yet know all of the factors necessary for life "to live." Further, even assembling the proper chemicals together does not produce life. The proper arrangement of amino acids to form protein molecules is only one small requirement for life. Most animals are constructed of millions of cells, and the cell itself is far more complicated than the most complex machine ever manufactured by humans.

The famous illustration "the probability of life originating from accident is comparable to the probability of the unabridged dictionary resulting from an explosion in a print shop" argues that information and complex systems *cannot come about by chance*, but can only be the product of an intelligent designer. Books likewise do not come about by chance, but are the product of both reasoning and intelligence (although some books may cause us to wonder about the author, but this is another problem!). Even Darwin admitted in his writings that it was extremely difficult, or impossible, to conceive that this immense and wonderful universe, including humans with our capacity of looking far backward and far into the future, was the result of blind chance.

Life from Non-Life?

An important part of the question, "Where did life come from?" is the issue of spontaneous generation, the concept that life could produce itself if the proper circumstances existed (Lewis, 1997). This idea is no longer accepted as possible by secular scientists — except only for the beginning of life, when some believe the first living organism somehow spontaneously generated itself once or, at most, a few times, and every living thing thereafter evolved from this "first" life. This principle of science that life only comes from life is called the "law of biogenesis." The term is from the Greek words *bios* (meaning life) and *genesis* (meaning birth, source or creation), and means that *living organisms are produced only by other living organisms*. Biologists know only that *all life derives from preceding life*, and that the parent organism's offspring are always of the *same* kind. The idea that life can come from non-life is called abiogenesis, which is assumed by evolutionists to have occurred only once or a few times at most in earth history. This conclusion is not a result of evidence, but is obtained because the current dominant world view in Western science, naturalism (atheism), *requires* a chance spontaneous origin of life.

The naturalistic view requires a set of unknown conditions to have existed in the distant past that operated to produce the first "living" thing. These unknown forces do not operate today to produce flies from decaying meat or bees from dead carcasses, as once believed. Scientists have demonstrated that the belief that "life" could come from "non-life," even if millions of years were available, is untenable (Overman, 1997). Darwinism demands a non-theistic explanation and therefore is forced to put much displaced faith in an unprovable "one-time" event that they reason must have occurred because life is here. Hoyle, in a review of the literature, concluded:

> There is not a shred of objective evidence to support the hypothesis that life began in an organic soup here on the earth. Indeed, Francis Crick, who shared a Nobel prize for the discovery of the structure of DNA, is one biophysicist who finds this theory unconvincing. So why do biologists indulge in unsubstantiated fantasies in order to deny what is so patently obvious, that the 200,000 amino acid chains, and hence life, did not appear by chance?
>
> The answer lies in a theory developed over a century ago, which sought to explain the development of life as an inevitable product of the purely local natural processes. Its author, Charles Darwin, hesitated to challenge the church's doctrine on the creation, and publicly at least did not trace the implications of his ideas back to their bearing on the origin of life. However, he privately suggested that life itself may have been produced in "some warm little pond," and to this day his followers have sought to explain the origin of terrestrial life in terms of a process of chemical evolution from the primordial soup. But, as we have seen, this [theory] simply does not fit the facts (Hoyle, 1983, p. 23).

This conclusion is not unique to Hoyle but common to thinkers not blinded by dogmatic naturalism. Einstein argued that the "scientist's religious feelings *take the form of rapturous amazement* at the harmony of natural law, which *reveals an intelligence of such superiority* that, compared with it, all the systematic thinking and acting of human beings is an utterly insignificant reflection" (Einstein, 1949, p. 29; emphasis mine). Scientists once argued that life was relatively simple, could spontaneously generate, and regularly did so. They now realize the human cell is the most complex machine known in the universe, far more complex than the most expensive computer. This realization has forced many persons to conclude life could not have evolved, but must have been created instantaneously as a fully functioning unit.

All of the extant evidence reveals that there is nothing living on earth, either animal or plant, that did not receive its life from previous life, its sexual or asexual parent. Since the law of biogenesis states that life proceeds only from pre-existing life, various forms of pre-existing life must have been parents of all living organisms. And since life cannot create itself, the source of life must be God: "O Lord. . . . For with you is the fountain of life" (Ps. 36:6–9). In the words of the well-known scientist, Robert Jastrow, "For the scientist who has lived by his faith in the power of reason, the story [of the quest for the answers about the origin of life and the universe] ends like a bad dream. He has scaled the mountains of ignorance; he is about to conquer the highest peak; as he pulls himself over the final rock, he is greeted by a band of theologians who have been sitting there for centuries (Jastrow, 1978, p. 116).

Readings

Annual Reviews of Astronomy and Astrophysics. 1982, 20:4–5.

Behe, Michael. Darwin's Black Box. New York: Free Press, 1991.

Branden, Carl and John Tooze. Introduction to Protein Structure. New York: Garland, 1991.

Crick, Francis. Life Itself. New York: Simon and Schuster, 1981.

Einstein, Albert. The World As I See It. New York: Philosophical Library, 1949.

Encyclopedia of Science and Technology. Vol. 3. New York: McGraw Hill, 1971.

Gould, Stephen Jay. Wonderful Life; The Burgess Shale and the Nature of History. New York: Norton, 1989.

Hickman, Cleveland, Larry Roberts, and Allan Larson. Integrated Principles of Zoology. Dubuque, IA.: Wm. C. Brown, 1997.

Hoyle, Fred. The Intelligent Universe. New York: Holt, Rinehart and Winston, 1983.

Irion, Robert. "Ocean Scientists Find Life, Warmth in the Seas." Science, 1998, 279:1302–1303.

Jastrow, Robert. God and the Astronomers. New York: W.W. Norton Company, 1978.

Kayzer, W. "A Glorious Accident," Understanding Our Place in the Cosmic Puzzle. New York: W.W. Freeman and Co., 1997.

Knight, Jonathan. "Cold Start; Was Life Kick-Started in Frozen Seas Rather Than Boiling Vents?" New Scientist, July 11, 1998, 2142:10.

Komfield, E.C. "The Evidence of God in an Expanding Universe." Look, Jan. 16, 1962.

Levy, David. "Four Simple Facts Behind the Miracle of Life." Parade Magazine, June 12, 1998, p 12.

Levy, Matthew and Stanley Miller. "The Stability of the RNA Bases: Implications for the Origin of Life." Proceedings of the National Academy of Sciences USA. 1998, 95: 7933–8.

Lewis, Ricki. "Primordial Soup Researchers Gather at the Watering Hole." Science, 1997, 227:1034–5.

Overman, Dean. A Case Against Accident and Self-Organization. New York: Rowman & Littlefield Pub., 1997.

Ruse, Michael. "Answering the Creationists," Free Inquiry, 1998, 18(2):28–32.

Spetner, Lee. Not by Chance! Brooklyn, NY: Judaica Press, 1997.

Trefil, James. 1001 Things Everyone Should Know about Science. New York: Doubleday, 1992.

Yockey, Hubert. Information Theory and Molecular Biology. Cambridge; Cambridge University Press, 1992.

Author's note: I wish to thank Steven Dapra for his comments on an earlier draft of this paper.

john k.g. kramer

Biochemistry

Dr. Kramer is a research scientist with Agriculture and Agri-Food Canada. He holds a B.S. (hons) from the University of Manitoba, an M.S. in biochemistry from the University of Manitoba, a Ph.D. in biochemistry from the University of Minnesota and completed three years of post-doctoral studies as a Hormel fellow at the Hormel Institute and as an NRC fellow at the University of Ottawa. Dr. Kramer has identified, characterized, and synthesized the structure of numerous food, bacterial, and biological components and has published 128 refereed papers and numerous abstracts and book chapters. He was one of the core scientists who evaluated the toxicological, nutritional, and biochemical properties of canola oil and demonstrated its safety. He presently serves as associate editor of the scientific journal *LIPIDS*.

Since completing my Ph.D. in 1968, I have spent 30 years doing lipid research. Although my work has not specifically addressed the "origin of life" or the "age of the earth," I believe these issues have far-reaching implications in the area of lipid biochemistry and nutrition research.

Early Background

I grew up in a Bible-believing home. Throughout high school I liked the sciences and excelled in these subjects. Therefore, it was natural for me to choose a career in scientific research. It was during my last year in high school that one of the pastors in our church approached me, concerned that I might lose my faith if I proceeded in a scientific career. He encouraged me to view the first chapter of Genesis without a time scale, since in his opinion it was more important to believe that God created all things, irrespective of how long it took. At first, this view seemed rather inconsistent with my interpretation of Scripture. But, I must admit, this thought raised sufficient doubt in my mind that I did not defend either position with much enthusiasm for several years. I was relieved that a critical confrontation never materialized in any of my classes throughout my BSc (Hons) and MSc program in chemistry and biochemistry at the University of Manitoba.

Confronted with a Choice

In 1964 I transferred to the University of Minnesota for a Ph.D. program in biochemistry with a minor in organic chemistry. It was there I was confronted with this very issue in my second year in a course in endocrinology. We were asked to write an essay on how life began, based on evolutionary principles. Weeks of reading and studying this subject provided me with no logical mechanisms for evolutionary processes. I was looking for the type of evidence familiar to me in biochemistry and organic chemistry. It was obvious to me that life could not form or be sustained in either a reducing or oxidizing atmosphere, never mind the unlikely association of inanimate molecules to form highly ordered structures containing information, fragile biological cells, and processes where several parts all need to be working together simultaneously.

Finally, I had to write the essay. I did. I described a possible scenario which I thought could be tested experimentally. However, after rereading the essay several times, I continued to see the weaknesses of my arguments. In total frustration and confusion, I added a few sentences at the end to the effect that it would be easier to believe in a Creator who made it all, than in favorable conditions acting on inanimate matter over time. The low mark on the essay was most discouraging, and all attempts failed to change the score. I realized I was found out!

Although I had committed my life to Jesus Christ and made a radical profession of my faith at the age of 16, at which time I was baptized, I now faced "my hour of decision." Should I believe in evolution or God? Having studied this area without the help of any Christian literature on this topic, I came to the firm conclusion that evolution lacked evidence to make it credible. I therefore determined to believe God's account for the time being and continued looking for evidence, one way or another.

In retrospect, that low mark on the evolution essay was the best thing that happened to me. I learned to critically evaluate the facts, irrespective of outside pressures. It was then that I began to see clear evidence for creation (Rom. 1:19–20). I took every opportunity to study Scripture and read books on beginnings. It was at this time I came across books by MacKay[1] and Morris and Whitcomb[2] which impressed me greatly. On the other hand, I became very disillusioned with evolutionists who managed to give good science followed by irrational conclusions that complex systems and processes just happened by some unexplained evolutionary mechanism plus time. No evidence. No logic. Just wishful dreaming. It also became evident to me that both views were strictly a matter of belief. To me the creation scenario appeared more logical than an explosion followed by self-propelled organization of matter which does not possess these properties.

Throughout this search I experienced an interesting transformation within myself. The Bible became alive and meaningful to me, and my relationship to God became real. I began to see an amazing order and design in nature, which was completely consistent with Scripture. One area which really fascinated me was the laws in the Old Testament regarding foods and hygiene, with its implications for nutrition, biochemistry, and bacteriology. How could these authors have known about modern science without divine revelation?

The Scientific Snow Job

In my scientific career I have observed an interesting principle. Whenever little is known on a subject, or is different from the norm, more speculations arise as to its evolutionary development. Instead of admitting "we do not know," and working towards discovering the unknown, some evolutionary comments are usually made. On the other hand, the more that is known about a certain subject, the more eagerness there is to describe it in detail, and classify such systems "irreducibly complex," as Michael Behe[3] refers to it.

No one has ever demonstrated macroevolutionary changes on a molecular level, yet many people readily speculate evolutionary links between bacteria, plants, animals, and man. Are the gross structures not made up of individual cells with complex molecules? If macroevolution is unlikely on a molecular level, how can the whole be changed? Endless DNA sequence comparisons do not explain evolutionary development. Furthermore, the changes (mutations) observed on a molecular level, such as DNA, are predominantly disruptive, and always with loss of, not gain in, information and complexity. This led Lee Spetner[4] to conclude "Whoever thinks macroevolution can be made by mutations that lose information is like the merchant who lost a little money on every sale but thought he could make it up on volume."

Evidence of Design in My Research

In the last few decades extensive work has been done on thermophilic and halophilic bacteria, which grow under extreme temperatures and salt conditions, respectively. These bacteria have been classified as archaebacteria because some scientists believe that these are earlier and simpler forms of life. The lipids of these bacteria have chemical linkages called ethers rather than esters, and the alkyl moieties are on position 2 and 3 of the glycerol backbone, rather than on the 1 and 2 positions, as in mammalian systems (see below).

(Position 1)	$CH_2\text{-}O\text{-}X$	$CH_2\text{-}O\text{-}CO\text{-}R$
	|	|
(Position 2)	$CH\text{-}O\text{-}R$	$CH\text{-}O\text{-}CO\text{-}R'$
	|	|
(Position 3)	$CH_2\text{-}O\text{-}R'$	$CH_2\text{-}O\text{-}X$
	Ether lipids	Ester lipids

where R and R' are alkyl groups, and X is H or a polar group

Furthermore, they produce their energy in the form of adenosine triphosphate (ATP) from a combination of sodium gradient plus a proton-motive force,[5] instead of only a proton-motive force as mammalian cells.[6] Fragile biochemical structures and processes in these bacteria, many of which are similar to mammalian cells, are protected. But how? Ether bonds are certainly more stable than ester bonds, but that may not be the whole explanation. From my research I believe an even greater stability is achieved by these ether lipids complexing with sodium ions. The integration of a sodium and proton gradient is still not understood, although the former initiates cell growth.[7]

Therefore, to view these bacteria as earlier and simpler forms of life is totally misrepresenting their complexity. These bacteria are just as complex as mammalian cells, and represent an amazing design suited for the extreme conditions of temperature and salt concentration. Each cell is produced according to the information in its respective DNA. Attempts to give these complex lipid structures common names containing the prefix "archae," to denote their evolutionary hierarchy,[8] does not provide scientific evidence. It states one's belief, but adds no scientific knowledge. In fact, it may even be misleading by implying that lipid structures and energy mechanisms may evolve differently under different environmental conditions. The evidence shows that *Methanobacteria thermoautotrophicum* remain *Methanobacteria thermoautotrophicum* through millions of generations, according to their genetic information, and growing under favorable conditions of high temperature and salt concentration.

Scriptural Principles Provide Helpful Directions to Solving Scientific Problems

In 1971 I was asked to participate in a research project on low erucic acid rapeseed oil (now known as canola oil) at Agriculture Canada, in Ottawa, Canada. A number of heart problems had been observed in rats fed rapeseed oil high in erucic acid, which continued to persist with the newly developed low erucic acid rapeseed oils.[9] There was concern that humans may be equally affected, and therefore there were discussions to consider recommending the removal of this oil for human consumption. A multidisciplinary team was established at Agriculture Canada to urgently address this issue and "let the chips fall where they may," as Dr. B. Migikovsky

(Director General of the Research Branch, Agriculture Canada) put it. I was faced with a choice. Should I approach this problem from the evolutionary point of view, development of animals to humans, or from the biblical point of view that animals and humans are created according to their kind? One's "Weltanschauung" certainly influenced the approach to this research. I chose the latter.

Based on the biblical perspective, I wanted to know the results from a number of different animal species, find a common toxicological denominator, determine its mechanism of action, then determine if a similar process occurred in humans, and above all be super-cautious on extrapolations. I was fully aware that my view was different from that of many others in the group, who occasionally expressed the view of looking for an evolutionary trend from one species to another, even though we were all aware of the pitfalls of such reasoning. Thalidomide, for example, showed no harmful effects in rats, yet showed fetal abnormalities in rabbits, mice, and humans.[10]

I have often been asked whether these two approaches are different. Strictly speaking, they are. However, I have found that scientists do not maintain a strictly evolutionary approach in the biochemistry–nutrition area. Generally scientists take a pragmatic approach in research. They look for order, consistency, a biochemical basis, and differences between species. Hence this great commonality between researchers from both camps. It is as though they know better but are afraid to sound religious. I am delighted to see that scientists are becoming brave and pointing out the inconsistency of evolutionary thought,[11] and suggesting that "intelligent design" might be a better conclusion to explain the physical and biological world.[12] But I feel it is sad that these authors, who clearly demonstrate the inconsistency of evolution, leave the reader in a vacuum. How did things come to pass? If there is evidence for "intelligent design," who is the Designer? The books by Gentry[13] and Parker[14] provide a more logical conclusion, by introducing the reader to the Designer.

The reason rapeseed oil affected the heart in such a unique way appeared to be a most challenging problem. I prayed that God would give me the wisdom to contribute to its solution. He did. The verse ruminating in my mind at the time was "For everything God created is good" (1 Tim. 4:4). I took this as a clue to consider the possibility that the observed phenomenon was possibly due to a nutritional imbalance because of the nature of the experiment. In toxicological studies a food component is generally fed to animals at the highest level possible. For a vegetable oil (such as rapeseed oil or canola oil, in this case) it meant giving the oil as the sole source of fat in the diet (20 percent by weight, or 40 percent of calories). Furthermore, was it possible that rapeseed oil contained a natural toxin which was exacerbated by the high content of this oil in the diet? These thoughts, together with testing for species differences, and checking for inappropriate methodologies used, became my driving force.

The answer to these questions took over ten years of intensive research with input by many scientists at Agriculture Canada. Proof accumulated slowly and in reverse order to the previous paragraph. As to the fourth point, yes, inappropriate methods were used to report the pathological findings, in the isolation of mitochondria, and the extraction of lipids. As to the third point: the fast-growing male rat was the only species which showed the characteristic heart problems. Female rats, pigs, monkeys, dogs, and a specific strain of rat which absorbs fat mainly via the portal system showed no specific response to canola oil. As to the second point, exhaustive fractionations and preparations of semi-synthetic oils led us to conclude that the so-called "toxic" factor was the oil itself. Therefore, after ten years, many experiments, thousands of analyses, and 50 publications, we arrived at the first point. We observed that these focal heart lesions in male rats were related to the fatty acid composition of the dietary oil. Fats high in saturated fatty acids showed the lowest incidence of heart lesions, while vegetable oils high in polyunsaturated fatty acids, specifically linolenic acid (one of the essential fatty acids), showed the highest incidence of heart lesions. I remarked at the time that we had developed a "biological gas chromatograph." It is of interest to point out that these results were just the opposite to those observed for atherosclerosis (hardening of the arteries).

Therefore, you may ask, what is the problem? The problem we believe is this: When we feed canola oil, the vegetable oil lowest in saturated fatty acids, to rats at 20 percent by weight (40 percent of calories), we depress the *de novo* synthesis of fats (mainly saturated and monounsaturated fatty acids) in the animal. But the growing animal requires saturated fatty acids for membrane synthesis, since the content of saturated fatty acids in membranes is about 40 percent. Therefore, by feeding on canola oil the animal becomes deficient in saturated fatty acids for membrane buildup during rapid growth. Saturated fatty acids are not provided by either the dietary oil or by *de novo* synthesis. The result is a more fragile membrane, more susceptible to break up during stress, resulting in focal heart lesions. These results also offer an explanation as to the reduced energy production observed in isolated heart mitochondria, and the high content of free fatty acids in the heart during lipid extraction.[15] Other vegetable oils and fats produce similar types of focal heart lesions, but the incidence and severity decreases rapidly with increased saturated fatty acids and decreased linolenic acid in the oil, that is, soybean oil > corn oil > sunflower oil > olive oil > lard. For humans consuming a mixed fat diet, and human infants not given a single vegetable oil low in saturated fatty acids as the sole source of fat in the infant formulas, these heart lesions would therefore not present a problem.

It was a real encouragement for me to see that a scriptural principle was consistent with science and provided me with a perspective that contributed to resolving this problem.

Why I Believe in Genesis 1

There is no one piece of evidence one can give. However, I believe the sum total of many facts would lead a person to reasonably conclude that the Genesis record may be the most plausible scenario. The Genesis record implies that this world is very young, possibly less than 10,000 years; that one should expect to see overwhelming evidence of design everywhere, in both physical and biological systems; and that there is a coherency and similarity between all systems, suggesting a common Designer.

The first evidence is that all life and non-life processes obey the first and second laws of thermodynamics. Therefore, the present world had a beginning and is measurably going downhill. Secondly, numerous pieces of evidence fit a young earth. To mention a few: the historical records, the population growth, the helium content in this world, the missing neutrinos from the sun, the oscillation period of the sun, the decline of the earth's magnetic field, the limited number of supernovas, radioactive halos, the mitochondrial DNA pointing to one mother, and the increase in genetic diseases, etc. Thirdly, the complexity of nature clearly points to a Creator. Every biological and physical system, once understood, shows incredible complexity. Archeologists have no problem identifying man-made objects. Why then do we have problems identifying a Creator-made world?

The only question I have is: why did He take so long — "six days"? Throughout Scripture God is shown as an instant Creator, not in six days or 20 billion years. To give but a few examples: a fish to swallow Jonah, the sun turning back, the parting of the Red Sea, water turning into wine, stilling of the storm, raising the dead, healing, etc. Therefore, why did He use six days? Scripture gives us the answer. He established a blueprint for our life, six days of work and one day of rest (Exod. 20:8). It must have been painstaking for God to slow down to our pace, to six days. It would have been more His nature to create everything instantly. I have often considered belief in Genesis chapters 1 to 11 as the "acid test" of believing in God, and in the salvation through Jesus Christ.

Therefore, why do I believe in a six-day creation? I believe in a Creator because I see the Creator's designs in nature everywhere and evidence of intelligence in the DNA of each cell. I believe in a "six-day creation" because I have experienced salvation from a truthful God, Jesus Christ, who has never disappointed me (Rom. 10:11). Therefore, why should I doubt Him if He said "I made it so"?

Notes

1 D.M. MacKay, *Christianity in a Mechanistic Universe* (Chicago, IL:The Inter-Varsity Fellowship, 1965).

2 Henry M. Morris and John C. Whitcomb, *The Genesis Flood* (Philadelphia, PA: Presbyterian and Reformed Co., 1961).

3 Michael J. Behe, *Darwin's Black Box, The Biochemical Challenge to Evolution* (New York:The Free Press, 1996).

4 Lee Spetner, *Not by Chance! Shattering the Modern Theory of Evolution* (Brooklyn, NY:The Judaica Press, Inc., 1997), p. 160.

5 F.D. Sauer, B.A. Blackwell, and J.K.G. Kramer, "Ion Transport and Methane Production in *Methanobacterium thermoautotrophicum*," *Proc. Natl. Acad. Sci. USA* 91, 1994, 4466–70.

6 Lubert Stryer, *Biochemistry* (NewYork:W.H. Freeman and Company,1995).

7 J.K.G. Kramer, F.D. Sauer, and D.R. Bundle, "The Presence of Tightly Bound Na^+ and K^+ in Glycolipids of *Methanobacterium thermoautotrophicum,*" *Biochem. Biophys. Acta* 961, 1988 285–92.

8 Y. Koga, M. Akagawa-Matsushita, M. Ohga, and M. Nishihara, "Taxonomic Significance of the Distribution of Component Parts of Polar Ether Lipids in Methanogens," *System.Appl. Microbiol,* 16, 1993 342–51.

9 J.K.G. Kramer, F.D. Sauer and W.J. Pidgen, eds., *High and Low Erucic Acid Rapeseed Oils, Production, Usage, Chemistry, and Toxicological Evaluation* (New York: Academic Press, 1983).

10 G.B. Gordon, S.P. Spielberg, D.A. Blake, and V. Balasubramanian, "Thalidomide Teratogenesis: Evidence for a Toxic Arene Oxide Metabolite," *Proc. Natl. Acad. Sci. USA* 78, 1981 2545–48.

11 Michael Denton, *Evolution, A Theory in Crisis* (Bethesda, MD: Adler & Adler Publishers Inc., 1986); see also footnotes 3 and 4.

12 C. Thaxton, "A New Design Argument," *Cosmic Pursuit* 1 (2) 1998 13–21; see also footnote 3.

13 Robert V. Gentry, *Creation's Tiny Mystery* (Knoxville, TN: Earth Science Assoc., 1988).

14 Gary Parker, *Creation: Facts of Life* (Green Forest, AR: Master Books, Inc., 1994).

15 Koga et al., "Taxonomic Significance of the Distribution of Component Parts of Polar Ether Lipids in Methanogens."

paul giem

Medical Research

Dr. Giem is assistant professor of emergency medicine at Loma Linda University. He holds a B.A. in chemistry from Union College, Nebraska, an M.A. in religion from Loma Linda University and an M.D. from Loma Linda University. Dr. Giem has published research articles in the areas of religion and medicine. His current research includes work on carbon-14 dating methods. He is author of the book *Scientific Theology*, which deals with a number of science–Bible areas, including dating methodology and biblical chronology.[1]

I grew up in a family in which science was greatly respected. My father was a physician, and I learned to enjoy physics, chemistry, and biology.

My family was also deeply religious. My parents believed the Bible, and were committed to following it.

Their belief in the Bible led to a belief in the creation of the world in six literal days of approximately 24 hours, as indicated by a straightforward reading of Genesis 1. This belief was reinforced by their reading of the fourth commandment, where the Sabbath is stated to memorialize a six-day creation with a rest on the seventh day. The Sabbath is a literal day, and this implied that the six days of creation were also literal days.

My parents solved the conflict between the majority of scientists and the Bible in this area by believing that science, if done properly, did not really conflict with a recent creation. It was only when science was misunderstood or misused that it conflicted with a recent creation. My father remembered the struggles he had had to integrate Piltdown Man into his world view, before it was discovered to be a fraud. Understandably, he did not fully trust evolutionary science.

The way I was taught science, it had no room for authority without evidence. Rather, the only acceptable authority was that which was backed up by evidence, and only precisely to the extent that it was backed up. My religious tradition was similar in some ways. Only tradition that could be backed up by Scripture was worth anything. The two attitudes were compatible, except at one point. The religious tradition was willing to accept Scripture without much question, whereas in principle, science might ask the question, why choose Scripture? Why not choose the Koran or the Vedas or the writings of Confucius? Or why not reject holy books entirely? And what does one do when science apparently conflicts with Scripture?

Many of my teachers in college had an answer to the latter question. They said that the evidence from science was equivocal at best. Scripture provided the additional evidence to allow one to choose a theist and Christian position. This way of answering the question at least did not require one to be a scientist to be saved. It seemed to me to be unsatisfying, but I had nothing better to suggest.

In college, I took a double major in theology and chemistry. For my senior chemistry seminar I wanted to examine a subject related in some way to theology, so I chose to review the experiments that had been done relating to the origin of life. It was popularly reported at the time that experiments had created life in a test tube, and had shown how life could have appeared on a prebiotic earth spontaneously. I was expecting some room for doubt, but was to find in the main a plausible scenario somewhat supported by the experiments.

I was stunned by the one-sidedness of the evidence I found. In fact, the evidence seemed (and seems) overwhelming that spontaneous generation did not happen. (A more detailed account, with general references, is in my book *Scientific Theology*, La Sierra University Press, 1997.) This evidence convinced me of two things. First, from that time on I never doubted that there was a God. I might not know whether He cared for me, but He certainly existed. Mechanistic evolution was dead. Second, at least in some cases, science can support theology. Theologians can expect the scientific evidence to come out strongly in their favor at least some of the time.

However, this evidence had no bearing on the dispute between theistic evolution, or progressive creation, and special creation. That discussion seemed to bog down in intractable disputes. It would be hard to decide whether a similarity between two groups (species, genera, families, etc.) of creatures was due to design or to common descent. How could one tell what a designer would not do? Or how could one tell what features could not be caused by common descent? And if one backed a theistic evolutionist into a corner, he would always reasonably respond that this is one area where God intervened. On the other hand, special creationists believed in some evolution on the lower group levels.

The major difference between theistic evolutionists and special creationists seemed to be time. This includes relative time and absolute time. Relative time includes questions such as how fast the Cambrian strata were formed, how much time passed between the

Ordovician and the Permian, and how fast the Grand Canyon took to form. Absolute time includes the absolute date of the Pliocene or the Jurassic or the Cambrian. These dates are almost exclusively based on evolutionary estimates and radiometric dating.

I decided to investigate radiometric dating. A summary of my results may be found in *Scientific Theology*. Very briefly, for potassium-argon dates, the assumption that argon is driven off is demonstrably not valid, and one cannot be sure that the clock is reset. This point is underlined by multiple dates that are too old, even for the evolutionary time scale. There are also problems with "too young" dates, which are not adequately explained as the result of argon loss. These dates suggest that the evolutionary time scale is too long. There is a gradient of argon in the geologic column, with more argon in the older rocks and less in the younger rocks, regardless of their potassium content, including in minerals with no potassium content. This creates a sort of instant time scale — just add potassium.

There was also a problem with selectivity, which could be documented from the literature. Other dating methods had similar problems. Rubidium-strontium dating isochrons could be mimicked by mixing lines, which require essentially no time to form. There were multiple examples of inaccurate dates by anyone's timescale, including ones that matched potassium-argon dates. Uranium-lead dating was also done by isochrons, and when incorrect dates were explained by discordia lines, these lines could also be reproduced by mixing lines. There were multiple examples of lower concordia ages which were not accurate by anyone's time scale. There was the data set on uranium dates on pleiochroic haloes in coal, which seemed to indicate an age for the coal (conventional age around 100 million years) of less than 300,000 years. Uranium disequilibrium dating, fission-track dating, and amino acid dating (which is not radiometric) all had their problems, as did other, less-established methods. Often the data were more easily explained on the basis of a short time scale rather than a long one.

Carbon-14 dating was the most fascinating method of all. Fossil carbon, with a conventional age of up to 350 million years, repeatedly dated to less than 55,000 radiocarbon years. This is compatible with a date of as low as 4,000 years in real time (the date of the Flood would have to be determined on other grounds). It is incompatible with an age of millions of years, or even realistically with an age of over 100,000 years or so. It basically forces one into accepting a short chronology for life on earth.

Thus, if one accepts a designer intelligent enough to produce life, and a short time scale, it becomes very difficult to avoid the claims of the Bible. There is also the inability to adequately explain the creation week on the basis of Mesopotamian or Egyptian legends or customs. This implies that Genesis 1–9 is not just myth, but an account of what actually happened.

I arrived at that conclusion by following the data. I am not afraid of further data. I welcome challenges and actually look for them. I believe that if we do our homework carefully enough, and without succumbing to bias, we will find that the Book, including a literal 6-day creation, will stand. When properly understood, nature testifies to the trustworthiness of God's Word.

Endnotes
1 Paul Giem, *Scientific Theology* (Riverside, CA: La Sierra University Press, 1996).

henry zuill

Biology

Dr. Zuill is Professor of Biology at Union College in Lincoln, Nebraska. He holds a B.A. in biology from Atlantic Union College, an M.A. in biology from Loma Linda University and a Ph.D. in biology from Loma Linda University. Dr. Zuill also serves as curator of the Joshua C. Turner Arboretum, which is an affiliate of the Nebraska Statewide Arboretum.

Abundant Life

The verandah at "High Sycamore" (named for a large, handsome sycamore tree at the foot of the hill upon which the house stands) overlooks a wide and wooded valley stretching southwestward toward a ridge of hills seven or eight miles away. This is a remote region to which we frequently come. It generally takes several days to wind down to nature's slower pace, but by then it is possible to see nature, really *see*, and listen and learn.

I was not seeing just the view of that wooded valley, however. There was another view as well. I was seeing the "view" that would become this chapter, and I was wondering how I should describe the ideas of which it was composed. As words came together, it turned out that the two views were not entirely isolated from each other. Threads of one became woven with the other until there was only one fabric.

In the view from the verandah, there are many colors and hues, varying light through the day, and under different weather conditions, highlights and shadows — an ever-changing panorama. We listen to audible sounds of wind in trees, beating rain, crackling thunder, and distinguishing calls of woodland creatures. One may also hear, if listening, the inner voice of the Creator teaching lessons through things He made. As a Christian ecologist, I need those times of renewal among our Creator's works.

Those mountains and valleys humble me. A large variety of plants and animals inhabit more than a million and a half acres of surrounding mountain forest land, meadows, lakes, ponds, rivers, and streams. I want to know how all of these creatures work with each other. This is a mixed hardwood and short-leaf pine forest. Trees include varieties of oaks, elms, and hickories, plus sweetgum trees and, of course, stands of short-leaf pine — especially on southern exposures. Wildflowers splash brilliant colors across the landscape from spring to autumn.

Birds from buntings and bobwhites to roadrunners and turkeys abound, as do many insect species, including butterflies and grasshoppers, cicadas, bees, beetles, and myriads more. Mammals include armadillos, squirrels, deer, bears, and coyotes. Amphibians and reptiles are common. In the evening, I often sit by the pond and listen to the frog chorus. In the morning, little lizards sun themselves on the verandah.

There are so many species, it would be impossible to see or recognize them all. I am amazed by, but will never fully understand, what is happening between them either. However, I am happy for the little I know — and I hope for additional insights. For in those hills I discover many marvellous relationships among different creatures. Is there a pattern among all of this biodiversity that can help me understand creation? Is it possible that I could know the Creator better, too?

As I sat on the verandah at "High Sycamore," I thought about the meaning of it all. Why did God make such abundance? Why was there so much diversity, so much *biodiversity*? What was the meaning of it all? What does this have to do with the six days of creation?

Thinking about Biodiversity

In recent years, much consideration and research has gone into studying biodiversity. In general, biodiversity studies have focused on conservation and how to preserve ecosystems. They have provided a whole new understanding and approach to saving endangered species. Instead of trying to save individual species, the approach now is to save intact ecosystems that are necessary for preserving and providing for endangered species — as well as for those not so endangered.

The word "biodiversity" was first used at a conference at the Smithsonian Institute in September 1986, and reported in the November 1986 edition of *Smithsonian Magazine*. The idea of biodiversity was understood much earlier by some ecologists, but it began to spread widely as a result of the conference.[1] Since then, it has been increasingly used and books have been written on the subject.[2] So, what is the idea of biodiversity?

"Biodiversity" obviously refers to plants, animals, and microbes, from bacteria to fungi, that collectively make up living systems — ecosystems. What are not so obvious are other meanings that have become attached to the word. It also refers to different populations of species, with their unique sets of genes and gene products.[3] Even more importantly, it includes the collective ecological services provided by those different species and populations working together for each other, keeping our planet healthy and suitable for life. Baskin describes the relationship this way: "It is the lavish array of organisms that we call "biodiversity," an intricately linked web of living things whose activities work in concert to make the earth a uniquely habitable planet."[4]

If I tried to completely list all ecological services, I would undoubtedly fail[5] and besides, it would be tedious for you. But a few examples may be helpful. We know plants and animals maintain relatively constant atmospheric levels of carbon dioxide[6] and oxygen through photosynthesis and respiration. Many decomposers keep soil fertile. Biodiversity services purify water, detoxify toxins, moderate climate, and pollinate flowers. All organisms provide habitats and niches for other creatures.

Some ecological relationships are so necessary that involved organisms could not survive without them. An example of this is the mutually beneficial relationship between plants and mycorrhizal fungi. As many as 90 percent of plant species interact with either generalized fungi that can service a variety of plants, or with others that are highly selective in the plants with which they interact.[7] Regardless, these fungi enable plants to obtain nutrients that would otherwise not be sufficiently available. Plants in turn provide carbohydrates for their fungi.

Several experiments[8] have been made to examine biodiversity.[9] Evidently highly biodiverse communities are more stable, more productive, have higher soil fertility, and are generally better off. Under stress, however, individual species populations may noticeably vary in size but, fortunately, redundant services appear to cover for immediate lacks. Nevertheless, when we look at the broad picture, higher diversity communities are more productive and more able to recover from stress.

As we look at the broad picture of biodiversity, it is clear that just as a body depends upon division of labor among cells, so an ecosystem depends upon division of labor provided by biodiversity. Just as there are important metabolic pathways in cells, so there are "ecochemical" pathways in ecosystems. The nitrogen cycle, among many possibilities, is an example of this. Different organisms, with different enzyme systems, are essential links in these ecochemical pathways.

Redundant Services

An interesting phenomenon in ecosystems is ecological services redundancy. This means that a service provided by one species may also be provided by other species. Some have suggested that redundancy may make some species unnecessary.[10] Research reveals that above a certain level of plant biodiversity, soil fertility or productivity did not increase, even when biodiversity continued to increase.[11] The "extra" biodiversity appeared redundant. Does this mean that some species really are expendable?

Since all plants generally contribute to both soil fertility and productivity, it is difficult to make a case for expendability based on these studies alone. What about other services provided by the same species? Are they not needed? As a result, ecologists have reportedly moved away from the species expendability position and may even refrain from using the word "redundancy."[12]

A single species may provide not just one, but several services, some of which may not be redundant. Consequently, with these variously overlapping and species-entwining redundancies, together with non-redundant services, it may not be possible to eliminate species with impunity after all.

Fundamentally, species making up an ecosystem need each other. As already seen, when under stress, populations of individual species may vary in size. Consequently, when one species is down, services it ordinarily provides will have to be provided by other species not as seriously affected. They cover for each other. Under different situations, of course, the roles may be reversed. Ecological backup is important and necessary for the long-range operation of ecosystems.

When we look at a species in terms of both the services it provides and those it requires, we are essentially referring to the "ecological niche," generally defined as the role of a species in its environment. Since no two occupied niches can be identical, or redundant, without one of the two species being competitively excluded,[13] it appears reasonable to say that two species cannot provide and require identical ecological services. There may be some overlap in services, however. When that happens, the niches of the two species may be compressed[14] and thereby avoid or reduce competition. Different niches could lead to changes in the species itself.

Ecological Resiliency

Ecosystems are dynamic! They can withstand a certain amount of abuse without ecological collapse. When one species becomes extinct, a few other species, but not *all* other species, become extinct.[15] Redundant systems prevent mass extermination. Lost services are provided by other species, as far as possible. Nevertheless, there is a limit to the abuse an ecosystem can withstand. Any loss weakens it. There is always a price to pay for environmental mistreatment. Continued species loss could eventually lead to ecosystem collapse, of course.

Two ecosystems may be functionally similar, but not identical in species biodiversity. Biodiversity is flexible and resilient. Those two ecosystems reflect available biodiversity. Opportunism must be taken into account when trying to understand differences that actually exist. Redundancy undoubtedly plays a part in ecosystem resiliency.

Species move into ecosystems when they can. Some species may not be found because they are not locally available. On the other hand, certain available propagules or offspring may not germinate, grow, or survive because necessary ecological services may not be available. When provided with those essential services, however, those species would be able to move into the ecosystem. The dynamic nature of ecosystems provides for making use of what species are available and able to function.

Biodiversity, redundancy, and resiliency permit an ecosystem to recover from severe damage and even ecosystem destruction. When this happens, the recovery is stepwise and may take a number of years. The process is called "ecological succession."

All of these necessary ecosystem qualities, in summary, allow ecosystems to function, to adapt, and to recover from injury.

Biodiversity and Creation

What does biodiversity tell us about creation? Does it tell us anything about the Creator? Does it have anything to say about why it was created? Does it support a six-day creation?

I believe there is a connection between biodiversity and creation, although I have seen no such connection made by other authors. All of the attention that I have seen has been directed toward the immediate problem of conservation. Without biodiversity and its ecochemical and ecophysical services, it is doubtful that ecosystems, or possibly even life itself, could exist. This much seems clear.

Behe noted complex biochemical relationships in cells and suggested design to explain their origin.[16] We tend to see the world through the "lenses" of our scientific disciplines. Thus Behe, a biochemist, understood cell complexity to result from design. If we jump to the ecological level, at the other end of the spectrum of life, our "ecology glasses" reveal unimaginable complexity there as well.

When we look broadly at the panorama of life and ecological relationships, we see that ecological complexity is built on layer upon layer of complexity, going all the way down through different hierarchical structural and organizational levels to the cell and even lower. Thus, if we think cytological complexity is impressive, what must we think when we realize the full scale of ecological complexity?

The biodiversity picture is still being developed. Some refer to biodiversity studies as an "emerging science."[17] Certainly there is much more to learn. It may not yet be possible to predict precisely what will happen when species are removed from an ecosystem, but we know an effect of some kind is certain. What has already been discovered, however, suggests that ecological relationships are essential. If biodiversity is as necessary for normal ecosystem operation as appears to be the case, it suggests that these services, and organisms providing them, had to have been simultaneously present right from the beginning. If these ecological interrelationships are really indispensable, then there is no easy evolutionary explanation. This suggests that ecology was designed.

The situation parallels what happened with the cell. As long as cells were visualized as mere sacks of nucleated protoplasm,[18] and little else, it was quite possible for many to be content with the assertion that it originated through natural processes, otherwise known as biochemical evolution! The development of the electron microscope and biochemistry changed all of that. Yet, the claim continues. Nevertheless, such a claim must now get by an overwhelming amount of information documenting an extremely high level of internal cell structure. Complexity of the cell is now just too daunting to flippantly assert biochemical evolution to explain it, unless you close your mind and press on blindly and boldly. It has now become quite a feat to think about cells originating through biochemical evolution. And if cells could not originate naturally, then nothing else could.

In the same way as with the cell, as long as ecology appeared to be only a loose collection of organisms without binding interrelationships, one could likewise think of it as possibly originating through natural processes. But now that ecosystems appear to be held together by essential and unbelievably complex biodiversity, about which information is steadily increasing, we have a dilemma similar to the one faced when the intricate structure of the cell was discovered. Since ecology is built upon so much underlying multispecies complexity, trying to explain the origin of ecology by chance events painfully stretches one's credulity.

Coevolution is often given as the way ecology came into existence. But, coevolution is defined as "joint evolution of two or more noninterbreeding species that have a close *ecological relationship*."[19] Note that ecological relationships had to precede coevolution. Consequently, coevolution appears to be no answer for understanding the origin of ecology.

I have no problem with two species finetuning an existing ecological relationship; I do have a problem with using coevolution to explain the origin of ecological services. That is an altogether different problem. Remember, we are talking about an essential multispecies integrated service system — an *entire* integrated system. There seems to be no adequate evolutionary way to explain this. How could multiple organisms have once lived independently of services they now require?

Systems of living things supporting each other, the *modus operandi* of biodiversity, is exactly what we would expect to find from the Creator who said, "Give, and it shall be given unto you" (Luke 6:38) and, "Freely ye have received, freely give" (Matt. 10:8). If this is the way heaven operates, would we not expect that it would also have been this way among creatures, including man, in the beginning? Sadly, in our fallen state, we have departed from this way of life. And what are the results?

> How long is the land to mourn And the vegetation of the countryside to wither? For the wickedness of those who dwell in it, Animals and birds have been snatched away (Jer. 12:4;NASB).

Nevertheless, we have hope:

> For the anxious longing of the *creation* waits eagerly for the revealing of the sons of God. . . . that the creation itself also will be set free from its slavery to corruption into the freedom of the glory of the children of God (Rom. 8:19–21).

Creation was said to be very good when it came from the Creator's hand, but ecosystems no longer function perfectly. They are degenerate. Scripture hints about original ecology, suggesting conditions that were far different from what we find today. It is hard to imagine ecology without death, for example. Nevertheless, that is exactly the picture painted in Scripture. Death and suffering came not only to man when he sinned, but to other creatures as well.

The woodland that I described at the beginning is a case in point. I can see it in the idealized way in which I described it, but there are problems there, too. Ticks and chiggers are abundant. For anyone not familiar with chiggers, they are tiny mites which may embed in your flesh, causing ugly raised and itching welts. Poison ivy is common, also. There are several species of venomous snakes.

None of these are what we would ideally expect. Where did these blights come from?

When humans sinned, it looks like they opened the "flood gates" of natural disaster. A global catastrophe ravaged earth's ecology. Genes were lost en masse, and mutations weakened those remaining. Degenerate environments, including degenerate occupants, stressed other degenerate inhabitants, which in turn reciprocated the stress, and so on. Some species disappeared, others adapted to new and trying conditions.

Predators and parasites developed as they and ecosystems became degenerate, and formerly abundant resources became scarce or were no longer available. Survivors turned to other sources for sustenance, including some not on the original menu. God predicted that thorns and thistles would result, as well as pain and death. Is this what God wanted? Was this punishment prescribed? No! But He foresaw it as an outcome of sin and life under Satan.

New species, as we now define species, developed from remnants of created "kinds." That is why species today tend to form similar species clusters — species of warblers, species of squirrels, species of roses, and so on. These similar species naturally provided similar, possibly even redundant, ecological services. On the other hand, as they adapted to new environments and niches, even those services could have become modified. It would be unsafe to suggest that, even within species clusters, there could be some expendable species.

Species clusters may help to explain some redundancy, but other species were undoubtedly made with redundant ecological skills. Some services may have been so widely needed that no single species would have been able to sufficiently provide it. Recycling of carbon and oxygen by plants and animals are examples of this.

Original created ecology must have been quite different from what we find now, but we can only speculate about details. The amazing thing about ecosystems today is that despite all they have suffered, they still continue to function. Redundant services, regardless of their original purpose, must play a part in this. We must appreciate the roles of both biodiversity and redundant services, even in the beginning, and as enabling forces in ecosystem resiliency and survival today.

Concluding Thoughts

The picture that emerges is one of ecosystems that do not now function optimally, but which still allow a glimpse of how things might have been. We can see that just as biodiversity is vital now, so it must also have been vital in the beginning. If this is so, then entire ecosystems, together with their ecological skills and backup systems, would have of necessity been present as well.

It appears that life on earth actually makes life on earth possible. That is, life on earth makes it possible for life on earth to continue. This is not saying that life *made* (past tense) life on earth exist, of course. It is saying that the whole system had to be present for *life to go on existing*. If this is true, there is no room for gradually unfolding ecology. Is that overstating the case? Although life is a gift of the Creator, He evidently gave His creatures important roles by which they were to contribute to each other.

Biodiversity, as well as Scripture, tells us that God placed humans in nature. We need the services that are there for us. Our services are needed as well. We *must* contribute *together* to the safe and smooth operation of nature because it nurtures all of us. Is this not what the Creator meant when He told man to tend and keep the garden? This is the way of heaven — to give and to receive without worry — as taught us by Jesus himself.

Biodiversity is a powerful testimony about the Creator that confirms Romans 1:20: "From the creation of the world, God's invisible qualities, his eternal power and divine nature have been clearly observed in what he made."

What does all this tell us about the six days during which God put ecosystems together? Biodiversity does not specify a six-day creation, it is not that finely focused, but it strongly supports such a possibility. It suggests that ecosystems were assembled during a very short time indeed. Otherwise, life could have failed for lack of mutually benefiting multi-species ecological services that are now requirements. Biodiversity consequently suggests that ecology was created.

Interestingly, much scientific energy has been devoted toward determining the age of earth, but little has been expended to investigate a six-day or even a short-duration creation. In fact, what of a scientific nature could be done to research this? Biodiversity studies, involving cross-species ecological integration, may be among the few scientific pursuits that have the potential for supporting what Scripture *emphatically* states:

> In six days the LORD made the heavens and the earth (Exod. 20:11).

This is the view from "High Sycamore."

Notes

1 The idea of biodiversity under different terminology had been understood for a longer period of time. For example, Paul and Anne Ehrlich had written about the importance of species in a book about the impact of extinction: *Extinction: The Causes and Consequences of the Disappearance of Species* (New York: Random House, 1981).

2 A book on the subject of biodiversity that I have read with much pleasure

and learning, and one I recommend is: Yvonne Baskin, *The Work Of Nature; How the Diversity of Life Sustains Us* (Washington, DC: Island Press, 1997).

3 C. Mlot, "Population Diversity Crowds The Ark," *Science News*, Vol. 152, Issue 17, 10/25/97, p. 260.

4 Baskin, *The Work of Nature*, p. 3.

5 The list of specific ecological services is certainly incomplete at this time.

6 Carbon dioxide has been rising for some years as a result of human activity. Until recently, the amount of CO_2 produced equalled the amount of CO_2 used. Some have asserted that humans only contribute around 5% of the total CO_2 produced, inferring that human influence in global warming is inconsequential. It turns out, however, that the 5% equals 100% of the amount of CO_2 above that needed to maintain equilibrium. It is the total amount contributing to global warming.

7 Baskin, *The Work of Nature*, p. 114.

8 Baskin's *The Work Of Nature* contains numerous examples of biodiversity services, aside from deliberate experimental work. Many discoveries have been made as a result of ecological blunders.

9 Several research reports are: J.J. Ewel *et al.*, "Tropical Soil Fertility Changes Under Monoculture and Successional Communities of Different Structure," *Ecological Applications* 1(3) (1991), p. 289–302; Shahid Naeem et al, "Declining Biodiversity Can Alter the Performance of Ecosystems," *Nature*, Vol. 368 (April 21, 1994), p. 734–737; and D. Tilman, "Biodiversity: Populations and Stability," *Ecology*, Vol. 77 (1996), p. 350–363.

10 B.H. Walker, "Biodiversity and Ecological Redundancy," *Conservation Biology*, 6: 1 (1992), p. 8–23.

11 See the papers by Ewel, Naeem, and Tilman cited in endnote 9.

12 Baskin, *The Work of Nature*, p 20.

13 This is in reference to Gause's principle, which one may find described in Robert Leo Smith, *Elements of Ecology*, 3rd edition (New York: HarperCollins), p. 219.

14 A compressed niche is generally called the "realized niche," while the niche that is not competitively compressed is the "potential" niche.

15 Peter Raven of the Missouri Botanical Garden, as reported by Baskin, *The Work of Nature*, p. 36–37, noted that when a plant becomes extinct, 10 to 30 others subsequently become extinct, also.

16 Michael Behe, *Darwin's Black Box: The Biochemical Challenge to Evolution* (New York: Free Press, 1996).

17 Baskin, *The Work of Nature*, p. 6.

18 Although the nucleus was easily observed, its internal complexity was not. Nor was its function understood.

19 Smith, *Elements of Ecology*, p. G–3 (see endnote 13).

jonathan d. sarfati

Physical Chemistry

6

Dr. Sarfati is a research scientist for Answers in Genesis in Australia. He holds a B.S. (Hons) in chemistry and a Ph.D. in physical chemistry from Victoria University of Wellington, New Zealand. Dr. Sarfati is a former New Zealand Chess Champion and represented New Zealand at the World Junior Championships and in three chess olympiads.

Science and Bias

Many people have the belief that "science" has proven the earth to be billions of years old, and that every living thing descended via evolutionary processes from a single cell, which itself is the result of a chance combination of chemicals. However, science deals with repeatable observations in the *present*, while evolution/long-age ideas are based on *assumptions* from *outside* science about the unobservable *past*. Facts do *not* speak for themselves — they must be interpreted according to a framework. It is not a case of religion/creation/subjectivity versus science/evolution/objectivity. Rather, it is the biases of the religions of Christianity and of humanism *interpreting* the *same* facts in diametrically opposite ways.

The framework behind the evolutionists' interpretation is *naturalism/uniformitarianism*: things made themselves; no divine intervention has happened; and God, if He even exists, has not revealed to us knowledge about the past. This is precisely what the chief apostle Peter prophesied about the "scoffers" in "the last days" — they claim "everything goes on as it has since the beginning of creation" (2 Pet. 3:4). Peter reveals the huge flaw of the uniformitarian scoffers: they are "willingly ignorant" of special creation by God, and of a cataclysmic globe-covering (and fossil-forming) flood.

The thinking inherent in the evolutionary mindset is illustrated by the following statement by Richard Lewontin, a geneticist and leading evolution promoter. It illustrates the implicit philosophical bias against Genesis creation, regardless of whether or not the facts support it.

> We take the side of science *in spite* of the patent absurdity of some of its constructs, *in spite* of its failure to fulfil many of its extravagant promises of health and life, *in spite* of the tolerance of the scientific community for unsubstantiated just-so stories, because we have a prior commitment, a commitment to materialism. It is not that the methods and institutions of science somehow compel us to accept a material explanation of the phenomenal world, but, on the contrary, that we are forced by our *a priori* adherence to material causes to create an apparatus of investigation and a set of concepts that produce material explanations, no matter how counter-intuitive, no matter how mystifying to the uninitiated. Moreover, that materialism is an absolute, for we cannot allow a Divine Foot in the door.[1]

Lewontin is typical of many evolutionary propagandists. Another good example is the National Academy of Science (NAS) in the

USA, which recently produced a guidebook for U.S. public school teachers, *Teaching about Evolution and the Nature of Science.*[2] A recent survey published in the leading science journal *Nature* conclusively showed that the National Academy of Science is anti-God to the core.[3] A survey of all 517 NAS members in biological and physical sciences resulted in just over half responding. Of those, 72.2 percent were overtly atheistic, 20.8 percent were agnostic, and only 7.0 percent believed in a personal God. Belief in God and immortality was lowest among biologists. The unbelief is far higher than the percentage among scientists in general, or in the whole U.S. population.

Commenting on the self-professed religious neutrality of *Teaching about Evolution and the Nature of Science* and the NAS, the surveyors comment:

> NAS President Bruce Alberts said: "There are many outstanding members of this academy who are very religious people, people who believe in evolution, many of them biologists." Our research suggests otherwise.

This atheistic bias is ironic, because the whole basis for modern science depends on the assumption that the universe was made by a rational Creator. Dr. Stanley Jaki has documented how the scientific method was stillborn in all cultures apart from the Judeo-Christian culture of Europe.[4] An orderly universe makes perfect sense if it was made by an orderly Creator. But if there is no Creator, or if Zeus and his gang were in charge, why should there be any order at all? No wonder that most branches of modern science were founded by believers in *creation*. The list of creationist scientists is impressive.[5]

C.S. Lewis also pointed out that even our ability to reason would be called into question if atheistic evolution were true:

If the solar system was brought about by an accidental collision, then the appearance of organic life on this planet was also an accident, and the whole evolution of man was an accident, too. If so, then all our thought processes are mere accidents — the accidental by-product of the movement of atoms. And this holds for the materialists' and astronomers' as well as for anyone else's. But if their thoughts — i.e., of Materialism and Astronomy — are merely accidental by-products, why should we believe them to be true? I see no reason for believing that one accident should be able to give a correct account of all the other accidents.[6]

The Bible claims to be the written Word of God, completely authoritative on everything it teaches (2 Tim. 3:15–17). There is excellent supporting evidence from archaeology, science, fulfilled prophecy, and the claims of Jesus Christ.

Scientific Evidence for Design

There is also evidence from nature. Romans 1:20 says, "For since the creation of the world God's invisible qualities — his eternal power and divine nature — have been clearly seen, being understood from what has been made, so that men are without excuse."

Upon seeing the wonderful works of design in this world, I believe that the intellectually honest person must conclude that they were made by a great designer. This is so, even though we live in a sin-cursed world (Gen. 3:16–19; Rom. 8:20–23), where many designs are no longer benevolent and others have deteriorated because of mutations. But even a fallen design is still a design.

And there are plenty of structures that still retain their physical perfection. Let me list a few of them:

- The dolphin's sonar system is so precise that it's the envy of the U.S. Navy. It can detect a fish the size of a golf ball 230 feet (70 m) away. It took an expert in chaos theory to show that the dolphin's "click" pattern is mathematically designed to give the best information.[7]

- This sonar system includes the "melon," a sound lens — a sophisticated structure designed to focus the emitted sound waves into a beam which the dolphin can direct where it likes. This sound lens depends on the fact that different lipids (fatty compounds) bend the ultrasonic sound waves travelling through them in different ways. The different lipids have to be arranged in the right shape and sequence in order to focus the returning sound echoes. Each separate lipid is unique and different from normal blubber lipids, and is made by a complicated chemical process, requiring a number of different enzymes.[8]

- Insect flight requires complicated movements to generate the patterns of vortices needed for lift. It took a sophisticated robot to simulate the motion.[9]

- Even the simplest self-reproducing organism contains encyclopedic quantities of complex, specific information. *Mycoplasma genitalium* has the smallest known genome of any free-living organism, containing 482 genes comprising 580,000 base pairs.[10] As for humans, the atheistic evolutionist Richard Dawkins admits, "There is enough information capacity in a single human cell to store the *Encyclopædia Britannica*, all 30 volumes of it, three or four times over."[11]

- Even more amazingly, living things have by far the most compact information storage/retrieval system known. To illustrate further, the amount of information that could be stored in a pinhead's volume of DNA is staggering. It is the equivalent information content of a pile of paperback books 500 times as tall as the distance from earth to the moon, each with a different, yet specific, content.[12]

- The genetic information cannot be translated except with many different enzymes, which are themselves encoded. So the code cannot be translated except via products of translation, a vicious circle that ties evolutionary origin-of-life theories in knots. These include double-sieve enzymes to make sure the right amino acid is linked to the right tRNA molecule. One sieve rejects amino acids too large, while the other rejects those too small.[13]

- The genetic code that is almost universal to life on earth is about the best possible for protecting against errors.[14]

- The genetic code also has vital editing machinery that is itself encoded in the DNA. This shows that the system was fully functional from the beginning — another vicious circle for evolutionists.

- Yet another vicious circle, and there are many more, is that the enzymes that make the amino acid histidine themselves contain histidine.

- There are complex rotary motors in living organisms. One type drives the flagellum of a bacterium. The vital enzyme that makes ATP, the "energy currency" of life, is a motor that can change gears, yet is so tiny that 10^{17} could fit inside a pinhead's volume.[15]

- The complex compound eyes of some types of trilobites,

extinct and supposedly "primitive" invertebrates, were amazingly designed. They comprised tubes that each pointed in a different direction, and had special lenses that focused light from any distance. The required lens design comprised a layer of calcite on top of a layer of chitin — materials with precisely the right refractive indices — and a wavy boundary between them of a precise mathematical shape.[16] The designer of these eyes is a master physicist, who applied what we now know as the physical laws of Fermat's principle of least time, Snell's law of refraction, Abbé's sine law, and birefringent optics.

- Lobster eyes are unique in being modelled on a perfect square with precise geometrical relationships of the units. NASA x-ray telescopes copied this design.[17]

- From my own specialist field of vibrational spectroscopy: there is good evidence that our chemical-detecting sense (smell) works on the same quantum mechanical principles.[18]

Chemical Evolutionary Theories Versus the Facts of Chemistry

Evolutionists believe that all life came from a chemical soup. However, while studying for my chemistry degree, I came across many well-known chemical laws that refute such "chemical evolution" theories.[19] For example:

- Life requires many *polymers*, large molecules built from many simple *monomers*. Polymerization requires *bifunctional* monomers (i.e., they combine with two others), and is stopped by a small fraction of *unifunctional* monomers (that can combine with only one other, thus blocking one end of the growing chain). All "prebiotic simulation" experiments produce *five times more* unifunctional molecules than bifunctional molecules.

- Many of life's chemicals come in two forms, "left-handed" and "right-handed." Life requires polymers with all building blocks having the same "handedness" (*homochirality*) — proteins have only "left-handed" amino acids, while DNA and RNA have only "right-handed" sugars. Living things have special molecular machinery to produce homochirality. But ordinary undirected chemistry, as in the hypothetical primordial soup, would produce equal mixtures of left- and right-handed molecules, called *racemates*. Racemic polypeptides could not form the specific shapes required for enzymes; rather, they would have the side chains sticking randomly. Also, a wrong-handed amino acid disrupts the stabilising a-helix in proteins. DNA could not be stabilized in a helix if even a small proportion of the wrong-handed form was present, so it could not form long chains. This means it could not store much information, so it could not support life.[20] A small fraction of wrong-handed molecules terminates RNA replication.[21] A recent world conference on "The Origin of Homochirality and Life" made it clear that the origin of this handedness is a complete mystery to evolutionists.[22]

- The chemistry goes in the wrong direction! Polymerization reactions *release* water, so by the well-known *law of mass action*, excess water *breaks up* polymers.[23] The long ages postulated by evolutionists simply make the problem worse, because there is more time for water's destructive effects to occur. While living cells have many ingenious repair mechanisms, DNA cannot last very long in water outside a cell.[24] Condensing agents (water absorbing chemicals) require acidic conditions and they could not accumulate in water. Heating to evaporate water tends to destroy some vital amino acids, racemize all the chiral amino acids, and requires geologically unrealistic conditions. Besides, heating amino acids with other gunk inevitably present in the hypothetical primordial soup would destroy them. A recent article in *New Scientist* also described the instability of polymers in water as a "headache" for researchers working on evolutionary ideas on the origin of life.[25] It also showed its materialistic bias by saying this was not "good news." But the real bad news is the faith in evolution (everything made itself), which overrides objective science.

- Many of the important biochemicals would destroy each other. Living organisms are well-structured to avoid this, but the "primordial soup" would not be. Sometimes these wrong reactions occur after a cell is damaged, for example, the browning of foodstuffs. This is often caused by a reaction between sugars and amino acids. Yet evolution requires these chemicals to form proteins and nucleic acids respectively, rather than destroy each other as per real chemistry.

- Fatty acids are necessary for cell membranes, and phosphate is necessary for DNA, RNA, ATP, and many other important vital molecules of life. But abundant calcium ions in the ocean would precipitate fatty acids and phosphate, making them unavailable for chemical evolution. This principle explains why washing with soap in hard water is so difficult.

I believe in a recent creation in six consecutive normal days because the only eyewitness tells us this is what He did, and He has shown that He should be trusted. He also makes it clear that no death (of the *nephesh* animals) occurred before Adam's. While this requires faith, it is a faith amply supported by science, as I can confirm from my own specialist field.

Notes

1 Richard Lewontin, "Billions and Billions of Demons," *The New York Review*, January 9, 1997, p. 31.

2 I have written a detailed rebuttal, *Refuting Evolution* (Green Forest, AR: Master Books, Inc., 1999).

3 E.J. Larson and L. Witham, "Leading Scientists Still Reject God," *Nature*, 394(6691):313, July 23, 1998. The sole criterion for being classified as a "leading" or "greater" scientist was membership of the NAS.

4 Stanley L. Jaki, *Science and Creation* (Edinburgh, Scotland: Scottish Academic Press, 1974).

5 A. Lamont, *21 Great Scientists Who Believed the Bible* (Australia: Creation Science Foundation, 1995), p. 120–131; Henry M. Morris, *Men of Science — Men of God* (Green Forest, AR: Master Books, 1982).

6 C.S. Lewis, *God in the Dock* (Grand Rapids, MI: Wm. B. Eerdmans Pub. Co., 1970), p. 52–53.

7 R. Howlett, "Flipper's Secret," *New Scientist*, 154(2088):34–39, June 28, 1997.

8 U. Varanasi, H.R. Feldman, and D.C. Malins, "Molecular Basis for Formation of Lipid Sound Lens in Echolocating Cetaceans," *Nature*, 255(5506):340–343, May 22, 1975.

9 M. Brookes, "On a Wing and a Vortex," *New Scientist*, 156(2103):24–27, Oct. 11, 1997.

10 C.M. Fraser et al., "The Minimal Gene Complement of *Mycoplasma genitalium*," *Science*, 270(5235):397–403, October 20, 1995; perspective by A. Goffeau, "Life with 482 Genes," same issue, p. 445–446.

11 Richard Dawkins, *The Blind Watchmaker: Why the Evidence of Evolution Reveals a Universe without Design*, (New York: W.W. Norton & Company, 1986).

12 W. Gitt, see "Dazzling Design in Miniature," *Creation Ex Nihilo*, 20(1):6, December 1997–February 1998.

13 Osamu Nureki et al., "Enzyme Structure with Two Catalytic Sites for Double-sieve Selection of Substrate," *Science*, 280(5363):578–82, April 24, 1998; perspective by A.R. Fersht, "Sieves in Sequence," same issue, p. 541.

14 J. Knight, "Top Translator," *New Scientist*, 158(2130):15, April 18, 1998.

15 H. Noji et al., "Direct Observation of the Rotation of F1-ATPase," *Nature* 386(6622):28–33, March 20, 1997; perspective in the same issue by S. Block, "Real Engines of Creation," p. 217–219; J.D. Sarfati, "Design in Living Organisms: Motors," *Creation Ex Nihilo Technical Journal*, 12(1): 3–5, 1998.

16 K. Towe, "Trilobite Eyes: Calcified Lenses," *Science*, 179:1007–11, March 9, 1973.

17 M. Chown, "X-ray Lens Brings Finer Chips into Focus," *New Scientist*, 151(2037):18, July 6, 1996.

18 L. Turin, "A Spectroscopic Mechanism for Primary Olfactory Reception," *Chemical Senses* 21:773, 1996; cited in S. Hill, "Sniff 'n' Shake," *New Scientist*, 157(2115):34–37, January 3, 1998. See also J.D. Sarfati, "Olfactory Design: Smell and Spectroscopy," *Creation Ex Nihilo Technical Journal*, 12(2):137–8, 1998.

19 See also Charles B. Thaxton, Walter L. Bradley, and Roger L. Olsen, *The Mystery of Life's Origin* (New York: Philosophical Library Inc., 1984).

20 W. Thiemann, ed., *International Symposium on Generation & Amplification of Asymmetry in Chemical Systems* (Germany: Jülich, 1973), p. 32–33; cited in: A.E. Wilder-Smith, *The Natural Sciences Know Nothing of Evolution* (Green Forest, AR: Master Books, Inc., 1981).

21 G.F. Joyce, G.M. Visser, C.A.A. van Boeckel, J.H. van Boom, L.E. Orgel, and J. van Westrenen, "Chiral Selection in Poly(C)-directed Synthesis of Oligo(G)," *Nature*, 310:602–4, 1984.

22 J. Cohen, "Getting All Turned Around Over the Origins of Life on Earth," *Science*, 267:1265–66, 1995.

23 Jonathan D. Sarfati, "The Origin of Life: The Polymerization Problem," *Creation Ex Nihilo Technical Journal*, (12:3), p. 281–284, 1998.

24 T. Lindahl, "Instability and Decay of the Primary Structure of DNA," *Nature*, 362(6422):709–715, 1993.

25 R. Matthews, "Wacky Water," *New Scientist*, 154(2087):40–43, June 21, 1997.

ariel a. roth

Biology

Dr. Roth is a former director of the Geoscience Research Institute in Loma Linda, California. He holds a B.A. in biology from Pacific Union College and an M.S. in biology and a Ph.D. in biology from the University of Michigan. His research has been supported by U.S. government agencies. During his career he held numerous university positions, including professor of biology and chairman, Loma Linda University. During the latter appointment, Dr. Roth directed a university team for underwater research on coral, which was sponsored by the U.S. National Oceanic and Atmospheric Administration. He has authored over 140 articles on origins issues and for 23 years edited the journal *ORIGINS*.

It is sometimes suggested that belief in creation is a matter of faith, while science, which usually endorses evolution, is considered to be more in the realm of reason. While concepts of faith and reason are different to evaluate and quantify[1] we generally recognize that we have to exercise a degree of faith to believe in anything, be it science, evolution, creation, or the Bible. However, there are many good reasons to believe in creation by God in six days. In fact, it seems to me that it takes a greater degree of blind faith (where there is no evidence) to believe in evolution than in the creation model of the Bible. The same problem applies to intermediate views between evolution and creation, such as theistic evolution or progressive creation, which have little support from either the data of nature or the Bible.[2]

The Origin of Life

Probably the most baffling problem which evolution faces is the question of the origin of life. How could living organisms which, even in their simplest forms, are extremely complex arise by themselves? The severity of the problem is well acknowledged by many competent scientists and need not be dwelt upon here.

The Problem of Complexity

The presence of complexity — interdependent parts that do not function unless other parts are also present — poses another major problem for evolution. For instance, a muscle is useless without a nerve going to the muscle to direct its contracting activity. But both the muscle and the nerve are useless without a complicated control mechanism in the brain to direct the contracting activity of the muscle and correlate its activity with that of other muscles. Without these three essential components, we have only useless parts. In a process of gradual evolutionary changes, how does complexity evolve?

Interdependent parts, which represent most of the components of living organisms, would not be expected from random, undirected changes (mutations) as is proposed for evolutionary advancement. How could these develop without the foresight of a plan for a working system? Can order arise from the turmoil of mixed-up, undirected changes? For complicated organs that involve many necessary changes, the chances are implausibly small.

Without the foresight of a plan, we would expect that the random evolutionary changes would attempt all kinds of useless combinations of parts while trying to provide for a successful evolutionary advancement. Yet as we look at living organisms over the world, we do not seem to see any of these random combinations. In nature, it appears that we are dealing largely, if not exclusively, with purposeful parts. Furthermore, if evolution is a real ongoing process, why don't we find new developing complex organs in organisms that lack them? We would expect to find developing legs, eyes, livers, and new unknown kinds of organs, providing for evolutionary advancement in organisms that lacked desirable advantages. This absence is a serious indictment against any proposed undirected evolutionary process, and favors the concept that what we see represents the work of an intelligent Creator.

The simple example of a muscle, mentioned above, pales into insignificance when we consider more complicated organs such as the eye or the brain. These contain many interdependent systems composed of parts that would be useless without the presence of all the other necessary parts. In these systems, nothing works until all the necessary components are present and working. The eye has an automatic focusing system that adjusts the lens so as to permit us to clearly see close and distant objects. We do not fully understand how it works, but a part of the brain analyzes data from the eye and controls the muscles in the eye that change the shape of the lens. The system that controls the size of the pupil so as to adjust to light intensity and to reduce spherical lens aberration also illustrates interdependent parts. Then there are the 100,000,000 light-sensitive cells in the human eye that send information to the brain through some 1,000,000 nerve fibers of the optic nerve. In the brain this information is sorted into various components such as color, movement, form, and depth. It is then analyzed and combined into an intelligible picture. This involves an extremely complex array of interdependent parts.

But the visual process is only part of our complex brains, which contain some 100,000,000,000 nerve cells connected by some 400,000 kilometers of nerve fibres. It is estimated that there are around 100,000,000,000,000 connections between nerve cells in the human brain. That we can think straight (we hope most of us do!) is a witness to a marvellous ordered complex of interdependent parts that challenges suggestions of an origin by random evolutionary changes. How could such complicated organs develop by an unplanned process?

The Search for an Evolutionary Mechanism

Movements of all kinds of things in nature tend to mix things up, be they molecules, huge boulders, or polluting substances poured into the ocean. This inexorable tendency runs counter to evolution, where organisms are supposed to have become more and more organized, from disorganized components, as the complexities of organisms evolved. How did evolution from simple to complex counter the tendency towards randomness that is so prevalent in nature? For two centuries evolutionists have been searching for a mechanism that would explain the origin of complexity, but so far this has been a virtually futile search.

At the beginning of the 19th century, the French naturalist Lamarck proposed that usage of an organ-caused evolutionary advancement, such as a neck becoming longer due to usage. His views have been largely rejected. About half a century later, Charles Darwin in England proposed a system of natural selection. In this process very small variations between organisms would be subject to the competition between organisms. This would result in the survival of the more advanced forms, while the weaker ones would be eliminated. Over long periods of time, this process would gradually evolve the advanced forms of life on earth.

While Darwin's model of natural selection is the one usually presented in basic textbooks of biology, it has been much criticized recently for a variety of reasons. It has a fatal flaw when it comes to the question of the gradual development of biological systems with interdependent parts, and this is the case for most if not all biological systems. The problem is that the very system of natural selection which Darwin proposed will tend to eliminate the interdependent parts of complex systems as these systems develop. The parts do not function until all the interdependent parts are present and the system works and provides some survival value to the organism. These non-functioning parts will tend to be eliminated by a natural selection process that should give preference to organisms that are not encumbered with extra useless parts. For instance, in our simple example of an evolving muscle-nerve-control interdependent system: if we are at the stage where we have evolved only a muscle, that muscle would be a useless encumbrance until the nerve and control mechanism have evolved. Until that time, natural selection would tend to eliminate those organisms with non-functioning parts of developing interdependent systems, and thus would interfere with evolutionary progress.

Half a century after Darwin proposed his views, the Dutch biologist de Vries vigorously challenged the idea that the small variations proposed by Darwin would have any significant evolutionary effect. He proposed much larger changes, called mutations. Unfortunately, his prime example, the dwarfing of the evening primrose plant around Amsterdam, turned out to be only the recombination of traits already present in the plants and not a new mutation. The same applies to the most commonly used example of evolution: the darkening of the English peppered moth. This darkening protected the moths from predators by making them less visible as the environment darkened during the Industrial Revolution. The moth has again becoming lighter as the environment has become lighter. These changes, which are sometimes called mutations,[3] are now acknowledged as representing only a fluctuation in different kinds of genes already present, and as such do not represent the novel changes of a real mutation.[4] However mutations, which represent more or less permanent genetic changes, were soon found in fruit flies and other organisms. But mutations are not a great breakthrough for evolution. They are almost always detrimental, and as such are more representative of a mechanism for degeneration than for advancement. One useful mutation out of a thousand is being generous to evolution.

In the middle of the 20th century, leading evolutionists proposed the "modern synthesis." Hailed as the final evolutionary model, it incorporated Darwin's natural selection, de Vries' mutations, and studies in population genetics. At the same time, other evolutionists were calling for much larger sudden changes than those noted for mutations.

These larger changes were needed because of major gaps between groups of organisms in assumed evolutionary lineages, as seen in the fossil record, and also because of the inadequacy of the survival value of small evolutionary changes while developing complex systems with interdependent parts.[5] The term "hopeful monster" was suggested for these proposed suddenly appearing new forms. But they would need matching mates to be able to breed with, and as one critic commented, "Who will breed with a monster, hopeful or otherwise?"[6]

The modern synthesis did not remain as the dominant evolutionary mechanism for very long, although a number of leading evolutionists still defend the model. One evolutionist comments, "And today the modern synthesis — neo-Darwinism — is not a theory, but a range of opinions which, each in its own way, tries to overcome the difficulties presented by the world of facts."[7] We are now in a period of diverse evolutionary opinions. A variety of new ideas and controversies have appeared. They revolve around such questions as: (1) Can one really identify the evolutionary relationships of organisms? (2) Are evolutionary changes gradual or sudden? (3) Is natural selection important to the evolutionary process? (4) How does complexity evolve without the advantage of foresight? Computer programs attempting to answer this have been only remotely related to the complexity of the real biological world. Many scientists who do not believe in creation are criticizing the evolutionary model.[8]

We are thus faced with the fact that after two centuries of conjecture, a workable mechanism for evolution has not been found.[9] While the perseverance of evolutionists is commendable, it would seem that by now it is time for science to give serious consideration to other alternatives of origins, such as creation.

The Evidence from the Fossils

The fossils which represent past life on the earth should have much to say about how that life originated. Some consider the fossil record that we find in the rock layers of the earth to be the strongest evidence for evolution, because there is an increase from simple to complex, as one ascends through the rock layers. However, if these layers were laid down by the great flood described in the Bible, one would also expect some sort of ascending complexity as the flood gradually destroyed the biological realms of the world that existed before it. On our present earth, we have simple life in the deep rocks, more complex life in the oceans and the most complex on land. Destruction of these realms by rising flood activity would result in a general increase in complexity.[10] More important to the question of origins are two aspects of the fossil record that pose serious problems for the evolutionary scenario. One is the great scarcity of intermediate forms, the other is the lack of geologic time for the major evolutionary changes postulated.

If evolution has proceeded over the eons of time postulated, we should expect a great number of intermediates between the major types of organisms, but we can scarcely find any. Charles Darwin was fully aware of the problem and openly admitted to it in his *Origin of Species*, stating, "Why then is not every geological formation and every stratum full of such intermediate links? Geology assuredly does not reveal any such finely graduated organic chain; and this, perhaps, is the most obvious and gravest objection that can be urged against my theory."[11] Darwin then attributed the problem to the "extreme imperfection" of the fossil record. We have found millions of fossils since Darwin's time, and the lack of intermediates remains as a major problem for evolution. The paleontologist David B. Kitts,[12] at the University of Oklahoma, points out, "Despite the bright promise that paleontology provides a means of 'seeing' evolution, it has presented some nasty difficulties for evolutionists, the most notorious of which is the presence of 'gaps' in the fossil record. Evolution requires intermediate forms between species and paleontology does not provide them." A very few missing links, like *Archaeopteryx*, which is considered to be intermediate between reptiles and birds, have been described, but these few examples do little to satisfy the many thousands expected there.

Some evolutionists have postulated that evolution proceeds by occasional rapid jumps (punctuated equilibria[13]), but these small jumps do not solve the problem at all. The problem for evolution is that it is between the major groups of plants and animals (phyla and divisions) that we would expect the greatest number of intermediates, and this is precisely where these intermediates are virtually absent. Any gradual process would be expected to leave all kinds of fossils between major groups as major changes evolve. It does not appear that evolution has taken place.

As one examines the details of the fossil record, it soon becomes apparent that if evolution took place, it had to proceed at a highly erratic rate of change. The model of a slow, gradually advancing evolutionary process is not supported by the fossil record as evolutionists interpret it. For instance, the simplest forms of life are assumed to have evolved around 3,500 million years ago. Yet almost 3,000 million years later, the fossil record shows little evidence of any evolutionary advancement. We are still virtually in the one-cell stage of life forms for the first 5/6 of evolutionary time. Then less than 100 million years later (1/35 of evolutionary time), virtually all the animal phyla have evolved. Some evolutionists suggest only 5–10 million years (1/350 of evolutionary time) for most of this.[14]

Evolutionists refer to this very brief period for the evolution of most animal phyla as the "Cambrian explosion." Samuel Bowring of the Massachusetts Institute of Technology comments, "And what I like to ask my biologist friends is: How fast can evolution get before they start feeling uncomfortable?"[15] The phenomenon of the Cambrian explosion fits remarkably well with a model of the biblical flood which postulates that this part of the fossil record represents the level of the seas before the flood where most of the animal phyla would be expected. Above the Cambrian explosion we have other smaller "explosions." For instance, evolutionists propose that most mammalian orders evolved in a mere 12 million years and living orders of birds in 5–10 million years. The fossil record as interpreted by evolutionists shows that the thousands of millions of years proposed for advancement are not there. Evolution needs all the time it can get, and the improbabilities it faces indicate that geologic time is far too short to accommodate these advancements. The rapid rates of evolution that would be required to accommodate the fossil record significantly reduce that time and accentuate even more the improbability problem of evolution.

The Time Questions

One of the most significant differences between creation and evolution is the question of the length of time life has been on earth. While evolution proposes that life has been evolving for thousands of millions of years, creation suggests that God created the various forms of life in six days a few thousand years ago. In the creation model the Great Flood described in the Bible provides the explanation for the fossil layers, while evolution suggests these were formed over eons of time. It is of interest that the recent trends in geological thinking favoring major rapid changes (catastrophism) provide interpretations that fit well with the biblical flood. However, geology is not moving toward a biblical interpretation. Nevertheless, the thousands of millions of years proposed for laying down of the fossil-bearing sedimentary layers of earth raise a number of interesting questions that challenge the long geologic ages suggested by current scientific interpretations.[16] Examples follow.

Animals require plants for food in order to survive. Yet in several of our important geologic formations we find good evidence for the animals, but little or no evidence for the plants necessary to support the animals. The fossil assemblages found represent incomplete ecosystems. How did the animals survive for the millions of years postulated for the deposition of these formations without adequate food? Examples include: (1) The *Protoceratops* dinosaur-bearing layers of the Gobi Desert of Mongolia, where the paucity of plants is considered "baffling."[17] (2) The Coconino Sandstone of the southwestern United States, which has many hundreds of good animal trackways, but no plants. (3) The important dinosaur-bearing Morrison Formation of the western United States, where "identifiable plant fossils are practically non-existent."[18] What did these behemoths eat as they evolved over the millions of years? It is estimated that a large dinosaur would eat 3½ tons of vegetation in one day. A more plausible scenario for these deposits is that they represent layers laid down rapidly during the biblical flood, with the waters of the flood sorting the organisms into various deposits, the plants forming some of our huge coal deposits.

When we look at our present earth, it appears that geologic changes are very slow. On the other hand, the creation scenario proposes very rapid changes during the biblical flood. It turns out that even if we ignore the flood, the relatively slow geologic processes we now observe are actually so fast that they challenge the thousands of millions of years proposed for the development of life on earth, as suggested for evolutionary processes.[19] As an example, the present rate of erosion of our continents by rain and consequent rivers into the ocean is so rapid that we would expect the continents to be eroded down to sea level in about 10 million years. Why are our continents still here if they are thousands of millions of years old? A number of geologists have alluded to this problem.[20] Even after correcting for man's agricultural activities, which hasten erosion, the rate is so fast that our continents could have been eroded to sea level over 100 times (if they could be revived) in a conservative postulated age of 2,500 million years for the continents. Renewal of the continents from below is sometimes proposed to resolve the dilemma. This does not seem to be a solution, since the geologic column which contains very ancient layers is still well represented on the continents, and we don't seem to have completed even one full cycle of continent erosion and uplift.

You are probably familiar with the usually flat-like sedimentary layers (strata) that are widespread over the surface of the earth. The Grand Canyon in Arizona exposes unusually good examples. What we are seldom aware of is that often between major sedimentary units there are gaps where, according to the standard geologic time scale, often scores to hundreds of millions of years of deposits are missing. A gap is recognized because there are layers representing these assumed millions of years elsewhere on the earth. They are identified by comparing the geologic column at various localities. The layer immediately above the gap is thought to be millions of years younger than the layer immediately below. If these millions of years really took place, why don't we see the abundant irregular erosion of the lower layer that is expected over such long periods of time? The contacts between the layers at these gaps are usually flat with little evidence of erosion. This suggests little time. This phenomenon is so common that it raises a significant question about the long geologic ages proposed for the geologic column.[21]

The incomplete ecological systems mentioned above which are postulated to have survived for millions of years, the rapid rates of erosion of the continents that should have washed them away long ago, and the scarcity of erosion at the gaps in the sedimentary layers of the earth — all these pose questions that demand answers if one is going to adopt any models proposing many millions of years for the development of life on earth. These data favor the biblical creation account.

Why Not Pick the Best of Science and the Bible?

Many have tried to reconcile the great differences between science's evolutionary model and the biblical model of creation. The Bible, which is accepted as a guide for life by so many, and science, which has enlightened us so abundantly about nature, are both highly respected. Many wonder which is true, and many have suggested various models that are intermediate between the two, so as to preserve parts of both science and the Bible.[22]

"Theistic evolution" is one of these intermediate models. It proposes that God used an evolutionary process over eons of time. The model preserves some kind of god, but he is not the kind of good God described in the Bible. God's creation described in the Bible is "very good." Furthermore, He is a God with concern for those who need help. The aberrant results, the competition, and the survival of only the fittest in the evolutionary process are very much out of character with the kind of God described in the Bible. Furthermore, the fossil record does not provide the intermediates expected from an evolutionary process.

Another model is "progressive creation," where God occasionally creates more and more advanced forms of life over eons of time. Here God is preserved as the Creator of all, but the model does not fit well with either the kind of God described in the Bible or the biblical creation account. The many thousands of fossil kinds that we find that are not now living imply numerous creation errors in the past. The presence of evil, in the form of predatory animals, earlier in the fossil record, long before the creation of man, negates the biblical account of God as a good Creator and the concept that evil in nature is the result of the fall of man. Furthermore, there is no suggestion in the Bible that God created over long periods of time. There is only one model of creation in the Bible: God does it all in six days.

Models such as progessive creation or theistic evolution suffer from lack of authentication. One can speculate that this or that happened in the past, but one would like some support from a respected source of information, such as the Bible or the data of nature, that this is actually the case. Neither nature nor the Bible indicate that these intermediate views between creation and evolution are the way God did it. One can find peripheral information to support many models, but one would like some more direct authentication before accepting speculative suggestions. One should not give up a more authenticated model for a more speculative one.

Why Believe in a Six-Day Creation?

We have the biblical concept of a six-day creation, we have the concept of evolution over thousands of millions of years, and we have a number of views intermediate between the two. Which is true?

Science is the best system devised by man to give us information about nature. However, the conclusions of science are not final. Science repeatedly revises and even reverses its conclusions. Science is more reliable in the experimental realm than when dealing with the past, especially when that past cannot be experimentally repeated. When it comes to answering the great questions of origins, meaning, and destiny, science has lost its credentials. This happened over a century ago when science decided to exclude God from its explanatory menu. If God exists, science will never find Him as long as it refuses to consider God as a part of reality. While a significant number of scientists believe in some kind of God, and their numbers are growing, we don't yet see God being incorporated as a reality into scientific research papers and textbooks. Science is still adhering to a narrow mechanistic approach to reality.

I believe science would not be facing some of the insurmountable questions about the origin of life mentioned earlier if it did not take such a narrow approach. Science would do well to return more towards the broader, open attitude it had several centuries ago, when the foundations of modern science were laid down, and noted scientists — such as Kepler, Boyle, Newton, Pascal, and Linn — believed in God as the Creator who established the laws of science.

The Bible, on the other hand, takes a more open approach, inviting us to consider nature as well as God (for example, see Ps. 19:1–4 and Rom. 1:19–20). As such, it has a broader base for addressing the questions of origins. The Bible is much more in demand by far than any other book. Current distribution is more than 17 times that of any secular book. It has a high degree of respect. This respect is based in part on the integrity and candor of its writers, as well as on the archeological, geographic, historical, and prophetic authentication that it holds. Its internal consistencey challenges any suggestion that it is a collection of invented stories. This is not a book that we can easily dismiss. When I consider the great questions of origins from a broad perspective, the biblical model makes the most sense to me; it leaves fewer unanswered questions.

Endnotes

1 A.A. Roth, "Do We Need to Turn Off Our Brains, When We Enter a Church?" *Origins* 23 (1996), p. 63–65.

2 For a detailed discussion of these various points see A.A. Roth, *Origins: Linking Science and Scripture* (Hagerstown, MA: Review and Herald Pub. Assoc., 1998).

3 For example: Carl Sagan, *The Dragons of Eden: Speculations on the Evolution of Human Intelligence* (New York: Ballantine Books, 1997), p. 28.

4 For example: T.H. Jukes, "Responses of Critics," in P.E. Johnson, *Evolution as Dogma: the Establishment of Naturalism* (Dallas, TX: Haughton Publishing Co., 1990), p. 26–28.

5 Richard Benedict Goldschmidt, *The Material Basis of Evolution* (New Haven, CT: Yale University Press, 1940).

6 C. Patterson, *Evolution* (London: British Museum and Ithaca, NY: Cornel University Press, 1978), p. 143.

7 Soren Lovtrup, *Darwinism: The Refutation of a Myth* (New York: Croom Helm, 1987), p. 352.

8 For a listing of 9 books by non-creationists that challenge evolution or Darwinism, see p. 140–141 in Roth, *Origins: Linking Science and Scripture*.

9 For the details see chapters 5 and 8 in Roth, *Origins: Linking Science and Scripture*.

10 This is discussed further in Roth, *Origins: Linking Science and Scripture*, chapter 10.

11 Charles Darwin, *The Origin of Species by Means of Natural Selection, or the Preservation of Favoured Races in the Struggle for Life* (London: John Murray, 1859), in the reprinted edition: J.W. Burrow, editor (Penguin Books, London and NY, 1968), p. 292.

12 D.B. Kitts, "Paleontology and Evolutionary Theory," *Evolution* 28 (1974), 458–472.

13 N. Eldredge and S.J. Gould, "Punctuated Equilibria: An Alternative to Phyletic Gradualism," in T.J.M. Schopf, editor, *Models of Paleobiology* (San Francisco, CA: Freeman, Cooper, and Co., 1972), p. 82–115.

14 S.A. Bowring, J.P. Groetzinger, C.E. Isachsen, A.H. Knoll, S.M. Pelechaty, P. Kolosov, "Calibrating Rates of Early Cambrian Evolution," *Science* 261 (1993), p. 1293–1298.

15 As quoted in M. Nash, "When Life Exploded," *Time* 146(23) (1995), p. 66–74.

16 For further discussion and examples, see chapters 13 and 15 in Roth, *Origins: Linking Science and Scripture*.

17 D.E. Fatovsky, D. Badamgarav, H. Ishimoto, M. Watabe, D.B. Weishampel, "The Paleoenvironments of Tugrikin–Shireh (Gobi Desert, Mongolia) and Aspects of the Taphonomy and Paleoecology of *Protoceratops* (Dinosauria: Ornithischia)," *Palaios* 12 (1977), p. 59–70.

18 T.E. White, "The Dinosaur Quarry," in E.F. Sabatka, editor, *Guidebook to the Geology and Mineral Resources of the Uinta Basin* (Salt Lake City, UT: Intermountain Association of Geologists, 1964), p. 21–28.

19. For some examples see chapter 15 in Roth, *Origins: Linking Science and Scripture*.

20 Robert H. Dott Jr. and Roger L. Batten, *Evolution of the Earth,* 4th edition (New York, NY: McGraw-Hill Book Co., 1988, p. 155; Robert M. Garrels and Fred T. Mackenzie, *Evolution of Sedimentary Rocks,* (New York: W.W. Norton & Co., 1971, p. 114; J. Gilluly "Geologic Contrasts Between Continents and Ocean Basins," in A. Poldervaart, editor, *Crust of the Earth*, Geological Society of America, Special Paper, 62: (1955), p. 7–18.

21 For a more extensive discussion, see A.A. Roth, "Those Gaps in the Sedimentary Layers" *Origins* 15 (1988), p. 75–92.

22 See chapter 21 in Roth "Do We Need to Turn Off . . ." for a discussion of a variety of these models.

keith h. wanser

Physics

Dr. Wanser is professor of physics, California State University, Fullerton. He holds a B.A. in physics from California State University, an M.A. in physics from the University of California, Irvine, and a Ph.D. in condensed matter physics from the University of California, Irvine. Dr. Wanser, who specializes in novel and ultrasensitive optical fiber sensor devices, components, and techniques, has published over 30 refereed and 18 other technical papers and holds seven U.S. patents. In 1996 he was the recipient of the School of Natural Sciences and Mathematics Outstanding Research Award.

Being raised from early childhood in a church that believed in a literal six-day creation and having read the Bible often as a teenager, I believed in creation, although I did not understand the importance and centrality to the Christian faith of the first ten chapters of Genesis. When I attended a state university as an undergraduate and talked with the physics professors, I was ridiculed for believing that the earth was young, and given many reasons from science showing that the Bible was in error, especially the first chapters of Genesis. As a young college student majoring in physics, I did not know enough science to be able to refute what these professors were saying, and since they knew so much more than I, gradually I lost faith in the literal accuracy of Scripture, although I still believed in God. This led me to a period of a few years where I was a "theistic evolutionist," morally adrift, and intensively reading a variety of scientific journals and books to try to find out the truth.

In 1976 I recommitted my life to Jesus Christ, and shortly thereafter began studying the scientific, historical, scriptural, and other evidence for a literal six-day creation and worldwide global flood, as described in Genesis. In the intervening 24 years since then, I have studied these bodies of evidence in some detail, and I am firmly convinced that there is far more scientific evidence supporting a recent, six-day creation and global flood than there is an old earth and evolution.

One of the major problems with the so-called theory of evolution is that the details depend on who is telling the story. Those details that become commonly accepted as "facts" are often changed in light of more recent discoveries. This has happened on numerous occasions, with little notice that the supposed prior facts were not facts at all. In other words, there is not one theory of evolution, but a body of opinions, speculations, and methods for interpretation of observational facts so that they fit into the philosophy of naturalism.

An example of a supposed fact demonstrating an ancient age of the earth is the rate of growth of stalactites and stalagmites in limestone caverns. As a young boy I toured Carlsbad Caverns in New Mexico and remember the tour guide informing us matter-of-factly that the limestone caverns and formations were formed over many millions of years, which did not seem to agree with what I had been taught in Sunday school. A sign above the entrance until 1988 said the caverns were at least 260 million years old. In recent years, the age on the sign was reduced to 7–10 million years, then 2 million years, and now the sign is gone — perhaps as a result of observations that stalactite growth rates of several inches a month are common.[1]

Creationists have performed a significant body of research demonstrating the rapid development of calcium carbonate formations under conditions likely following the Noahic flood. In May 1998 I observed stalactites longer than six inches growing from the edge of the concrete boarding platform at the Arlington, Virginia, metro rail station, which was only completed in June 1991. Another example of a supposed fact was the slow rate of petrifaction of wood, requiring long periods of time to occur. Petrifaction of wood has been shown to occur rapidly in highly silicified waters, and would likely have been accelerated by the conditions of a worldwide flood. Indeed, a U.S. patent has been granted on a process to rapidly petrify wood so as to make it fire-and-wear resistant.[2]

Over the last 35 years, scientists who believe in a recent, six-day creation have made some very interesting discoveries and convincing arguments for a young earth and worldwide Noahic flood. In essentially all cases, their research has not been supported by government funding. This is in contrast to the many millions of dollars of government-funded research by scientists who hold evolutionary pre-suppositions, which has been used to support their beliefs. In spite of these handicaps, a remarkable body of evidence refuting evolutionary notions has been assembled by creationists.[3] They demonstrate that several processes which formerly were thought to require long periods of time actually occur rapidly, and testify to a young earth and recent creation. Furthermore, creationists are beginning to make testable predictions based on their theories, as well as become more quantitative in their modelling.

The catastrophic plate tectonics model that has been developed[4] has served to help explain several geologic features that are associated with the Flood, as well as geomagnetic reversals and the post-Flood ice age. Early creationist work on the rapid, free induction decay of the earth's magnetic field was able to explain the observed decay of about 7 percent in the field over the last 130 years, with no adjustable parameters, and set an upper limit to the age of the field of about 10,000 years.[5] This theory was later modified to include local and rapid geomagnetic reversals associated with catastrophic plate tectonics and Noah's flood, and extended to include the size of planetary magnetic fields.[6] Predictions based on this recent and biblical creation model were made about rapid geomagnetic reversals and planetary magnetic fields, which have been verified experimentally.[7]

The explanation of the planetary magnetic fields is in surprising agreement with the creationist theory and there is no evolutionary counterpart to it. Similarly, the predictions of rapid geomagnetic reversals have been verified by analysis of lava flows in Steen's Mountain in Oregon, which indicate geomagnetic polarity reversals occurring in a matter of a few weeks, much to the bewilderment and surprise of evolutionary scientists.[8]

Major problems with evolutionary scenarios of origins occur at several stages. One very interesting problem occurs right at the beginning in theories of quantum cosmology, which predict that the big bang originated from a quantum fluctuation of the vacuum.[9] Unfortunately, this speculation is nothing more than that, since in all experimentally observed processes involving elementary particles and nuclear reactions, something called Baryon number is conserved. The conservation of Baryon number insures that when particles are brought into existence from energy, they occur in equal numbers of matter/anti-matter pairs. Thus, in pair production, an electron and positron are produced; similarly, a proton and antiproton are produced. On the other hand, as far as we are able to observe, the universe appears to have an extreme dominance of matter over anti-matter, which contradicts the notion that a big bang produced the matter that we see in the universe around us.

Because of this problem, elementary particle physicists have proposed Grand Unified Theories or GUTs which hypothesize terms in the mathematical equations of the theory which violate Baryon number conservation, in order to produce a dominance of matter over anti-matter as a result of the big bang. Unfortunately, these theories predict that the proton is unstable and will decay, which has led to considerable experimental efforts to detect proton decay[10]. However, such searches have failed to find proton decay and have set lower limits on the proton lifetime of at least 10^{+31} years.[11] The fact that there is no experimental evidence for violation of Baryon number conservation strongly calls into question any big-bang scenario for the origin of matter in the universe. There are several other problems with theories of quantum/big-bang cosmology, which have been discussed by Morris.[12]

An intriguing creationist theory has been proposed[13] which involves a white hole cosmology, a bounded universe, an initial water mass, and Einstein's theory of general relativity. This cosmology allows for a literal six-day creation in the frame of reference of the earth (which is taken to be somewhere in the vicinity of the center of the universe), while long periods of time could elapse in other portions of the universe, thus allowing sufficient time for starlight to have travelled distances of billions of light years to reach the earth. It also allows for an expanding universe and red shifts, such as are observed. Other predictions of this theory, such as the temperature of the cosmic background radiation, have yet to be worked out in detail; nevertheless, this theory offers a viable alternative to naturalistic big-bang cosmology and solves the longstanding problem of light travel time in recent creation cosmologies.

Another creationist alternative to big-bang cosmology has recently been proposed,[14] which not only accounts for observed cosmological red shifts, but can also explain the 2.7 kelvin cosmic background radiation. Although these recent cosmological models are in their early stages, as compared to more than 50 years of refinement of the standard big-bang model, they do demonstrate that the observed experimental facts may be understood without requiring a big bang. In addition, they demonstrate the originality and productivity of creationist scientists, contradicting claims by some evolutionists that creation scientists do not develop any new science.

One of the biggest stumbling blocks to belief in six-day creation is associated with radioisotope dating methods and the exceedingly old ages of rocks and fossils inferred from such methods. Recent work by creationists has shown that the widely used potassium-argon dating method suffers from fatal flaws in its assumption of no initial argon trapped in volcanic rocks at the time of their solidification.[15] There have been various creationist proposals for accelerated radioactive decay and experimental searches for evidence that this has occurred in the past.[16] Possible scenarios of intense neutrino and/or gamma ray fluxes due to various supernova and stellar disturbances (possibly during Noah's flood) may have contributed to the appearance of age when radioactive substances are examined by causing substantial radioactive decay in a very short time period, rather than over long periods of time at currently observable rates. Besides causing additional radioactive decay, such fluxes or increases in cosmic radiation could also have resulted in the rapid decrease in the human lifespan following the flood, as recorded in Genesis. It is believed that the decrease of the earth's magnetic field associated with catastrophic plate tectonics during Noah's flood also contributed to a dramatic increase in cosmic ray flux in the upper atmosphere and an attendant increase in the production of carbon 14.

An extremely large flux in gamma rays flooding the solar system was recently observed and is believed to be a relatively "common" occurrence.[17] These extremely intense gamma ray emissions were attributed to a type of neutron star known as a magnetar. Magnetars are expected to dissipate their energy in about 10,000 years, an indication that they themselves are young.

In addition to proposals for accelerated nuclear decay, there has recently appeared experimental evidence that the decay of unstable quantum mechanical systems is non-exponential.[18] On very general grounds, one may show that the decay of an unstable quantum mechanical system is non-exponential at short times. It is one of the largest extrapolations in science to assume that the decay of radioactive isotopes with half-lives of more than 10^{+9} years is exponential, when the exponential decay law for radioactive isotopes has only been experimentally verified for short-lived isotopes with half-lives less than 100 years. This is an extrapolation of at least 7 orders of magnitude in time! There are reasons to believe that the longer-lived radioisotopes should exhibit significant deviations from the exponential decay law. The rigorous quantum mechanical theory of the decay of long-lived radioisotopes is currently under investigation, in order to determine the size of the deviation from the exponential decay law at times short compared to the half-life. If significant deviations are found, this will completely alter the interpretation of radioisotope data and the inferred ancient chronologies, which are based on the assumption of the validity of the exponential decay law over unobservably large times.

Cited in this brief article is just a small sample of the interesting work that has been and is being done by scientists who believe in creation. The inquisitive reader is urged to study the books in the bibliography by Morris (see note 3). In addition, there are many internet web sites[19] with numerous articles which give scientific, historical, and biblical evidences for a recent, six-day creation and the worldwide Noahic flood.

Notes

1 G.W.Wolfram, "Carlsbad 'Signs Off,' " *Creation Research Society Quarterly*, vol. 31, June 1994, p. 34; E.L. Williams, "Cavern and Speleotherm Formation — Science and Philosophy," *Creation Research Society Quarterly*, vol. 29, Sept. 1992, p. 83–84; E.L. Williams, "Rapid Development of Calcium Carbonate Formations," *Creation Research Society Quarterly*, vol. 24, June 1987, p. 18–19.

2 E.L. Williams, "Rapid Petrifaction of Wood," *Creation Matters*, vol. 1, Jan. 1996, p. 1; E.L. Williams, "Fossil Wood from Big Bend National Park, Brewster County Texas: Part II," *Creation Research Society Quarterly*, vol. 30, Sept. 1993, p. 106–111; H. Hicks, "Sodium Silicate Composition," U.S. Patent #4,612,050, Sept. 16, 1986.

3 Henry M. Morris, "A Young-Earth Creationist Bibliography," Institute for Creation Research *Impact* article No. 269, November 1995; http://www.icr.org

4 S.A. Austin et al., "Catastrophic Plate Tectonics: A Global Flood Model of Earth History," proceedings of the Third International Conference on Creationism, 1994, p. 609–621; C. Burr, "The Geophysics of God," *U.S. News and World Report*, July 16, 1997; http://www.usnews.com/usnews/issue/970616/16terr.htm

5 Thomas G. Barnes, *Origin and Destiny of the Earth's Magnetic Field* (El Cajon, CA: Creation Research Society, 1983), p. 132.

6 R. Humphreys, "The Earth's Magnetic Field is Young," Institute for Creation Research *Impact* article No. 242, August 1993; http://www.icr.org

7 D.R. Humphreys, "Physical Mechanism for Reversals of the Earth's Magnetic Field During the Flood," proceedings of the Second International Conference on Creationism, 1990, vol. 2 (Creation Science Fellowship, Pittsburgh, PA, USA), p. 129–142, and references therein.

8 R.S. Coe, M. Prevot, and P. Camps, "New Evidence for Extraordinarily Rapid Change of the Geomagnetic Field During a Reversal," *Nature*, vol. 374, April 20, 1995, p. 687–692.

9 D. Atkatz, "Quantum Cosmology for Pedestrians," *American Journal of Physics*, vol. 62, July 1994, p. 619–627.

10 Graham G. Ross, *Grand Unified Theories* (Menlo Park, CA: Benjamin/ Cummings, 1984), p. 212–216, 438–444.

11 R. Mathews, "Rock Solid," *New Scientist*, May 22, 1999, p. 48–52.

12 Henry M. Morris and John D. Morris, "The Heavens Don't Evolve Either," *The Modern Creation Trilogy*, vol. 2, Science and Creation (Green Forest, AR: Master Books, Inc., 1996), p. 203–232.

13 D. Russell Humphreys, *Starlight and Time* (Green Forest, AR: Master Books, 1994), p. 83–133.

14 R.V. Gentry, "A New Red Shift Interpretation," *Modern Physics Letters A*, Vol. 12, No. 37, 1997, p. 2919–2925. Also see e-prints "The New Red Shift Interpretation Affirmed," http://xxx.lanl.gov/abs/physics/9810051 and "The Genuine Cosmic Rosetta," http://xxx.lanl.gov/abs/gr-qc/9806061

15 A. Snelling, " 'Excess Argon': The 'Achilles Heel' of Potassium-Argon and Argon-Argon 'Dating' of Volcanic Rocks," Institute for Creation Research *Impact* Article No. 307, January 1999 and references therein. Available online at http://www.icr.org

16 J.W. Bielecki, "Search for Accelerated Nuclear Decay with Spontaneous Fission of ^{238}U," proceedings of the Fourth International Conference on Creationism, 1998, p. 79–88.

17 R. Cowen, "Crafts Finds New Evidence of Magnetars," *Science News*, vol. 154, Sept. 12, 1998, p. 164. See also http://www.magnetars.com

18 S.R. Wilkinson et al., "Experimental Evidence for Non-exponential Decay in Quantum Tunneling," *Nature*, 387, June 5, 1997, p. 575–577.

19 Three Internet web sites with information on creation/evolution are: Institute for Creation Research, http://www.icr.org; Christian.Answers Net, http://www.ChristianAnswers.Net; and Answers in Genesis, http://www.answeringenesis.org

timothy g. standish

Biology

Dr. Standish is associate professor of biology at Andrews University in Berrien Springs, Michigan. He holds a B.S. in zoology from Andrews University, an M.S. in biology from Andrews University, and a Ph.D. in biology and public policy from George Mason University (University of Virginia), Charlottesville, Virginia. He teaches genetics at Andrews University and is currently researching the genetics of cricket (*Achita domesticus*) behavior.

Reading *The Blind Watchmaker* by Richard Dawkins was a pivotal experience for me. I had recently started my Ph.D. program at George Mason University and eagerly signed up for a class entitled "Problems in Evolutionary Theory." *The Blind Watchmaker* was required reading, and with growing enthusiasm I noted glowing endorsements printed on the cover. According to *The Economist*, this book was "as readable and vigorous a defense of Darwinism as has been published since 1859." Lee Dembart, writing for the *Los Angeles Times*, was even more effusive: "Every page rings of truth. It is one of the best science books — of the best of any books — I have ever read." A book that was "Winner of the Royal Society of Literature's Heinemann Prize, and the Los Angeles Times Book Award" must contain nothing but undistilled brilliance. I felt smug with confidence as I paid for the book and left the store, brimming with ebullience to start reading.

After wading through all the hyperbole, I was stunned by the ideas put forward by Dawkins in *The Blind Watchmaker*. Rhetoric burnished the arguments with a glittering sheen, briefly giving the impression that pebbles were gems. But once each metaphor was stripped aside, the core ideas did not support the idea that natural selection could account for the origin of life and the meaningful complexity of organisms. Most startling to me was the realization that, one of the book's core theses, in fact, violated the principle of natural selection.

Dawkins wove two ideas together in supporting Darwinism. The first idea was that, given enough chances, the improbable becomes probable. For example, flipping a coin ten times in a row and getting heads each time is very unlikely; one would only expect it to happen about 1 in 1,024 tries. Most of us would not sit around flipping coins just to see it happen, but if we had a million people flipping coins, we would see it happen many times. This phenomenon is publicized in the newspapers when lottery winners are announced. Winning a million-dollar jackpot is unlikely, but with millions of people purchasing tickets, eventually someone wins.

Dawkins admits that the odds on life starting from a random collection of chemicals is very slim, but given an immense universe and the billions of years it has existed, the improbable becomes probable. In this is echoed the logic of Ernst Haeckel, who wrote in his book *The Riddle of the Universe*, published in 1900:

> Many of the stars, the light of which has taken thou-
> sands of years to reach us, are certainly suns like our own
> mother-sun, and are girt about with planets and moons,

just as in our solar system. We are justified in supposing that thousands of these planets are in a similar stage of development to that of our earth . . . and that from its nitrogenous compounds, protoplasm has been evolved — that wonderful substance which alone, as far as our knowledge goes, is the possessor of organic life.

Haeckel was optimistic about the presence of conditions that could support life on planets other than earth, and it is in this that one of the problems with Dawkins' argument emerges. While the universe is immense, those places where life as we know it could survive, let alone come into being, seem to be few and far between. So far, only one place has been discovered where conditions for life are present, and we are already living on it. Thus, there is not much cause for optimism that the universe is teeming with planets bathed in a primordial soup from which life might evolve. Dawkins wrote glibly of the immensity of the universe and its age, but failed to provide one example, other than the earth, where the unlikely event of spontaneous generation of life might occur. Even if the universe were teeming with proto-earths, and the spans of time suggested by modern science were available, this is still not a great argument, as if something is impossible — in other words, the odds of it happening are zero — then it will never happen, not even in an infinite amount of time. For example, even if we had our million people flipping coins, each with ten flips in a row, the odds on any one of them flipping and getting 11 heads in ten tries is zero because the odds of getting 11 heads in ten tries with one person is zero. The bottom line is that the odds on life evolving from non-living precursors is essentially zero. Ironically, this was the stronger of the two ideas, or arguments, presented by Dawkins.

The second argument was presented as an analogy: Imagine a monkey typing on a typewriter with 27 keys, all the letters in the English alphabet and the space bar. How long would it take for the monkey to type something that made any sense? Dawkins suggests the sentence spoken by William Shakespeare's Hamlet who, in describing a cloud, pronounces, "Methinks it is like a weasel." It is not a long sentence and contains very little meaning, but it works for argument's sake. How many attempts at typing this sentence would it take a monkey, which would presumably be hitting keys randomly, to type the sentence?

As it turns out, the odds can be easily calculated as the probability of getting each letter or space correct raised to the power of the number of positions at which they have to be correct. In this case, the probability of the monkey typing "m" at the first position of the sentence is 1/27 (we won't worry about capitalization). The sentence has 28 characters in it, so the probability is $(1/27)^{28}$ or 1.2×10^{-40}. That is about one chance in 12,000 million million million million million million! You would want a lot of monkeys typing very fast for a long time if you ever wanted to see this happen!

To overcome this problem with probability, Dawkins proposed that natural selection could help by fixing each letter in place once it was correct and thus lowering the odds massively. In other words, as a monkey types away, it is not unlikely that at least one of the characters it types will be in the correct position on the first try. If this letter was then kept and the monkey was only allowed to type in the remaining letters until it finally had the correct letter at each position, the odds fall to the point that the average diligent monkey could probably finish the task in an afternoon and still have time to gather bananas and peanuts from admiring observers. Dawkins got his computer to do it in between 40 and 70 tries.

Luckily I had taken biochemistry before reading *The Blind Watchmaker*. Organisms are made of cells, and those cells are composed of little protein machines that do the work of the cell. Proteins can be thought of as sentences like "Methinks it is like a weasel," the difference being that proteins are made up of 20 different sub-units called amino acids instead of the 27 different characters in our example. The evolution of a functional protein would presumably start out as a random series of amino acids one or two of which would be in the right position to do the function the protein is designed to do. According to Dawkins' theory, those amino acids in the right location in the protein would be fixed by natural selection, while those that needed to be modified would continue to change until they were correct, and a functional protein was produced in relatively short order. Unfortunately, this ascribes an attribute to natural selection that even its most ardent proponents would question, the ability to select one non-functional protein from a pool of millions of other non-functional proteins.

Changing even one amino-acid in a protein can alter its function dramatically. A famous example of this is the mutation that causes sickle cell anemia in humans. This disease causes a multitude of symptoms, ranging from liver failure to tower skull syndrome. It is caused by the replacement of an amino acid called glutamate, normally at position number six, with another amino acid called valine. This single change causes a massive difference in how the alpha globin sub-unit of hemoglobin works. The ultimate sad consequence of this seemingly insignificant mutation in the protein causes premature death in thousands of individuals each year. In other proteins, mutations to some, but not all, areas can result in a complete loss of function. This is particularly true if the protein is an enzyme, and the mutation is in its active site.

What Dawkins is suggesting is that a very large group of proteins, none of which is functional, can be acted on by natural selection to select out a few that, while they do not quite do the job yet, with some modification via mutation, can do the job in the future. This suggests that natural selection has some direction or goal in mind, a great heresy to those who believe evolutionary theory.

This idea of natural selection fixing amino acids as it constructs functional proteins is also unsupported by the data. Cells do not churn out large pools of random proteins on which natural selection can then act. If anything, precisely the opposite is true. Cells only produce the proteins they need to make at that time. Making other proteins, even unneeded functional ones, would be a wasteful thing for cells to do, and in many cases, could destroy the ability of the cell to function. Most cells only make about 10% of the proteins they are capable of producing. This is what makes liver cells different from those in the skin or brain. If all proteins were expressed all the time, all cells would be identical.

In reality, the problem of evolving life is much more complex than generation of a single functional protein. In fact, a single protein is just the tip of the iceberg. A living organism must have many functional proteins, all of which work together in a coordinated way. In the course of my research, I frequently physically disrupt cells by grinding them in liquid nitrogen. Sometimes I do this to obtain functional proteins, but more often to get the nucleic acids RNA or DNA. In any case, I have yet to find that the protein or nucleic acid I was working on was not functional after being removed from the cell, and yet, even though all the cell components were present and functional following disruption, I have never observed a single cell start to function again as a living organism, or even part of a living organism. For natural selection to occur, all proteins on which it is to act must be part of a living organism composed of a host of other functional protein machines. In other words, the entire system must exist prior to selection occurring, not just a single protein.

"Problems in Evolutionary Theory" was a class that made me realize the difficulties those who discount the possibility of a Creator have with their own theories. The problems with evolutionary theory were real, and there were no simple convincing resolutions.

Progressing in my studies, I slowly realized that evolution survives as a paradigm only as long as the evidence is picked and chosen and the great pool of data that is accumulating on life is ignored. As the depth and breadth of human knowledge increases, it washes over us a flood of evidence deep and wide, all pointing to the conclusion that life is the result of design. Only a small subset of evidence, chosen carefully, may be used to construct a story of life evolving from non-living precursors. Science does not work on the basis of picking and choosing data to suit a treasured theory. I chose the path of science which also happens to be the path of faith in the Creator.

I believe God provides evidence of His creative power for all to experience personally in our lives. To know the Creator does not require an advanced degree in science or theology. Each one of us has the opportunity to experience His creative power in re-creating His character within us, step by step, day by day.

john r. rankin

Mathematical Physics

Dr. Rankin is senior lecturer in the Department of Computer Science and Computer Engineering, La Trobe University, Australia. He holds a B.S. (hons) with first class honors in applied mathematics from Monash University, a Ph.D. in mathematical physics from the University of Adelaide, and a postgraduate diploma of computer science from the University of Adelaide. He has taught in tertiary institutions for more than 17 years.

When we ask about the origins of everything, what are the choices? We basically really only have two choices: evolution or creation. Evolution has its problems and no scientist denies that. But that doesn't answer the question of why I believe in creation. Theories can be easily patched up with extra assumptions and more circuitous explanations and couldn't the problem areas simply be put down to our present state of knowledge? Could we not simply hope that in the not-too-distant future, with further research, each particular thorny problem in evolution will eventually get resolved satisfactorily, one by one? In my perspective, however, if we think of the problem areas in evolution as "holes" in the theory, these holes are getting bigger with time, and they are not going away.

Evolution covers such a wide span of scientific disciplines that no one area is sufficient to disprove the theory. In earlier days, scientists accepted the assurance that although they had insurmountable difficulties with evolution in their own area of scientific work, evolution "works" and makes sense in other areas of research and in basic science in general. But as time has gone on, the problem areas for evolution in the various disciplines of science have not gone away but remained and are standing out like "sore thumbs." With this situation, scientists have become aware of the difficulties for evolution in all other areas, in addition to their own. Now they are starting to say that maybe there are fundamental problems with the evolution explanation itself.

Let me describe my original area of research and how it related to evolution theory. My early research work was in the area of cosmology. This involves a deep study of mathematics and astronomy and, in particular, Einstein's theory of general relativity. In cosmology we have a number of "cosmological models" that we study. These are mathematical solutions of the Einstein equations that describe different possible universes allowed according to the laws of physics. My research project was to pursue the question: If the universe started off as a homogeneous distribution of atomic gases and plasma, would the typical small statistical fluctuations in density grow and condense under the known laws of gravity to form protogalaxies, the precursors of galaxies with all their complex constituents of globular clusters, stars, planets, moons, asteroids, and comets of today?

This is the current belief of evolution theory: that an initially homogeneous and uninteresting universe became differentiated over billions of years into the complex and beautiful structure of interrelated objects that we know and see today. The attitude of my research supervisor was, "We are here; therefore, we must have evolved!"

and by assumption everything evolved from a uniform gaseous state.

This is certainly a big question and to tackle it I looked into the initial phases of this supposed process. So the question I tackled was: Would statistical fluctuations in the cosmological models currently believed to be realistic representations of the cosmological structure of the universe grow under the gravitational laws of general relativity to the level of becoming statistically significant? Linearized equations are suitable for the expected background random density fluctuations. If these equations say that, for standard cosmological models, initial random (insignificant) fluctuations will grow over cosmological time (measured in billions of years) to become statistically significant — at which point the linearized equations break down and a fully non-linear mathematical treatment is required — then we have established the foundations for the evolution theory.

After five years of heavy mathematical research concentrated on this one question, the answer came back: No. Indeed, there was some growth in the initial fluctuations but, even over 10 or 20 billion years, the initial statistical fluctuations in density were still at the level of fluctuation that could be expected on statistical grounds in a homogeneous universe. Previous research had seemed to indicate that statistical fluctuation would condense rapidly. However, these calculations had been done in the background of unrealistic cosmological models, namely models that were static and mostly non-relativistic. These static models could not be justified — either from the point of view of physical theory or from cosmological observations and what we now know about the universe.

Of course, this result was a great disappointment to the strong believers of evolution theory. It seemed obvious that gravity would do this simple chore required at the foundation of evolution theory.

What was counteracting the natural force of gravity in condensing fluctuations was the expansion of the universe itself, which is also a product of the laws of gravitation. The standard reaction to such a negative result is to search for alternative considerations, apart from gravity, that could be involved to generate statistically significant fluctuations. For example, thermodynamics, that is, fluctuations in heat distribution and the flow of heat, could "assist" gravity to do its job. Another idea is to invoke the interaction between the different fluid components in the cosmological model: radiation, plasma types, and dust. Perhaps the point of decoupling between radiation and matter is a significant enough stimulus to accelerate the process of protogalaxy formation. A third type of mechanism is to resort to turbulence to counteract the disruptive effect of the expansion of the universe on the protogalaxy formation process.

Each of these additional mechanisms in support of galaxy formation brings much greater mathematical complexity to the problem. It is easy to maintain the standard line of evolution theory that a homogeneous gaseous universe evolved into a hierarchically structured galactic universe by invoking complex mechanisms such as these, for which the proof is still outstanding and must remain so for quite some time, because of the enormously increased complexity of the mathematics involved in the new explanations. However, the indications are quite clear that the effects of heat, energy transfers between fluid components, and turbulence are all disruptive to the growth of density fluctuations.

This is an example from one area of research of a major flaw in the evolution explanation from which evolution has never recovered. And yet books still continue to come out in increasing numbers saying that the evolution explanation is correct and incorporating the idea that, early in the universe, gases condensed to form protogalaxies, which further condensed into galaxies of stars and planets with the emergence of life. Do we hear of any of these supporters being willing themselves to spend years of their lives pursuing the complex mathematics involved in their patched-up but unproven theories? Alternatively, are they willing to pay others to do this work and approach the problems objectively, that is, willing to accept that physical theory could result in a negative answer, indicating that their modified explanations are also wrong?

Unfortunately, the supporters of evolution now seem to be less willing to support or pursue this research themselves. As a result, there are few researchers left in the field, with the exception of the changing population of final-year research students. After all the research to date, we are still unable to explain the origin of galaxies as inhomogeneities in the universe from the perspective of evolution. We seem, in fact, to be further away from a satisfactory explanation of evolutionary galactic origins than we were when we started to study the subject, using modern physical theory. As in one field of science, so in all others, we are unable to explain the origin of the beautiful and complex realities of this world from an evolutionist approach.

The burden of evolution is to explain everything, including the mathematics, the logic and the thinking processes involved. This is a burden that increases in size as knowledge continues to grow. It is a burden that takes away our firm foundations for thought and scientific explanation. Maybe the evolutionist approach is wrong, then?

The creationist approach allows us to have an exceedingly intricate and beautiful world at the outset, ready for us to explore its wonders scientifically. This is the approach that puts us on a firm foundation, and this is why I believe in creation rather than evolution.

bob hosken

Biochemistry

11

Dr. Hosken is senior lecturer in food technology at the University of Newcastle, Australia. He holds a B.S. in biochemistry from the University of Western Australia, an M.S. in biochemistry from Monash University, a Ph.D. in biochemistry from the University of Newcastle and an M.B.A. from the University of Newcastle. Dr. Hosken has published more than 50 research papers in the areas of protein structure and function, food technology, and food product development.

My first year at university was one of the most challenging and exciting times in my life. Suddenly I was no longer a child; I was independent, having to interpret the world for myself, planning my own future and determining my own life values. I was unsure of what I should study, and my high school peer group disintegrated as some friends chose to study arts, while others went into law, dentistry, or commerce. While I had many memorable lectures in the first year, some of which are best forgotten, it was the one lecture on glycolysis and the Krebs cycle which stood out, opening up to me a whole new world: the marvels of biochemistry and molecular biology. I found the metabolic steps involved in the synthesis and release of chemical energy through photosynthesis and oxidative phosphorylation absolutely marvellous. I could not get enough of it, I had to become a biochemist.

In this subject we also had several lectures on evolutionary biology, and while the concepts were interesting, they did not excite me intellectually or emotionally. To me, unlocking the secrets of metabolism was like opening the book of life. There had to be a designer for this system to work, and to me this was not chance, but the hand of God.

After graduating in chemistry and biochemistry, I began my postgraduate career, focusing on the biosynthesis, structure, and function of proteins. I worked with a team to determine the amino acid sequences of myoglobin and hemoglobin from a range of Australian marsupials and monotremes, with the aim of determining the phylogenetic relationships of these unique animals. Marsupials are pouched animals and include the kangaroos, while the monotremes lay eggs and include the echidna and the platypus, and it is these features that make the latter so interesting to the taxonomist. Given that the platypus lays eggs, has a duck-like beak, webbed feet, and a furry tail, it is not surprising that some people have viewed it as a missing link in the evolution of animals.

It was found that the amino acid sequences for myoglobin and hemoglobin from various species of kangaroo, echidna, and platypus were different, and the sequence information could be used to evaluate the phylogenetic relationships of these animals. This could then be linked to the radiation of animals associated with continental drift and the evolutionary record.

While these findings were very interesting, the most exciting thing for me about this work was the opportunity it provided for relating the molecular architecture of each species of hemoglobin to the unique physiological requirements of the animal species studied.

In other words, in a study of the relation between the structure and function of hemoglobin in various marsupial and monotreme species, I found it more meaningful to interpret hemoglobin structure in relation to the unique physiological demands of each species. A marsupial mouse has a greater rate of metabolism than a large kangaroo, so small marsupials need a hemoglobin with a structure designed to deliver oxygen to the tissues more efficiently than that required in large animals, and I found this to be actually the case. I also investigated the relation of hemoglobin structure and oxygen transport in the echidna and platypus, and again found the oxygen delivery system of the platypus was well suited to diving, while in the echidna it was suited to burrowing. The bill of the platypus has been found to be equipped with incredibly sensitive electro-receptors, capable of sensing muscular contraction of tiny prey, including dragonfly or mayfly larvae. This enables the platypus to find food in the murky waters in which it lives. These kinds of findings indicate to me that each animal is in some way uniquely designed to suit its particular environment, and I cannot help but attribute the complexity of the design to a Creator, rather than to random evolutionary forces.

The argument of design in nature as an evidence for a Creator is not new. William Paley, in his *Natural Theology* in the 1860s, used this kind of general argument. He was, however, not able to draw on the insights provided by modern molecular biology. While these arguments are in part based on non-scientific paradigms, what's new? Most people, in fact, make their most important decision in life on non-scientific paradigms. Today as we ponder the unique architecture of the molecular systems that make up life, I am sure that I will not be the last person to conclude that "there must be an architect."

I have regarded my early research experience in the area of

protein structure and function as a privilege, not only because it provided me with wonderful insights into molecular design and function, but also because it provided the insights to appreciate the subsequent advances that were to take place in biochemistry and molecular biology. I could now appreciate more than ever the complexity of the molecular control mechanism involved in metabolism and the immunological defense systems of the body. The one-hour lecture in first year university studies of glycolysis and the Krebs cycle, which had initiated my interest in biochemistry, could now be expanded to fill many books, and I cannot possibly conceive how such a system could ever evolve. There has to be an intelligent designer, and this is my personal God.

james s. allan

Genetics

Dr. Allan is a former senior lecturer in genetics at the University of Stellenbosch in South Africa. He holds a B.S. in agriculture from the University of Natal, an M.S. in agriculture from the University of Stellenbosch and a Ph.D. in genetics from the University of Edinburgh, Scotland. He currently serves as an international consultant in the field of dairy cattle breeding.

As a biologist in the field of population and quantitative genetics, I had believed in the theory of evolution for nearly 40 years. During that period of my life, the long-time requirements of the theory did not really concern me. Chance (genetic drift) and natural selection in response to gene mutation and/or environmental change seemed to be logically acceptable mechanisms for the assumed extent of adaptive radiation.

My research involved using biometrical methods of analysis. I was concerned to predict rates of genetic change as a result of applying artificial selection procedures of varying intensities, based on different kinds and amounts of information. The accuracy of prediction of the rate of genetic change can be assessed theoretically and the results can, in many cases and in the short term, be checked empirically. The change in genetic merit (and associated phenotypic merit) from one generation to the next is due to changes in the relative frequencies of the underlying genes.

Over all those years, because I accepted the "fact" of evolution, I saw no reason to differentiate in principle between changes in relative gene frequency as a consequence of either short-term or long-term natural selection. To me, these forms of selection resulted in just the one simple principle of change in relative gene frequency, and the essence of the theory of evolution is change in relative gene frequency as a result of genetic drift and of natural selection in response to gene mutation and/or environmental change.

When, at a fairly advanced stage of my career, I became a Christian I began to read the Bible reverently and as intelligently as I was able. At that time most of my reading was focused in the New Testament and, as my main concern was to know more of Christ as my Savior, my opinion concerning the theory of evolution remained unchallenged. I did not, in fact, give it much thought.

One day, after I had been expounding on the universality of DNA as evidence for the theory of evolution, my wife, who had been a Christian much longer than I, asked me whether there was any reason for God to have used other genetic systems. Just one simple question, but it stimulated me to ask myself many more.

Was there any reason for God to have created life forms on the basis of ABC . . . PQR . . . and XYZ as well as DNA? Were that so, would it have influenced my belief in the theory of evolution, or would I have interpreted it as a number of independent origins of life?

Was there any reason why God should not have created all forms of life as "variations on themes" and so have provided the observed orderly degrees of genetic and phenotypic resemblance as evidenced in taxonomic classification? Relatives tend to resemble one another in physical, functional, and behavioral characteristics. This is a phenomenon which is basic to the science of genetics. The resemblance is due to the fact that relatives, sharing in the common gene pool of a reproducing population, have genes in common. The closer the relationship, the greater is the proportion of genes in common and, therefore, the greater is the degree of resemblance. The theory of evolution assumes a common origin for all forms of life and, therefore, infers that species, genera, families, orders, etc. are genetically related. They all do carry some genes with similar structure and function, yes, but did this imply genetic relationship in the normal, within-species sense, and was one at liberty to assume a common origin for all forms of life? Was there any reason why God should have created different species, genera, etc. in completely different ways and with completely different genes?

I then felt a need to ask questions of a more scientific nature about the validity of evolutionary assumptions. I present here two aspects arising out of such questions concerning the claimed evolution of man.

1. Cytochrome-c is a protein and is a gene product. It functions as a key enzyme in oxidation reactions and seems to occur in practically every living organism. There are 20 different amino-acids. Cytochrome-c consists of a chain of 112 amino-acids, 19 of which occur in exactly the same sequential order positions in all organisms tested. Differences in the identity and positions of the remaining 93 amino-acids are considered to be the result of mutational substitution during the course of evolution. The amino-acid constitution of human cytochrome-c differs from that of many but not all other species. There are no differences in the cytochrome-c taken from humans and from chimpanzees, and only one difference between human cytochrome-c (the amino-acid isoleucine in position 66) and that from the Rhesus monkey (threonine in that position). The numbers of differences in the cytochrome-c of various species compared with that of humans are: cow, pig, and sheep (10), horse

(12), hen and turkey (13), rattlesnake (14), dogfish (23), fly (25), wheat (35), yeast (44), etc.[1] Information of this nature is used to construct phylogenetic trees of assumed genetic relationship. This is presented as evidence for evolution on a molecular level and, among other things, it is concluded that man and the chimpanzee have a relatively recent common ancestor. Assuming for the sake of argument that this is correct, does the constitution of cytochrome-c provide valid evidence for evolution?

The fact that cytochrome-c has a fixed number of 112 amino-acids is an indication of the importance of the three-dimensional structure of the molecule, i.e., there is a structural constraint on the total number of amino-acids. On the other hand, only 19 of the 112 are identical in all organisms tested. Since the identity and positions of the remaining 93 amino-acids differ among organisms except, for example, in the case of man and chimpanzee, it is reasonable to conclude that there are no functional constraints on the substitution of these remaining amino-acids.

Apart from the single gene controlling the constitution of cytochrome-c, humans and chimpanzees differ in many thousands of other genes. As a conservative estimate, let us say 5,000. What the theory of evolution is saying is that while humans and chimpanzees have evolved independently from a common ancestor so as to now differ in these 5,000 genes, there has been no change in the 93 amino-acids specified by the cytochrome-c gene, and this in spite of there being no functional constraint on change in any of the latter. I find this to be an unacceptable claim.

According to Weaver and Hedrick,[2] however, the lack of differentiation in the constitution of cytochrome-c between humans and chimpanzees is due to the very slow (0.3×10^{-9}) estimated rate of amino-acid substitution in cytochrome-c. How is this rate determined? It is estimated on the basis of the assumed time since the species diverged, i.e., the claim is assumed proven on the assumption that it is true. Must I accept this kind of reasoning? Is there any reason why God should not have created them in virtually the same form as we see them now?

2. The theory relating to the evolution of humans from their assumed ancestor in common with the chimpanzee requires millions of years of mutation, genetic drift, and natural selection prior to the appearance of "modern man." However, when I consider mutation rates, the "cost" of the substitution of each new mutant gene in a population in terms of the number of "genetic deaths," the assumed number of mutant gene differences between evolutionary stages, and the population size necessary to accommodate such a large number of successive mutations, I find that there is a remarkable lack of evidence for the "evolution of man." My reasons are as follows.

Haldane[3] considered this kind of information and came to the conclusion that the number of genetic deaths needed to secure the substitution of one gene for another by natural selection is in the region of 30 times the number of individuals in a generation.[4] Using this figure, the cost of substituting 5,000 successive, independent mutant genes in a population of constant size can be calculated. On the basis of an average mutation rate of 10^{-6}, the size of the population must be at least in the order of one million. This implies some 150,000,000,000 forerunners of "modern man," forerunners who are often represented as belonging to small groups of cave-dwelling hunters called australopithicenes who roamed the African savannah. Why is there such a shortage of evidence in the form of fossils, tools, or whatever, for the existence of such vast numbers of australopithicene-like pre-humans?

It could, of course, be argued that such vast numbers of individuals were spread over millions of years, but I find difficulty with this when I look not only at the lack of evidence, but at the reality of total population numbers.

According to the 23rd General Population Conference in Beijing in 1997, the total human population of the earth in that year was assessed to be in the region of 6,000 million, showing that there has been a remarkable increase over the past 200 years. Estimates of the population numbers back to the year 1500 and a prediction for the year 2080 are given in the following table.

YEAR	1500	1650	1800	1900	1950	1997	2080
No. (millions)	300	550	1000	1700	2500	6000	10000

Extrapolation further into the past gives the following approximate numbers:

YEAR	-2000	-1000	0	1000
No. (millions)	1	50	100	250

I find these figures to be in close agreement with what one would expect from the biblical specification after the Flood in 2344 B.C. The assumed existence of thousands of millions of "pre-humans" is both physically and scripturally unrealistic.

Creation in Six Days

I must admit that the six days of the creation presented some difficulty for me. The apparent logic of conclusions from observations and measurements in various fields of science had previously led me to doubt the little I had known of the Word of God, to the extent that I had agreed with attempts to replace it with an alternative concept of time. But God does not say aeons or years or months or weeks — he says days, and we generally understand days to be 24-hour periods.

I then realized that had God wanted to say a billion years rather than six days, He could have said it, very simply, in the way He spoke to Abraham: "I will make your offspring like the dust of the earth, so that if anyone could count the dust, then your offspring could be counted" (Gen. 13:16). In the same way He could have said, "I took as many years as there are particles of dust on the earth to create the heavens, the earth, the seas, and all that is in them" — and it would have sounded very impressive — but He said *six days*. Would He have said this if it were of no concern?

I now believe that God means literally what He says and writes, and that there is no reason to look for symbolism. The word day is used so often and with such a clear implication of being a normal 24-hour period that to interpret it otherwise requires, to my mind, an unbelievable stretch of the imagination. (See also Jer. 33:20.)

It is also clear to me that if one wishes to believe in the theory of evolution, a great deal of Scripture, including Jesus' own spoken word (Matt. 19:4, 25:34; Mark 13:19; John 5:46–47), has to be discounted. So, whom must we believe, God or man? I believe that God gives us the answer when He says, "Stop trusting in man, who has but a breath in his nostrils. Of what account is he?" (Isa. 2:22).

Notes
1 Data from Charlotte J. Avers, *Genetics* (New York: Van Nostrand, 1980), Fig. 16.12.
2 Robert F. Weaver and Philip W. Hedrick, *Genetics* (Dubuque, IA: Wm. C. Brown Publishers, 1989).
3 J.B.S. Haldane, "The Cost of Natural Selection," *J. Genet*, 1957, 55:511–24.
4 See also J.F. Crow and M. Kimura, *An Introduction to Population Genetics Theory* (New York: Harper and Row Publishers, 1970), Section 5.12.

george t. javor

Biochemistry

Dr Javor is Professor of Biochemistry, School of Medicine, Loma Linda University, in Loma Linda, California. He holds a B.S. in chemistry from Brown University, a Ph.D. in biochemistry from Columbia University, New York, and completed post-doctoral studies at Rockefeller University. Dr. Javor has published over 40 technical papers and abstracts in the area of biochemistry and a similar number of articles on science-Bible topics.

I am a practicing scientist and a believer in a six-day creation. It is probably safe to assume that the majority of contemporary scientists do not accept the authenticity of the creation account of Genesis chapters 1 and 2. The reason for this is not hard to guess. There is no evidence that the writer of the Book of Genesis was aware of the existence of gravitational force, of atoms, neutrons, protons and electrons, of the mass of the earth, or of the dimensions of the solar system. In other words, from a modern perspective, the creation account of the Book of Genesis was written in a background of scientific ignorance.

So let us look at the world from our modern perspective, and ask whether it is reasonable to suppose that it came into being in six days. We now know that ours is an immensely complex world. Its inanimate components, the gigantic masses of land, water, and air, are in a continuous flux, and there is yet much to learn about their dynamics. This is painfully clear when we see how inadequate are the efforts to forecast the weather, hurricanes, or earthquakes.

We notice the springs in the mountains give rise to rivers, which flow into lakes and oceans. The waters of the oceans then return into the mountains by means of rain and snow and through underground paths. The cycling of water bathes the earth's surface and is indispensable for the existence of life. So are the cycles of the elements carbon, nitrogen, and sulfur through the biosphere.

The cycle theme in fact is everywhere — from the movement of the electrons around the atomic nucleus to the rotation of the earth around the sun. Cycles do not have beginnings or ends. In order to bring them into existence, the forces responsible for the cycles have to be balanced, and if there are multiple steps required for the completion of a cycle, *all of the components of the cycle have to be in place.* Cycles speak of organization, of design, of *rapid implementation,* and of a *designer.*

The complexity of the animate world is orders of magnitude greater than that of inanimate nature. The earth is covered with multitudes of different forms of life. With the exception of some micro-organisms, all life forms are running on solar power, either directly or indirectly. Plants capture the sun's light energy by their green solar panels and package it into stable chemical entities such as carbohydrates. These sugars become the energy source for all organisms that are "photosynthetically challenged."

Having photosynthetic capacity does not render plants completely self-sufficient. In the absence of soil micro-organisms that convert the air's nitrogen gas into useful nitrates, plants cannot grow. The existence of plants completely depends on nitrogen-fixing microbes. Other soil micro-organisms degrade dead organic matter, thereby recycling the precious elements of carbon, nitrogen, sulfur, and phosphorus.

Photosynthesis makes oxygen available for all non-bacterial organisms. Oxygen, of course, is used by the organisms to burn carbohydrates. This is done at such slow rates that the sun's energy is not lost as heat, but is trapped in the form of the universal "currency" of energy, adenosine triphosphate or ATP. One of the products of this slow combustion, carbon dioxide, is not lost but used by plants for their growth. By these means, every living organism is linked into a giant solar-energy-utilizing network.

What we have here is a seamless integration of earth's rotation around the sun with the phenomenon of life on our planet. Is it far-fetched to suggest that the Creator of the sun and the earth is also the engineer who designed the solar-powered living organisms?

Recent advances in biology permit us to ask whether it is still reasonable to suppose that living organisms evolved on a hypothetical primordial earth from mixes of organic chemicals. At the time when the modern versions of these theories were first entertained, in the 1920s, so little was known about the biochemical realities that undergird living organisms that such proposals seemed reasonable. But now we know that even the simplest of living cells, bacteria (that are not parasitic), must contain thousands of complex structural and catalytic proteins, a variety of nucleic acids, hundreds of small bio-molecules, all in a *dynamic non-equilibrium steady state*.

Within live cells, we see numerous series of interconnected chemical conversions ("pathways") that are functioning uninterrupted. Their continuous activities are due to steady supplies of starting material and the ongoing utilization of end products. The recycling of waste to biosynthetic precursors completes the *cycling* of matter through living systems.

The absence of any component of these complex series of chemical changes will cause defective operation or even death to the cell. Is it reasonable, then, to suppose that when living cells were first brought into existence, *all of their components* must have been present and functioning? If this is so, then living cells had to be made rapidly.

The same suggestion may be made for all of the components of the ecological system, where mutual support and interdependence exist. It is sensible to suppose that these were created simultaneously. (To be sure, the picture is muddied by predation, which was not part of the original created order.)

If we had complete knowledge of every aspect of our physical world, both animate and inanimate, we could calculate the number of inventions that are represented in them. When we assert that our world has been created by a Creator, we imply the existence of a mind that not only invented nature but brought it all into existence. The greatness of such a God cannot be exaggerated.

If we don't understand how a world like ours could be created in six days, we need to ask how a world like ours could be created at all. We will have to admit that we just do not know. The difference between a late 20th-century believer in the Creator God and one living in 1500 B.C., at the time of Moses, boils down to the fact that now we have a better perspective on the greatness of the Lord.

For the believer who is also a scientist, the words of the Bible: "For in six days the Lord made the heaven and the earth, the sea, and all that is" (Exod. 20:11) still make wonderful sense.

dwain l. ford

Organic Chemistry

Professor Ford is Emeritus Professor of Chemistry, Andrews University, Berrien Springs, Michigan. He holds a B.A. in chemistry from Andrews University and a Ph.D. in chemistry from Clark University, Worcester, Massachusetts. Over an academic career spanning more than 30 years at Andrews University, Professor Ford served in various positions including chairman of the Department of Chemistry and dean of the College of Arts and Sciences. He was the recipient of five awards for excellence in teaching as well as three National Science Foundation fellowships.

As a boy growing up on a farm in Minnesota, I came to appreciate the Bible stories at home and at church. In spite of my mild case of dyslexia, I completed reading the entire Bible by about the time I graduated from elementary school. My faith in God was strengthened by numerous answered prayers.

When I entered graduate school in 1958 to work toward a Ph.D. in chemistry, my faith in Scripture was seriously challenged by my major professor. I wondered if it were possible that I had been wrong all my life and my professor right. He seemed very certain about his ideas and he wanted me to do research toward the development of his theory of biochemical evolution. Since I was skeptical of his theory, I was asked to witness each of the significant findings of another graduate student working on evolutionary research next to me in the lab.

As a scientist and a Christian, I have been forced to weigh the evidence available from both science and the Scriptures in an area in which experimental proof is impossible to achieve. After examining both sides of this issue for 40 years, I submit the following reasons why I have retained my faith in God as the Creator.

Chemical evolution, based on random activity of molecules, fails to adequately account for the origin of the proteins required for even the simplest known free-living organism, *Mycoplasma genitalium*. This bacteria has one chromosome, a *cell* membrane, but lacks a cell wall and has the smallest genome of any known self-replicating organism. It has 470 genes, which contain an average of 1,040 nucleotide base pairs (bp). This implies that the average size protein coded for by these genes contains about 347 amino acids. The probability of forming, by a random assembly method, one such average-size protein molecule containing the amino acid residues in a required sequence is only $1/10^{451}$.

If the earth were made of pure carbon it would contain only about 10^{50} carbon atoms, but more than 10^{451} carbon atoms would be needed in order to make enough amino acids to form the proteins to achieve the probability of producing one protein molecule with the prescribed sequence. In other words, it would require an amount of carbon about 10^{401} times the size of the earth in order to achieve the probability of forming one required protein molecule with the specifications above! Realizing that the probability of producing proteins by a random assembly method is exceedingly small, some have proposed that DNA was formed by chemical evolution first and then it was used to direct the synthesis of the protein. This trades one problem for another. The random assembly of a gene containing 1,040 bp to code for a specified protein would be likely to require as much or more carbon than it would to make the protein directly by a random assembly method.

With a problem this great in forming one gene, imagine the problem of forming the 470 specific genes found in the one chromosome containing 580,070 bp: *M. genitalium*. Michael Behe, in his 1996 book *Darwin's Black Box*, uses the term "irreducible complexity" to refer to such situations where all conditions must be met simultaneously in order for the organism to survive.

In spite of the excitement in the 1950s and early 1960s generated by research based on chemical evolution theory, the net result today is a clearer understanding of the magnitude of the problem of the origin of protein, DNA, and life, without having found the answers. Since the only known method in nature for efficiently producing protein involves DNA, mRNA, and tRNA interacting with proteins such as RNA polymerase, tRNA synthetases, and ribosomal proteins, it seems reasonable to consider the possibility that all were formed simultaneously as part of intelligent design.

Even though there is general acceptance of the evidence for small genetic changes which may be referred to as microevolution, hard evidence for the formation of any new species by macroevolution is lacking.

Evidence for intelligent design is widespread in nature. For example:

a. The motorized rotating flagellum of some bacteria.
b. Blood clotting and its control.
c. The high degree of organization within a typical cell.
d. Cell division and its control.

e. The system for protein synthesis.

f. The human eye.

g. The respiratory chain based in the highly organized mitochondria.

h. The biosynthetic pathway in which acetyl CoA is the key compound.

Acetyl CoA is derived primarily from fatty acids and glucose and can also serve as an intermediate in the conversion of excess carbohydrate into fat. Oxidation of acetyl CoA in the citric acid cycle results, through the electron transport system, in the storage of energy in the form of ATP for chemical syntheses or muscular contraction. The acetyl CoA can also serve as the starting material for the synthesis of a wide variety of products, such as natural rubber, fragrance of lily of the valley flowers, oil of roses, menthol, oil of ginger, oil of celery, oil of cloves, carotenes, vitamins A, D, E, and K, plus all the steroids, such as cholesterol, the female hormones progesterone and estradiol, the male hormone testosterone, etc. This is a small sample of the wide variety of natural products derived from acetyl CoA.

Why don't we humans produce natural rubber in our bodies instead of about 50 kinds of steroids? The types of products, from this carefully regulated pathway, are determined by the specific enzymes in that species which are present at that time. The predominant products from this pathway may vary with time for a given species. The delicate balance that exists in this pathway can be illustrated by the fact that women make their female hormone estradiol from the male hormone testosterone, which they also produce. This does not cause a problem unless a woman develops adrenal cancer, which increases the amount of adrenal tissue capable of producing testosterone as well as other steroids. The first symptom usually observed by a woman with adrenal cancer is that she suddenly has to shave every day and her voice lowers in pitch, due to the production of testosterone faster than her body can convert it to estradiol. It seems very unlikely that an extremely complex pathway as this one, with all of its interconnecting processes and required enzymes, could arise purely by chance without an intelligent designer. I see no compelling arguments, based on chemical evolution or Darwinian evolution, which make it more reasonable for *me* to believe in evolution than in creation.

Just as scientific theories based on interpretation of data obtained by observation of the natural world are never absolutely proven, likewise I can never prove that the Genesis account of creation is true. I was not an eyewitness but, as a Christian I can, by faith, search for the testimony given by eyewitnesses. Who were those eyewitnesses of the creation events? God (Gen. 1:1), the Holy Spirit or Spirit of God (Gen. 1:2), Jesus Christ the Word (John 1:1–14).

The writers of the Bible were under the inspiration of God (eyewitness) as they wrote and they were moved by the Holy Spirit (eyewitness). God's daily progress report during the creation week stated that "it was good" or "very good." Christ (eyewitness), the Creator of all things, endorsed the Genesis creation report by quoting from it and chiding others for their ignorance of it. God wrote in stone that He had created in six days, and He is quoted twice in Exodus telling Moses to tell the Israelites that fact as well . . . and I believe Him.

angela meyer

Horticulture Science

Dr. Meyer is a former research scientist at Hort Research, Mount Albert Research Centre in New Zealand. She holds a B.S. in botany from the University of Auckland, an M.S. with first class honors in botany from the University of Auckland and a Ph.D. in horticultural science from the University of Sydney. Dr. Meyer (née Snowball) has published 11 refereed papers in the area of seasonal effects on fruit production and in 1994 was awarded the New Zealand Science and Technology bronze medal for excellence in kiwi fruit research and service to science.

There are several reasons I believe in the biblical account of creation.

Firstly, I believe the Bible to be the Word of God, accurate and truthful in all that it says. It has been tested and found to be true in history, archaeology, and fulfilled prophecy. As we continue to test it in areas of science, I believe we will find it to be true there, also. I believe we can accept the Bible's authority in the account of the origin of life.

Secondly, I believe the biblical account of creation because it is the best explanation for the complexity of life. I have never seen any evidence for evolution. All that I see around me in nature points to a divine designer.

In my own field of research, the control of flowering in crop plants, I see a wonderful precision demonstrated. The internal processes which govern flowering in each species are complex, interrelated, and designed to produce the best outcome for the individual plant, in terms of numbers, position, and quality of flowers and, therefore, fruit load.

Controlling factors, such as temperature, day length, light quality, and various hormones, act upon the flowering process to different degrees, depending on the species, plant age, position, growing conditions, and season. The whole system is not at all well understood by us mere humans — although we attempt to modify and maximize the system to our benefit in horticulture. This is all so complex and so interdependent that these systems cannot have come about gradually by chance. All plant life systems must have been complete and operative at the same moment in time — on day 3. It is also significant that for pollination and seed distribution, many plant species need animals which were created on days 5 and 6. A thousand-year gap between the days would not provide for the survival of many plants.

In addition, the extravagance of shape variation, color, and patterns of flowers is a clear expression of a divine artist. Evolutionary processes would most likely produce a much more restricted, conservative, and utilitarian display (if evolutionary processes were, in fact, possible).

Here I see the wisdom, greatness and power of our Creator God displayed.

stephen grocott

Inorganic Chemistry

16

Dr. Grocott is general manager, Research and Development, Southern Pacific Petroleum. He holds a B.S. (hons) in chemistry from the University of Western Australia and a Ph.D. in organometallic chemistry from the University of Western Australia. Dr. Grocott has worked in the field of mineral processing research for 17 years, holds 4 patents, and has published about 30 research papers. He is an elected fellow of the Royal Australian Chemical Institute.

I am a practicing scientist. Why do I believe in the supposedly thoroughly disproved, simpleton's story given in the Genesis account of creation? Why would I want to risk the criticism, alienation, and mirth of my peers in industry, universities, and professional societies?

The ultimate answer is that I am a Christian, but perhaps that is the subject of another essay. Instead, let me answer the following question from a purely scientific viewpoint, "Why do I as a practicing scientist believe in a 6-day creation, a young earth, and a global flood as described in a literal reading of Genesis?" I'll call this view the Creationist View and I'll call the main alternative view held by most scientists the Evolutionary View.

Now before I answer this question, let me tell you that as a scientist, I have no problems whatsoever in such a belief (the Creationist View). Nor have I encountered in my work anyone who has been able to counter such arguments with science. Furthermore, I enjoy discussing this subject with other evolution-believing scientists. Why? Because there are few substantive counters to a creationist belief but innumerable counters to evolutionary belief.

Anyway, on to the answer. There are so many "science-based" reasons for belief in creation that I will only touch upon a few that intellectually appeal to me.

What Is Science?

The first place to start is with a definition of science. Many exist, but most of them come down to something like, "If something is scientific, it is observable and testable (i.e., able to be repeated)."

Now it might surprise readers without a scientific background to hear me say that very few scientists have any real idea what science is. However, if you are a scientist you will probably acknowledge the truth of this seemingly nonsensical statement. In my undergraduate studies and postgraduate research, I can't ever recall anyone telling me what science is (and isn't!), showing me what it is, or providing me with an explanation of how it operates. If you are studying science or working with scientists and you doubt me, I challenge you to ask them for a definition of what is "scientific." After a pause, most of them would not be able to give an answer much deeper than "It is what scientists do."

As an undergraduate, I was taught to remember, not to think. Sure, I was given tools which I could *use* to think, but I wasn't actually *taught* to think. Then, as a Ph.D. researcher I worked in a very narrow field (as do all Ph.D. researchers), and so the breadth of a question like "What is the definition of scientific?" was absolutely irrelevant to me. Upon graduation and working as a research scientist for 17 years and as a leader of other scientists, the question has never arisen, nor apparently needed to have been asked. My point is that most scientists don't really know what is or isn't scientific, because it rarely affects what they do.

Why make a big deal of this? The reason is because creation and evolution are actually both outside the realms of science and, to know this, you need to know what science is — and as we have seen, most scientists don't.

Neither "process" is currently observable, testable, or repeatable. Please note that when speaking of evolution, I am talking of the appearance of new (not rearranged) genetic information leading to greater and greater complexity of genetic information. I am also talking about the appearance of life starting from inanimate chemicals. When talking about evolution, I am not speaking of natural selection, which leads to a reduction in genetic information in those species. Creationists, of course, have not the slightest problem with natural selection. After all, it has been practiced by farmers for centuries in their breeding of plants and animals through selecting preferred offspring and mating or propagating these. Anyway, the theory of natural selection was described by creation-believing scientists long before Darwin boarded the *Beagle*.

Evolution needs increasing complexity, increasing information. We don't see it occurring today and no one was there to observe it in the past. Evolutionists counter by saying that it is too slow to observe. Even if this were true, it still means that evolution is non-scientific because it is not observable or testable. Similarly, creation is not scientific. Obviously we don't see it occurring today and only God was there to see it in the past (assuming that one believes in a Creator God).

Summary. Given that creation and evolution are both outside the realms of science, why should I, as a scientist, have problems with belief in creation while really being "scientific"? I don't. This is not to say that many of the implications of creation and evolution can't be scientifically evaluated. They can, but neither belief can be proven. Nonetheless, as a scientist, after thoroughly studying this subject, I have been left feeling very satisfied with the scientific legitimacy of creation, and very uncomfortable with the leaps of faith required by many of my colleagues in order to believe in evolution.

Origin of Life

If one believes in evolution, then one has to also account for the origin of life — the very first step. Without this, the whole subject of evolution hangs on nothing.

Now this is a subject about which I have read much. And the weight of evidence against the spontaneous origin of life on earth is, in my opinion, overwhelming. One can make some basic calculations about the chemical equilibria of molecules essential to life. These calculations show that the formation of biochemically necessary molecules at even minuscule concentrations is highly unfavorable. Furthermore, the assembly of these molecules into more complex biochemical precursors such as proteins, polysaccharides, nucleic acids, or cell walls is beyond vanishingly small and is, in fact, statistically "impossible." The invocation of influences such as the catalytic effect of minerals, concentration of precursors in evaporating ponds, occurrence below ground, etc. is fiction of the highest order. Theories such as these are usually sought because the hypothesizing scientist starts with the premise that life evolved from non-life and, therefore, at some time in the past, lifeless simple molecules climbed Mount Impossible and multiplied.

Suppose that you could go back in your time machine to a time when, according to evolutionists, a lifeless world existed. Assume that you have taken with you an ocean full of organic precursors of life. What would happen to them? They would all decompose to simpler and simpler molecules and mostly would end up as lifeless common inorganic substances. Sterilize a frog and put it in a sterile blender — buzzzz. Seal up the mixture in a sterile container and leave it as long as you want. You won't get life, despite the fact that you started with the best possible mixture of so-called precursors to life. Repeat the experiment a million times — in the sun, in the dark; with oxygen, without; with clay, without; with UV, without. It won't make any difference. Thermodynamics clearly states that the mixture will decompose to simpler, lower energy, less information-containing molecules.

The complexity of the simplest imaginable living organism is mind-boggling. You need to have the cell wall, the energy system, a system of self-repair, a reproduction system, and means for taking in "food" and expelling "waste," a means for interpreting the complex genetic code and replicating it, etc., etc. The combined telecommunication systems of the world are far less complex, and yet no one believes they arose by chance.

Summary. I am afraid that as a scientist I simply cannot say strongly enough that spontaneous origin of life is chemical nonsense and, therefore, I am left with no alternative but to believe that life was created.

I could write many, many pages, adding more scientific arguments to this essay. I could write pages of references. Instead I will conclude with a few neat examples of consistency between a biblical world view and the world in which we live.

Neat Science in the Bible

*Familial marriages:*You've just fallen in love with a close relative. Why aren't you allowed to marry and have children? We all know why. It is because of the high risk of genetic malformation in the children. This comes about because close relatives have very similar mutations in their genetic information. Therefore, when the mother's and father's DNA comes together in the child, when there is a mistake on one gene, it is much more likely to also be present on the spouse's matching gene and lead to a baby with genetic defects. If the child is a product of "non-relatives," it is far more likely that a mistake on one gene will be paired with a correct gene, so that no abnormality will be manifest from that gene pair. Well, what has all this got to do with creation and evolution?

Well, if in the beginning Adam and Eve were created perfect (no gene damage), then their children would also have been genetically almost perfect. Therefore, there were no problems with marriage between even brothers and sisters (guess where Cain got his wife). In fact, close marriages weren't outlawed by God until the time of Moses — many hundreds of years later. This biblical account fits perfectly with observed accumulation of genetic mistakes over time (not improvement in the species). It explains why it was okay for Cain to marry a close relative and explains why God didn't outlaw it until much later. Neat, heh?

*Sedimentary deposits:*What do you see in the geology of the world? Massive sedimentary deposits. How did they form? Primarily through moving water. Belief that these formed through gradual erosion over millions of years does not fit with common sense or good science. The lateral extent of identical deposits (i.e., hundreds of kilometers of exactly the same rocks) implies catastrophism. So do features like the Grand Canyon (as more long-age geologists are starting to consider) and Ayers Rock, the largest single rock in the world, which is in Australia. The belief that it was a little bit of water over a long time (versus a lot of water over a little bit of time) is a faith-based position that is not supported by science, since it lies outside science. Was anyone there to record it and is it being repeated anywhere in the world today? On the contrary, modern-day catastrophes have been observed to cause massive local sedimentary deposits and other geological features. The Bible devotes three whole chapters to describing a worldwide flood with massive vulcanism and tectonic activity. This fits very well with what we see.

Fossils: How are fossils formed? In school I was told that fossilization occurs gradually over years. Nonsense! Let's use our common sense. The recently dead (or living) organism must be rapidly buried in sediment that can harden and exclude oxygen. Again, just what you'd expect from a catastrophic worldwide flood. Fossilization and rapid formation of deep strata must occur rapidly. How else do you explain vertical fossilized trees (without roots!) or a dinosaur's neck sticking through strata that are allegedly millions of years old? Tell me how the tree or dinosaur stayed alive for millions of years while the strata slowly formed around it. There are thousands of examples. A catastrophic flood fits the evidence quite well.

Other Reasons I Feel Comfortable with a Belief in Creation

Apart from the scientific reasons given above, I have many, many other reasons I am intellectually more satisfied by my belief in creation. I've listed a short selection of these.

Flood stories: How else do you simply explain the Flood stories shared by dozens of cultures around the world (stories recorded long before they were "contaminated" by Bible-carrying westerners).

Chinese pictograms: Ancient Chinese characters clearly and explicitly describe the Genesis creation and flood accounts.

Scientists changing their views: Although the scientists who believe in creation are decidedly in the minority, they are growing in number, as represented by scientist-members of creationist organizations around the world. Furthermore, increasing numbers of scientists who previously believed in evolution, while not becoming "creationists," are discarding evolutionary viewpoints because they appear to be inconsistent with science. Non-Christian scientists now openly discuss evidence for:

- rapid (years, not millions of years) formation of coal, oil, and natural gas
- catastrophic formation of geological features such as the Grand Canyon
- the apparent impossibility of the spontaneous formation of life from non-living matter
- the growing evidence of the flaws in the theory of evolution.

The moral consequences of a belief in evolution: If no one created me, if I am just highly evolved pond scum, then surely I am my own authority. Who or what determines right or wrong? Isn't it just relative? Isn't it different for different people and changing as society evolves? If I can get away with something for my benefit (i.e., for my evolutionary advantage), if genes are "selfish" as I have been taught, then why not push beyond the limits? Why care about the poor people, the old, the maimed, the victims in other countries? Why not abort the babies in utero, why not kill the old and useless, why not kill the dumb ones and also the unemployed if we have enough machines to do the labor?

If there are no absolutes (i.e., set by something outside man and not by man) then why not agree with one Australian philosopher (working at an Australian University) who proposes infanticide for excess children? How can you logically argue against this if man really does set his own rules? I know that at the moment this is against man's rules but man's rules change. Remember, a generation ago abortion and euthanasia were both illegal and taboo subjects.

A belief in creation, on the other hand, implies that there are absolutes imposed on us by a Creator, to whom we are accountable. This fits well with what I feel and see.

Emotions: We've all felt love. Is this an evolutionary artifact? Do I deeply love my children because I want my gene line to continue? Is that all there is to being a parent — survival of the species? Does my heart melt when I think of my wife simply because I want to propagate more and I want her to look after my little two-legged gene-bundles? When I witnessed the births of my two children, did I cry because those babies meant my gene line would continue? I guess that you can try to believe that I was (and that we all are) tricked by evolution.

Alternatively, you can believe in a Creator who describes himself as love and says that He made us in His image, able to discern right from wrong, and able to love both Him and others for no logical reason other than that is the way we were made. Yes, you can believe that your life has no higher purpose than to propagate the species and then die, but in your heart and head, does that fit with the world you see?

Conclusions

Science is a wonderful thing. I enjoy it a great deal. As a scientist, I count myself lucky to be able to do science and to be good at it.

And as a scientist, I have far more trouble trying to perform the mental gymnastics necessary to explain the world from an evolutionary, long-age viewpoint than I do from the young-earth, creationist viewpoint.

Although neither viewpoint can be proven (since they are both outside science), the circumstantial evidence, the consistency of the evidence and the foundation upon the most fundamental laws of science lead me to be much more comfortable believing in creation.

andrew mcintosh

Mathematics

Dr. McIntosh is Reader in Combustion Theory, Department of Fuel and Energy, University of Leeds in the United Kingdom. He holds a B.S. with first class honors in applied mathematics from the University of Wales, a Ph.D. in the theory of combustion from the Cranfield Institute of Technology, and a D.Sc. in mathematics from the University of Wales. He has contributed chapters to 10 textbooks dealing with combustion theory and published over 80 research papers. Dr. McIntosh is the author of *Genesis for Today: Showing the Relevance of the Creation/Evolution Debate to Today's Society.*[1]

World Views

As a scientist, I look at the world around me, and observe engineering mechanisms of such remarkable complexity that I am drawn to the conclusion of intelligent design being behind such complex order.

No scientist is entirely objective. We are always governed by our assumptions. If a scientist does not believe in God, then his starting point of atheism will be bound to affect his judgment as he looks at the world around him. If his mind is closed to the possibility of a designer, his own assumption will force him to adopt what to many will seem an "unlikely" explanation for what he observes.

(These matters of the philosophy behind the science of today are amplified in my book *Genesis for Today*.[2])

In my view we need to get back to the attitude of Einstein who, though he himself did not believe in an anthropomorphic deity, had a deep awe for the harmony of the universe. There was a humility in his brilliant scientific career which led to the discovery of the theory of special relativity and the consequent realization of the equivalence of energy and mass (through the famous equation $E=mc^2$). This was followed by the momentous discovery of the theory of general relativity which showed for the first time the connection between gravity and time, and led to the demonstration of the curvature of the space-time continuum in the universe. He said in an interview in 1929:

> We are in the position of a little child entering a huge library filled with books in many different languages. The child knows someone must have written those books. It does not know how. It does not understand the languages in which they are written. The child dimly suspects a mysterious order in the arrangement of the books but doesn't know what it is. That it seems to me, is the attitude of even the most intelligent being toward God. We see a universe marvellously arranged and obeying certain laws, but only dimly understand those laws. Our limited minds cannot grasp the mysterious force that moves the constellations.[3]

Such humility has been all but lost in our scientific world today. Many hold tenaciously to a strange view that theism is by definition excluded by science. Such a position is not logical, since theism or atheism is a product of one's assumptions. I unashamedly start not only from a theist position (which rather than be contradicted by my scientific enquiries, is confirmed by them), but also recognize that God can reveal himself to us — this I believe He has done in Jesus Christ.

Order and the Second Law of Thermodynamics

There is a fundamental law in the universe to which there is no known exception. That is, that when there is any work done due to energy conversion, there is always some dissipation of useful energy. In purely thermodynamic terms, this means that, for a closed system, the measure of energy no longer available for useful work is increasing. This is called entropy.[4] Thus, in a closed system, the overall entropy is increasing.

However, the law applies not only to the area of mechanics and engines. It applies to any system, since entropy is effectively a measure of the disorder in that system. In overall terms, disorder increases, cars rust, and machines wear out. No spontaneous reversal of this process has ever been observed for a closed system.

For living systems, this law still applies. That which is dead (such as a stick or leaf from a tree) has no information or teleonomy within it to convert the sun's energy to useful work. Indeed, it will simply heat up and entropy will increase.

Despite attempts by G. Nicolis Prigogine and co-workers to find auto-organization by random processes within living creatures, sustained order can never be achieved, because no new information is available. Indeed, after arguing that auto-organization by random processes may be possible in non-equilibrium systems, Prigogine states in the first reference:

Unfortunately, this (self-organization) principle cannot explain the formation of biological structures. The probability that at ordinary temperatures a macroscopic number of molecules is assembled to give rise to the highly ordered structures and to the co-ordinated functions characterizing living organisms is vanishingly small.[5]

Entropy, Information, and the Living World

The major obstacle to evolutionary theories as to origins is that information cannot be defined in terms of physics and chemistry. The ideas of a book are not the same as the paper and ink which constitute the book. Indeed, those same words and thoughts can be transmitted through an entirely different media (such as a computer CD-ROM, floppy disk, or a tape recorder). The chemicals do not define the message they carry. Meaning cannot spontaneously arise, since meaning presupposes intelligence and understanding.

One of the greatest discoveries was that of DNA by Francis H. Crick (UK) and James D. Watson (USA) in 1953. This molecule was found to be the universal storage medium of natural systems. A length of DNA is formed in such a way that two deoxyribose sugar-phosphate strands together form a double helix 2nm (10^{-9}m) in diameter with a pitch of 3.4nm. Between these two strands are hydrogen bridges, across which four types of nucleotides are placed: Adenine (A), Thymine (T), Cytosine (C), and Guanine (G). Effectively these four nucleotides are the chemical alphabet for writing "words" on the chemical "paper," which is the two sugar-phosphate strands. The helix enables a 3-dimensional storage of information formed by the patterns of the chemical letters used. The DNA string is like a sequence of dots and dashes in a coded message. The coded information using the letters (ACG, GUC, CAU, etc.) rides on the complicated chemical molecules, but is not defined by it. Information does not equal energy or matter.

In radio signals there is a carrier wave of lower frequency than the information signal which rides on the back of the carrier wave. Once received, the carrier wave is not important and the message is converted to sound and speech. In exactly the same way, the information concerning one cell could have been written using entirely different coding, that is, a different ordering of the nucleotides. As long as the rules stay the same, it is unimportant. Alternatively, completely different chemisty could be involved, that is, a different "alphabet" leading to a completely new language structure. What is paramount in this discussion is that information (that is the setting of the rules, the language, code, etc.) has been there from the beginning. To argue that this came by chance is scientifically preposterous. As Professor Gitt has stated, "No information can exist without an initial mental source. No information can exist in purely statistical processes."[6]

Though Dawkins has argued for a seemingly endless series of small advantageous mutations singled out by natural selection operating at the micro level[7] there are formidable arguments against his position. Denton, in his book *Evolution — A Theory in Crisis*,[8] discusses the problem of pleiotropy, that is, one gene affecting a number of seemingly totally unrelated functions in living organisms. For example, changes in the coat color genes in mice also affect body size. The microbiologist Behe has also ably rebutted Dawkins in his book *Darwin's Black Box*,[9] where he has shown that behind the many words of this arch-defender of Darwin, there is no mechanism in Darwinian evolution to add new information to a species at the macro level by a meaningful set of changes to the DNA letters, because "forward information" as to what the changes are aimed at is needed. Otherwise the intervening mutations have no advantage. Indeed, to form the code to begin with, it is vital that the sender and the receiver part of the cell both have prior agreement as to the meaning of the code, else there can be no communication. But Darwinian evolution only has chance mutations at its disposal. Because no "advance thinking" can possibly be allowed, there is no way that the nucleotides can arrange themselves in a "pre-defined code," since this assumes prior knowledge. Thus, the very existence of the DNA-coded language stalls evolution at the first hurdle.

Flight in the Natural World — Complexity All Can Observe

Examples of complexity in the natural world are not hard to come by. Living creatures all have examples of irreducible complexity as very ably demonstrated by Behe in his book *Darwin's Black Box*. One of the best examples of complexity, which defies a series of "gradual" changes (as advocated by Dawkins in his book *Climbing Mount Improbable*), is flight. For controlled, heavier-than-air flight, there are four fundamental requirements: (1) a correct wing shape to give a lower air pressure on the upper surface, (2) a large enough wing area to support the weight, (3) some means of propulsion or gliding, and (4) extra surfaces, or a means of altering the main surfaces, in order to change direction and speed.

Flight occurs in many branches of the living world: (a) birds; (b) insects: flies, bees, wasps, butterflies, moths; (c) mammals: bats; (d) reptiles: the extinct pterodactyls. Each class of creature is anatomically different, with no connection made even by the most ardent evolutionist. A tenuous connection has been attempted between reptiles (dinosaurs) and birds: it is seriously proposed that there was a "pro-avis" dinosaur that flapped scales on its arms to catch insects, and then changed its scales to feathers to gain airborne advantage on its prey. Even if one accepts the fossil record as a guide to change over millions of years, there is no evidence of any "pro-avis" creature ever existing in the fossil record. For the evolutionist, there is the scenario of flight evolving at least three times independently! The wings of the three main current groups of flying creatures today are substantially different: birds' wings are made of feathers; insect wings are made of scales, membranes, or hairs; and bat wings use skin spread out over a skeleton. So the evolutionist is faced with not just one impossible hurdle — that some reptiles grew feathers and began to fly — but two further hurdles. These are that flight evolved again when some rodents (mice? shrews?) developed a skin-like surface over their front legs to become bats, and then, quite separately, some insects grew very thin wings of scales, membranes, or hairs to becomes flies, bees, and butterflies!

Birds

A bird's wings are made of feathers. A feather is a marvel of light-weight engineering. Though light, it is very wind-resistant. This is because there is a clever system of barbs and barbules. Each barb of a feather is visible to the naked eye and comes off the main stem. What is not generally realized is that on either side of the barb are further tiny barbules which can only be seen under a microscope. These are of different types, depending on whether they are coming from one side of the barb or the other. On one side of the barb, ridged barbules will emerge, while on the other side, the barbules will have hooks. Thus, the hooks coming out of one barb will connect with ridges reaching in the opposite direction from a neighboring barb. The hooks and ridges act like "velcro," but go one stage further, since the ridges allow a sliding joint, and there is thus an ingenious mechanism for keeping the surface flexible and yet intact.

The next time you see a flight feather on the ground, remember it is a marvel of lightweight, flexible, aerodynamic engineering.

Reptile scales have no hint of such complicated machinery. Stahl has freely admitted, "No fossil structure transitional between scale and feather is known, and recent investigators are unwilling to found a theory on pure speculation."[10]

There is no genetic information within reptile scales to allow such a unique device as the sliding joint of a feather to be made. The tortuous route suggested by some of small "advantaged mutations" to scales leads to clumsy structures which are, in fact, a disadvantage to the creature. Not until all the hook and ridge structure is in place is there any advantage, even as a vane for catching insects! Unless one invokes some "thinking ahead" planning, there is no way that chance mutations could produce the "idea" of the cross-linking of the barbules to make a connecting lattice. Even if the chance mutation of a ridge/hook occurs in two of the barbules, there is no mechanism for translating this "advantage" to the rest of the structure. This is a classic case of irreducible complexity which is not consistent with slow evolutionary changes, but quite consistent with the notion of design.

But that is not all. Even if one had the feather, the delicate lattice structure would soon become frayed, unless there was also oil to lubricate the sliding joint made by the hooked and ridged barbules. Most of us realize that once the barbs of a feather have been separated, it is difficult to make them come back together. The feather becomes easily frayed in the absence of oil, which a bird provides from its preening gland at the base of its spine. Some of this oil is put on its beak and spread throughout the feathers, which for a water bird also gives waterproofing of its surface (thus, water slides off a duck's back). Without the oil the feathers are useless, so even if a supposed land-dwelling dinosaur got as far as wafting a wing, it would be no use after a few hours!

As one might expect, however, the story does not end there either, for a bird can fly only because it also has an exceedingly light bone structure, which is achieved by the bones being hollow. Many birds maintain skeleton strength by cross members within the hollow bones. Such an arrangement began to be used in the middle of this century for aircraft wings and is termed the "Warren's truss arrangement." Large birds, such as an eagle or a vulture, would simply break into pieces in midair if there were some supposed halfway stage in their skeletal development where they had not yet "developed" such cross members in their bones.

Furthermore, birds breathe differently. The respiratory system of a bird enables oxygen to be fed straight into air sacs, which are connected directly to the heart, lungs, and stomach, bypassing the normal mammalian requirement to breathe out carbon dioxide first before the next intake of oxygen. Human beings breathe about 12 times a minute, whereas small birds can breathe up to about 250 times a minute. This is thus a perfect system for the high metabolic rate of birds, which use up energy very quickly. In fast forward flight particularly, birds could not sustain exhaling against the oncoming airstream. Note also that birds are warm-blooded, which presents a vast biological hurdle for those who maintain a reptile ancestry for birds.

Consider the wing-flapping motion of a bird. This motion requires a bird to have strong wing muscles, with a forward-facing elbow joint to enable the foreshortening of the wing used much in the upward stroke of most species, and in the dive of birds of prey.

The versatility of the swivel joint at the base of the wing, coupled with the elbow joint on the wing itself and the smooth feather structure overlaying all, leads to great flexibility in the aerodynamics of the wing. Lift and drag can be balanced with instant movements, which in aircraft still require comparatively cumbersome changes of flap and ailerons.

Suppose we have an "almost" bird with all the above structures — namely feathers, preening gland, hollow bones, direct respiration, warm blood, swivel joint, and forward-facing elbow joint — but no tail! Controlled flight would still be impossible. Longitudinal stability can only be achieved with a tail structure, which most small boys soon realize when making paper airplanes! But what possible advantage do all of the above have for any land-based "almost" bird? Such a creature would be easy prey to any hunting animal.

In the list of mechanisms (feathers, preening gland, etc.), all are essential. Attempt to drop one and the whole project fails! The tail is essential, and with the tail must come another muscle to operate the variable small, but all-important wing surface — for instance, holding the plumage spread out and downwards when coming in to land. In other words, the tail is no use as a static "add-on." It must have the means of altering its shape in flight. All these mechanisms are controlled by a nervous system connected to the on-board computer in the bird's brain, all pre-programmed to operate within a wide envelope of complicated aerodynamic maneuvers.

Hummingbirds

One of the most delightful demonstrations of all of the above principles coming together involves the hummingbird. These small birds have the ability to beat their wings at up to 80 beats per second and, as is well known, can hover, fly backwards, forwards, and sideways with ease (much of the information here is drawn from an excellent article by Denis Dreves[11]). Speeds of 50 miles an hour are commonplace for these flying marvels. Fuel must be replenished very quickly because of the great turnover of energy. Consequently, the bird must feed on a food which can be broken down quickly into energy.

All this is achieved by feeding on the nectar of flowers, which requires the ability to hover and a thin long beak to get into the flower (e.g., a fuchsia for the rufous hummingbird). The bird also has a special tongue with two furrows, enabling the nectar to be stored on it. The long tongue goes in and out of the bill, at an unbelievable rate of 13 times per second and, when retracted, is curled up at the back of the head.

One can envisage the odd scenario of the supposedly half-evolved hummingbird either with the ability to hover and a sparrow beak, unable to feed, or the long beak but no ability to hover, which would mean flying into the flower with no ability to stop! All the requirements must be there to begin with.

The extreme maneuverability of hummingbirds is due to their having the ability to swivel the wing through a much greater angle than other birds. Consequently, the hummingbird can produce a power stroke on the upward motion of the wing as well as the downstroke, and the motion of the wing tip of a hummingbird in flight sweeps out a figure eight as the joint swivels round some 90 degrees first in one direction, and then about 90 degrees in the other direction. Further rotation is possible which means that the wing can thus beat a power stroke in any direction, with small asymmetries enabling sideways movements as well.

Flight cannot be explained by supposed evolutionary change.

The attempts to find any transitional forms have all failed. *Archaeopteryx* has been shown to have fully developed flight feathers (thus, no half-bird), with other recognizable birds found fossilized at a lower level. Other supposed "pro-avis" creatures (half reptile/half bird) have never been found. The evidence is overwhelming that birds have always been birds, and is entirely consistent with their being created right at the beginning on day 5, just as the Bible says.

It is not scientific to argue, on the one hand, for the obvious design of a Boeing 747, and then rule design "out of court" when considering the far more versatile flight of an eagle, falcon, or the remarkable hummingbird. Modern minds within the secular media are presenting an unscientific duality of thought when praising engineering complexity in man-made machines, glorying in the great creative advances of mankind, but presenting the complexity in the world around us (of often far greater intricacy than man-made machines) as due to a gigantic unplanned cosmic experiment, with no Creator.

Flying Insects

Flying insects have no connection whatsoever with birds, and yet flight is fully developed in all the fossils of flies, moths, and butterflies. There is not any contender at all for any transitional forms. The wings of such creatures are exceedingly fragile, made of scales, membranes, or sometimes hairs or bristles. They start as larvae or grubs, with some feeding on totally different substances than the adult (e.g., caterpillars and butterflies). The best example is the dragonfly, which starts as a nymph underwater, obtaining oxygen from the water; yet no adult dragonfly could possibly exist in the same surroundings. It is quite common for dragonflies to reach speeds of 30 miles per hour, but no transitional fossils exist. The evidence is, in fact, of much larger, fully developed dragonflies with a wingspan of two to three feet in the past,[12] indicating decline today, rather than advance. The related damselfly has the remarkable ability to hover as well, such that the sophisticated aerodynamics of the four wings operating independently inspired the design of early forerunners of the modern helicopter.

The complexity of the life cycle of creatures such as the butterfly (caterpillar to chrysalis to butterfly) and the dragonfly (water nymph to dragonfly), and their perfect wing structure as adults, points to intricate design which cannot be explained by small changes. The survival of each species is dependent on all the mechanisms being present to begin with.

Migrating Butterflies

The monarch butterfly of North America migrates 2,000 miles from California in the northwest (or Ontario in the northeast) to the over-wintering site of central Mexico. More amazing is the following fact: some adults who make the journey back are fully mature, so that some females lay eggs and die en route northward.

These offspring, after going through the caterpillar/chrysalis stage, continue the migration northward. More remarkable still is the fact that not all these make it back to the northeast of America, so another generation, the third, then finally completes the journey, fulfilling the aspiration of grandma! This, of course, means that a remarkable system of information is bound up in the genetic coding of each butterfly, such that it "knows" at what stage of the migrating cycle the group of butterflies is in. This information is passed on to each generation. Such a delicate mechanism shouts intelligent design!

Furthermore, it has been established that magnetite has been found in the bodies of monarch butterflies (and also honeybees), indicating that they are able to orientate themselves by sensing the earth's magnetic field. Their eyes are also sensitive to polarized light from the sun, again giving them a direction cue. The two eyes, far from being simple, are actually each made of 6,000 separate lenses! There are no half-formed butterflies in the fossil record. They are similar to modern ones — fully formed and ready to go!

Flying Mammals — Bats

Bats are entirely different from birds and insects, with wings made of skin and a radar system of echo-sounding with pinpoint accuracy, enabling the bat to find insect food on the wing, with unbelievable precision. No half-bat has ever been found in the fossil record, and it would be hard to imagine how such a halfway creature could survive. Flight alone is only possible with fully developed wings. This combined with the sophisticated radar is yet another example of irreducible complexity.

Combustion and the Bombardier Beetle

Lastly, an example from combustion — the bombardier beetle. This creature requires an explosive mixture (hydrogen peroxide and hydroquinone), a combustion chamber to contain the chemicals, exhaust nozzles to eject the mixture into which two catalysts are also injected (the enzymes catalase and peroxidase) — all this at the right moment to make the violent reaction take place as the mixture leaves the back end. The bombardier beetle manages it all with ease, along with the capacity to send four or five bombs in succession into the face of a predator, controlled by muscles and directed by a reflex nervous system. This is combustion theory and practice par excellence! Even the combustion chamber of the latest Rolls

Royce Trent Gas Turbine would not reach the complexity of this little creature.

All the above requirements would have to be in place at the same "evolutionary moment"! There is no way any "intermediate" could survive because of the risk of either (1) blowing him/herself to smithereens (because he has the combustible mixture and the catalyst, but no exhaust system), or (2) slowly eroding his/her insides by having a combustible mixture, all the necessary exhaust tubes, but no catalyst, or (3) being eaten by predators despite trying to blow them away with catalysts through a fine exhaust system, but no combustible mixture! For the creature to function, everything must all be in place together — as a good Rolls Royce engineer knows — for aircraft gas turbines to work!

Consistency with a Biblical World View

As a scientist, I see nothing to discount straightforward belief in Scripture, when considering the mechanisms in nature. Those which have been considered in this chapter could be added to by many more intricately balanced mechanisms which overwhelmingly testify to a creative hand.

Many, of course, refuse to acknowledge the evidence for design in nature because they make the untestable assumption of atheism. If someone seriously did doubt the design of a modern airliner, that person could be convinced by taking him into an aircraft factory and introducing him to the teams of design engineers. In the same way, man's prejudice against design in creation can only really be answered by a radical change of heart and by personally meeting the author of all. In the end the difference between these two world views is due to religious differences. I believe that it is because humans do not want to be accountable to a Creator God that they persist with a theory which has little evidence to support it.

Furthermore, in the view of this author, there is much in the fossil record which is entirely consistent with catastrophic destruction in a worldwide flood. We have for too long underestimated the forces of nature, and only perhaps in recent decades have geologists (some reluctantly) returned to a catastrophic view of many rock layers.

In June 1991 the volcano Pinatubo in the Philippines erupted with a cloud of ash 130,000 feet (over 24 miles) high and 10 miles wide. Pyroplastic flows devastated the landscape, with later further volcanic ash and mud flowing for thousands of square miles. The volcanic blast in 1883 at Krakatau (in between the Sumatra and Java islands of Indonesia) was even greater; this was heard 2,900 miles away, with rocks thrown 34 miles high into the atmosphere and dust falling 3,313 miles away ten days after the explosion. A tsunami (tidal wave) 100 feet high was created, which travelled right across the Indian Ocean at 450 mph, and volcanic mist circled the earth and turned the sun blue and green.

On May 18, 1980, probably the most well-documented recent volcanic eruption took place at Mount St. Helens in Washington state. The top of the mountain was completely removed and a hot blast ripped away 150 square miles of forest. The movement of the mountain caused a wave nearly 900 feet high to move across Spirit Lake, with the effect that approximately one million tree trunks found their way into the lake. Many others were pushed further down into lower regions by mud flows and were actually observed upright, roots down, moving at great speed in the mud flows.

Not until this eruption had it been quite appreciated what the immediate aftermath of volcanic eruptions can sometimes cause. Sediments 600 feet thick were exposed by subsequent mud flows carving their way through the initial sediments before they had hardened. The Toatle River canyon, formed in 1980, is effectively a miniature 1/40th version of the Grand Canyon. The implication is that the Colorado River is not the way the world's greatest canyon was formed, that is, by slow erosion. All the evidence is consistent with massive volcanic and sedimentary upheaval on a continental scale, followed by the bursting of great dams of water, and clay breaking and causing subsequent massive mud flows, entirely consistent with the description in the Book of Genesis of the Great Flood.

When the Bible speaks historically (and literary experts agree Genesis is written as history), I believe we can trust what it says.

Endnotes

1 Andrew McIntosh, *Genesis for Today: Showing the Relevance of the Creation/ Evolution Debate for Today's Society* (Epsom, United Kingdom: Day One Publications, 1997).

2 Ibid., chapter 2, "Genesis and Science."

3 Denis Brian, *Einstein: A Life* (New York: J. Wiley, 1996), p. 186.

4 McIntosh, *Genesis for Today,* Appendix A.

5 I. Prigogine, G. Nicolis, and S. Babloyant, "Thermodynamics of Evolution," *Physics Today*, 25 (11), 1972, 23–8; G. Nicolis and I. Prigogine, *Self Organization in Non-equilibrium Systems* (New York: Wiley, 1977).

6 *Siemens Review*, vol. 56, part 6, 1989, p. 36–41.

7 See Richard Dawkins, *The Selfish Gene* (New York: Oxford University Press, 1989); *The Blind Watchmaker* (New York: Penguin, 1991); and *Climbing Mount Improbable* (New York: Norton, 1996).

8 Michael Denton, *Evolution — A Theory in Crisis* (Bethesda, MD: Adler and Adler, 1986), p. 142–156.

9 Michael Behe, *Darwin's Black Box* (New York: Free Press, 1996), p. 220–221.

10 Barbara J. Stahl, *Vertebrate History: Problems in Evolution* (New York: McGraw-Hill, 1974), p. 349.

11 *Creation Ex Nihilo*, 14(1), 1992, 10–12.

12 see David Attenborough, *Discovering Life on Earth* (Boston, MA: Little, Brown, 1981), p. 60–61.

john p. marcus

Biochemistry

Dr. Marcus is research officer at the Cooperative Research Centre for Tropical Plant Pathology, University of Queensland, Australia. He holds a B.A. in chemistry from Dordt College, an M.S. in biological chemistry and a Ph.D. in biological chemistry from the University of Michigan. Dr. Marcus's current research deals with novel antifungal proteins, their corresponding genes, and their application in genetic engineering of crop plants for disease resistance.

My belief in a literal six-day creation of the universe is based primarily on the teaching of the Bible and my understanding that this is God's Word and is true. This faith, however, does not close my eyes to scientific evidence; rather, it opens my eyes so that I can make sense out of all the data. Two things that confirm my belief in creation are the clear evidence of design in nature, and the vanishingly small probabilities of life coming about by chance.

Evidence of Design

The clear evidence of deliberate design in living organisms strongly confirms our faith in God's Word. Psalm 104:24 states "O LORD, how manifold are thy works! in wisdom hast thou made them all: the earth is full of thy riches." God's creation clearly reflects the infinite wisdom which He used to design and create it. The order-liness of living things and their mind-boggling complexity are surely unmistakable indications that this creation did not come about by random and disorderly chance processes. There are many ways to illustrate that a simple examination of an object will reveal the presence or absence of design. One can easily appreciate that certain items are extremely unlikely to come about by chance operations acting over time.

When archaeologists come across a smooth, cylindrical clay structure with walls consistently about the same thickness, a flat bottom that allows the structure to stand upright, and an opening in the top, it is a sure sign to them that some type of intelligent civilization was responsible for producing that clay pot. It is such a simple deduction to make — it is obvious that an ordered structure such as a clay pot could not have come about by chance. One can see that even the smallest amount of order exhibited in a simple clay pot is almost completely beyond the reach of random processes. That is why archaeologists know that a clay pot is a clear signature of civilization; orderliness is evidence of design.

Step back now and consider: how is this different from the formation of life from non-living chemicals? To be sure, there is a difference; the generation of a living organism from simple non-living chemicals is infinitely *less* likely to occur. Living organisms are so much more complex than is a clay pot that an adequate comparison cannot even be made. What person would want to believe that a clay pot arose by chance processes? Only a person bound and determined to exclude the possibility that civilization might have been responsible for making that pot. One can appreciate that evolutionists are also bound and determined to exclude God from the picture! It seems that they don't even ask whether the evidence is consistent with creation. They simply insist that all explanations for the existence of the universe must come from within the universe and not from a God who stands above it. In the case of living organisms, as in the case of clay pots, the presence of orderliness gives the game away. Plainly, this orderliness could not have come about by chance — not even if chance were helped along by natural selection! It must have been arranged by an outside intelligence. Design needs a designer.

DNA[1] evidence is often claimed to give support to the evolutionary theory; in reality, DNA illustrates God's handiwork of design in a powerful way. Let us consider the complexity of this important component of living systems in order to see how absurd it is to believe that life could come about by chance. DNA is the primary information-carrying molecule of living organisms. The beauty and wonder of this molecule can hardly be overstated when one considers its properties. Being the blueprint of living cells, it stores all the information necessary for the cell to feed and protect itself, as well as propagate itself into more living cells, and to cooperate with other living cells that make up a complex organism.

If the DNA of one human cell were unravelled and held in a straight line, it would literally be almost one meter long and yet be so thin that it would be invisible to all but the most powerful microscopes. Consider that this string of DNA must be packaged into a space that is much smaller than the head of a pin[2] and that this tiny string of human DNA contains enough information to fill almost 1,000 books, each containing 1,000 pages of text.[3] Human engineers would have a most difficult time trying to fit one such book into that amount of space; one thousand books in that amount of space boggles the mind! For compactness and information-carrying ability, no human invention has even come close to matching the design of this remarkable molecule.

Amazing as the DNA molecule may be, there is much, much more to life than DNA alone; life is possible only if the DNA blueprint can be read and put into action by the complex machinery of living cells. But the complex machinery of the living cell requires DNA if it is going to exist in the first place, since DNA is the source of the code of instructions to put together the machinery. Without the cellular machinery, we would have no DNA since it is responsible for synthesizing DNA; without DNA we would have no cellular machinery. Since DNA and the machinery of the cell are co-dependent, the complete system must be present from the beginning or it will be meaningless bits and pieces.

In order to emphasize this co-dependence of the cellular machinery and DNA, let us examine some proteins (i.e., the machinery) that are directly involved in the conversion of the DNA blueprint into more proteins. Before we list the processes and proteins associated with converting DNA information into proteins, we should emphasize the following points: (1) each and every step in the overall process absolutely requires protein(s) that are unique and extremely complex; and (2) these unique and complex proteins can only be produced by the overall process in which they themselves are critically involved.

The making of RNA[4] from a DNA template is a critical first step in the process of protein formation. For RNA to be synthesized, no fewer than five different protein chains[5] must cooperate. Four of these proteins form the RNA polymerase complex and the last one tells the RNA polymerase where to start reading the DNA template. This enzyme complex must recognize where to start transcribing DNA into RNA; it must then move along the

DNA strand, adding individual building blocks[6] to the growing RNA chain; and lastly, it must know where to finish the transcription process.

It is not enough, however, simply to make one kind of RNA; three different types of RNA are required in the process of making proteins, messenger RNA (mRNA), ribosomal RNA (rRNA), and transfer RNA (tRNA). Molecules of mRNA carry the information extracted from the DNA blueprint which encodes the protein to be synthesized; rRNA molecules make up a critical component of ribosomes (discussed below); and tRNA is responsible for carrying individual amino acids to the site where they will be added to a new protein. Before tRNA molecules can serve their proper function, however, they must be charged with a suitable amino acid in order that it can be added on to a growing protein chain at the appropriate time. At least 20 different aminoacyl–tRNA synthetase proteins are necessary to attach individual amino acids to the corresponding tRNA molecules (at least one for each type of amino acid).

Once mRNA, tRNA and rRNA molecules have been synthesized, it is then necessary to translate the information from the mRNA into a protein molecule. This process is carried out by a huge complex of proteins called the ribosome. These amazing protein synthesis "machines" contain multiple different proteins, together with various ribosomal RNA molecules all associated into two main subunits. In a simple bacterium such as *E. coli*, ribosomes are composed of some 50 different proteins[7] and three different rRNAs!

The reactions mentioned above are only the core reactions in the process of synthesizing proteins; we have not even discussed the energy molecules that must be present for many of these reactions to proceed. Where is the energy going to come from to produce these energized molecules? How will the cell harvest energy unless it has some sort of mechanism for doing so? And, where is an energy-harvesting mechanism going to come from if not from pre-encoded information located in the cell?

A quick summation will reveal that the process of converting DNA information into proteins requires at least 75 different protein molecules. But each and every one of these 75 proteins must be synthesized in the first place by the process in which they themselves are involved. How could the process begin without the presence of all the necessary proteins? Could all 75 proteins have arisen by chance in just the right place at just the right time? Could it be that a strand of DNA with all the necessary information for making this exact same set of proteins just happened to be in the same place as all these proteins? And could it be that all the precursor molecules also happened to be around in their energized form so as to allow the proteins to utilize them properly?

Needless to say, without proteins life would not exist; it is as simple as that. The same is true of DNA and RNA. It should be clear that DNA, RNA, and proteins must *all* be present if any of them are going to be present in a living organism. Life must have been created completely functional, or it would be a meaningless mess. To suggest otherwise is plain ignorance (or perhaps desperation). So, we truly have a "which came first?" problem on our hands. I believe the answer is, of course, that none of them came first! God came first; He designed and then created all of life with His spoken Word. DNA, RNA, and protein came all at exactly the same time. It is extremely difficult to understand how anyone could believe that this astoundingly complicated DNA-blueprint translation system happened to come about by chance.

Meaningful Molecules Could Not Have Arisen by Chance

Now let us consider the probability of just one of the above 75 proteins coming about by chance. Consider a smaller than average protein of just 100 amino acid residues. *If* all the necessary left-handed amino acids were actually available, and *if* the interfering compounds, including right-handed amino acids, were somehow eliminated, and *if* our pool of amino acids were somehow able to join individual amino acids together into protein chains faster than the proteins normally fall apart, then the chances of this random 100 amino-acid protein having the correct sequence would be 1 in 20^{100} possible sequence combinations; 20 available amino acids raised to the power of the number of residues in the protein, i.e., 1 in 1.268×10^{130}, or 1 in 12, 680, 000, 000, 000, 000, 000, 000, 000, 000, 000, 000, 000, 000, 000, 000, 000, 000, 000, 000, 000, 000, 000, 000, 000, 000, 000, 000, 000, 000, 000, 000, 000, 000, 000, 000, 000, 000, 000, 000, 000!!!

To put this number in some perspective, we must do some calculations. The reader may wish to skip ahead if the absurdity of chance giving birth to order is already appreciated. Let us take a more-than-generous scenario and see how desolate the theory of evolution becomes in view of the probabilities. The earth has a mass of around 5.97×10^{27} grams. If the entire mass of the earth were converted to amino acids, there would be in the order of 3.27×10^{49} amino acid molecules available.[8] If all of these molecules were converted into 100-residue proteins,[9] there would be 3.27×10^{47} proteins. Since there are 1.27×10^{130} possible combinations of amino acids in a 100-mer protein (see above), a division of the number of possibilities by the number of proteins present on our hypothetical globe shows that the chances of having just *one* correct sequence in that entire globe of 100-mer proteins is 1 in 3.88 x 10^{82}!!![10]

Even if each of these 3.27 x 10^{47} 100-mer proteins could be rearranged many times over into different sequences during the time span of the earth, the chances that one correct sequence would be produced are still not close to being realistic. Consider that there are "only" 1.45 x 10^{17} seconds in the mythical evolutionary age of the earth.[11] It can be calculated that each and every 100-mer protein in that hypothetical earth would need to rearrange itself an average of 2.67 x 10^{65} times per second in order to try all possible combinations![12] The 100-amino-acid molecules could not even come close to assembling and disassembling that quickly. It is physically impossible.

An age of 4.6 billion years is an extremely long time, to be sure, but I suspect evolutionists wish they had picked a much larger number for the age of the earth and of the universe. It becomes obvious why evolutionists are never quick to point out the actual numbers associated with the probabilities of life coming about by chance. Remember, we have only examined a small protein of 100 amino acids. The very same calculations could be performed considering that we need at least the 75 proteins mentioned above in order to have a self-replicating system. For 75 proteins of the same size, the probability of obtaining the correct sequences for all of them comes to 20^{7500} or 3.7779 x 10^{9700}!!! (That is correct, almost 9,700 zeros.)

Even if there were oceans full of amino acids just trying all kinds of different combinations, a correctly formed molecule in the Indian Ocean is not going to be able to cooperate very easily with another correctly formed molecule in the Atlantic Ocean. Nor would a correct sequence of amino acids be able to interact with another functional protein which happened to occur in the same physical location but a mere one year later. Truly, the thought of even one single functional protein arising by chance requires blind faith that will not or cannot grasp the numbers! Such thoughts are pure fantasy and have nothing to do with science.

It is no wonder that evolutionists have not come up with any specific scenarios that would explain how life arose from non-living chemicals. The stories that are put forward are like fairy tales with some science thrown in to make them sound educated. One popular biochemistry textbook admits that there is no physical evidence for the transition of life from non-life:

> Our hypothetical nucleic acid synthesis system is therefore analogous to the scaffolding used in the construction of a building. After the building has been erected the scaffolding is removed, leaving no physical evidence that it was ever there. *Most of the statements in this section must therefore be taken as educated guesses.* Without having witnessed the event, it seems unlikely that we shall ever be certain of how life arose[13] (emphasis in the original).

Far from being educated guesses, the many deceptive evolutionary scenarios seem to be nothing short of biased myths arising from the desperate desire to exclude God from lives and consciences.

How do evolutionists respond to the zero likelihood of life arising by chance? The biochemistry text quoted above asks and then answers the question: "How then did life arise? The answer, most probably, is that it was guided according to the Darwinian principle of the survival of the fittest as it applies at the molecular level."[14] The key fact to note here is that natural selection simply cannot act unless there are functional, self-replicating molecules present to act on. We have already seen that no such system could possibly appear by chance. Life in its totality must have been created in the beginning, just as God told us.

Notes

1 DNA stands for deoxyribonucleic acid.

2 About 1/100th of a millimeter in diameter.

3 One human cell contains 3×10^9 nucleotide bases (genetic letters) in just one of the two copies of DNA present in the cells.

4 RNA stands for ribonucleic acid, which is very similar to DNA but contains an additional oxygen molecule in the sugar backbone.

5 This figure is for "simple" prokaryotic systems; in more complex eukaryotic systems, not only are there more proteins involved in forming the RNA polymerase complex (i.e., 9–11 proteins), there are three different RNA polymerase complexes, specialized for the synthesis of various RNAs, including mRNA, rRNA, and tRNA.

6 Nucleoside triphosphates: ATP, GTP, UTP, and CTP. These building blocks are relatively complex chemicals and require energy, precursor chemicals, and proteins in order to be made available for RNA synthesis.

7 This is the figure for prokaryotes; for eukaryotes there are 73 different proteins involved and 4 rRNAs.

8 Take the mass of the earth 5.9728×10^{27}g divided by 110g/mole, the average mass of amino acids, to determine that there would be approximately 5.4298×10^{25} moles of amino acids; multiply this number by Avogadro's number (6.023×10^{23}) to determine the number of amino acid molecules present.

9 That is, proteins containing 100 amino acids each. The size of our hypothetical protein is actually smaller than most proteins that occur in nature.

10 The number of possible sequences (1.268×10^{130}) divided by the number of 100-mers available $(3.27 \times 10^{47}) = 3.88 \times 10^{82}$.

11 Sixty seconds per minute x 60 min/hr x 24 hr/day x 365.26 days/year x 4.6 billion years $= 1.45 \times 10^{17}$ seconds.

12 The 1.268×10^{130} sequence combinations to try divided by 3.27×10^{47} proteins that can be rearranged $= 3.88 \times 10^{82}$ rearrangements necessary for each 100-mer protein if all combinations are to be tried. 3.88×10^{82} rearrangements per protein divided by 1.45×10^{17} seconds $= 2.67 \times 10^{65}$ rearrangements per protein per second. This is an over-simplification, since it assumes that each 100-mer would actually never try the same sequence twice and that all the possibilities would necessarily be tried.

13 Donald Voet and Judith G. Voet, *Biochemistry* (New York: John Wiley and Sons, 1995), p. 23.

14 Ibid.

nancy m. darrall

Botany

Dr. Darrall is a speech therapist at the Bolton Community Health Care Trust in the United Kingdom. She holds a B.S. with first class honors in agricultural botany from the University of Wales, a Ph.D. in botany from the University of Wales, Abery-stwyth, and an M.S. in speech and language pathology and therapy from the University of London. For 14 years Dr. Darrall worked in the area of environmental research at the National Power, Technology, and Environmental Centre, at Leatherhead, studying the environmental impact of electricity generation, and in particular the physiological effects of gaseous air pollutants on agricultural crops and trees.

In the north of England, in a small industrial town called Helmshore, is some grass that has made it famous throughout the world of air pollution research. It looks much the same as any other grass of the same species, ryegrass — or *Lolium perenne* to the biologist — but there are certain differences that have enabled it to survive in an area highly polluted by sulphur dioxide during the days of heavy industry. Similarly, groups of individuals from various species survive in industrial areas with high levels of lead and zinc in the soil. Many authors of the scientific papers describing these findings have referred to the evolution of resistance to pollution. As a biologist involved in research on air pollution, I have had good opportunity to study much of this work, for example, Bell and Mudd (1976), Horsman et al. (1978), Roberts et al. (1983), and Taylor (1978). Bradshaw and McNeilly (1981) comment that the almost universal occurrence of metal tolerant populations on mine spoils shows the remarkable power of natural selection as a force for evolutionary change in response to environmental factors — evolution in action! Is this true? Can examples like these be used to prove that all life evolved by mutation and natural selection? I would suggest that there is too much scientific evidence around today to leave us in doubt about the answer to that question.

I would like to discuss those areas that have particularly influenced my own perspective on the origin of living things, the character of God, evidence of irreducible complexity, the origin of information, and the probability of a new species appearing. The complexity of the natural world is beyond doubt; the origin of such complexity, by evolution or design, requires careful evaluation of information from all sources. The essence of neo-Darwinian evolution is that new species, new designs, new organs such as the eye, the wing, and the ear, can arise by chance. More than that, it says that life originated spontaneously from chemical matter and, over millions of years, all the different life forms came into being by the processes of mutation and natural selection. The origin of life is matter and only matter; anything else is irrelevant and unnecessary, excluded from debate by definition, before that debate is started (Johnson, 1995). The process is unguided and mindless, unpredictable in its outcome; man is the result of a purposeless and natural process that did not have him in mind (Simpson, 1967).

Evolution — an Added Extra

During my time at university studying agricultural botany and pure botany, there were no courses in evolution.

I studied the nature of DNA, genes, and chromosomes and went on to look at gene expression in individuals and populations and the transfer of genetic information to subsequent generations. We learned to classify plants by traditional methods and modern techniques. The professor who lectured this last course commented that evolutionary theory had provided no new techniques or procedures for constructing classifications and that speculative attempts to produce phylogenetic trees and systems without much valid evidence actually retarded the progress of taxonomy (Heywood, 1967).

In ecology, the complex interrelationships between plants and animals within various environments were explored, and the evolution of these complex webs of interaction was stated as a fact.

However, in no subject area was experimental or observational evidence given or theoretical arguments provided to support such a statement. In other subjects — plant anatomy, biochemistry, physiology, crops of agriculture, plant breeding, crop pests, and diseases — no reference was made to the topic of evolution. Clearly, the complexities of all these fields of study can stand alone and develop without the evolutionary basis that is claimed to underpin all areas of biological science. Little has changed in biochemistry and biological sciences, judging by the scientific texts today.

Planned, Purposed and Designed

At university, I also had the opportunity of benefiting from systematic study of the biblical Christian faith. I was already a Christian with a knowledge of God's saving power before I went to university. However, during this time, my understanding of the character of God developed. There came a point where I could see a non-conformity between the God revealed in the Bible and the nature of a god who would be compatible with the processes of evolution. Evolution with an add-on module of belief in God was very unsatisfactory and would contradict and downgrade the revelation of God in Scripture. The purposeful, supernatural being revealed in the Bible, who is all powerful, the originator of all things, including all material objects, of all design and of all the rules by which the natural world operates, would have to give way. I would have to admit to a god of limited power; things might come into being independent of his will.

Outcomes may not necessarily be of his choosing and autonomous self-sufficient nature might just happen to produce something else instead.

God planned, purposed, and designed the perfect result, the world as originally created, and He achieved it by the perfect means, with flawless precision (Tozer, 1961). Creation is an expression of the being of God and will therefore reflect the character of God. However, to be consistent with the principles of evolution, I would have to acknowledge a wisdom with a source in things, in matter, in molecules, and also in processes in the natural world that might change or improve on God's beginnings of a task. This would involve agreeing with the view of neo-Darwinists, that science is the only reliable path to knowledge. As a consequence, I would have to accept that science has a monopoly on the production of knowledge and that the boundaries of science are the boundaries of knowledge and reality. A God who is all-knowing and planned our salvation before the foundation of the world cannot be allowed alongside a naturalistic interpretation of the world. At best, a god might be tolerated who is a remote being who set things in motion, but then watched helplessly from the sidelines as things unfolded. In this case, I would have to consider the Bible no longer as an inerrant source of knowledge about God's dealings with man, about the origin of sin and suffering, but as writings merely of tradition, irrelevant to today's world, because we have evolved beyond God's plans.

The historical accuracy of the accounts in the early chapters of Genesis, dealing as they do with the creation of Adam and Eve, corruption of the natural world and death as a result of the Fall, would also be unacceptable. This would have to be replaced with a view of evolutionary progression of plants and animals, a gradual improvement upwards to better things. This, then, would deal a death blow to the authority of the New Testament, as the authors use the historicity of these early people as a basis for developing arguments about salvation and judgment.

As my Christian faith is part of my everyday life, I found that it was impossible to relegate faith to a separate sphere from my observations and understanding of science. Professor Edgar Andrews has discussed the illogical nature of compartmentalizing faith and science in his book *Christ and the Cosmos* (1986) and I found his arguments helpful in clarifying my own position. He points out that we make observations and perform experiments using our natural senses to collect scientific information. From this factual information we use our powers of reason to develop an understanding of the natural world. However, this understanding excludes knowledge of spiritual things. Our five senses enable us to observe the natural world, but faith enables us to observe the spiritual realm of God. To develop our spiritual understanding, we use our faith.

We cannot use faith on its own, so our powers of reason look at the information, using our faith to come to spiritual understanding. Reason works on faith plus information to give spiritual understanding, just as reason acts on the observations of the five senses to develop our understanding of the way the natural world functions today. Faith is not an alternative pathway to a different form of knowledge unrelated to the material world in which we live. Both routes lead to understanding. However, by the use of reason plus faith plus information, we come to a growing understanding of the way God works in the world, "the wisdom of God." I realized that His work in the natural world would be no less a reflection of His character than His dealings with men and women. These would be consistent with His direct revelation through Scripture, although they might not be as complete. To believe that God created the world by evolution would mean that the God of the Bible would have to step aside for some lesser being.

This was something I was not prepared to accept. I needed to start evaluating the evidence and looking at the arguments for evolution and also those for creation by an intelligent being.

A New Examination Technique?

One argument that I found particularly helpful came from information theory (Wilder-Smith, 1981). A major difference between living and inanimate things is the power to reproduce. This is possible because of the genetic blueprint, the genes, that are contained within all cells of living things. Usually they are made up of molecules of DNA, and the identification of the structure of this molecule has been one of the great achievements of science in this century. DNA strands found in ribbon-like structures, chromosomes, are duplicated before cell division. These copies are passed on to succeeding generations, which can then develop the same form and function, anatomy, physiology, and biochemistry as their ancestors. Three units of coding are the basis of DNA, just as the English language has 26 letters in the alphabet, and these letters are combined in various ways to mean different things when the code is translated. These units of coding in the genes provide the instructions to make strings of amino acids that are the building blocks of proteins. Many of these proteins are enzymes that catalyze biochemical reactions and make the other constituents of the cell.

The DNA double helix is analogous to the paper and ink of my biology textbooks. Anyone who has sat down in front of a blank piece of paper in an examination will be aware of the need for something more than paper and ink in order to pass. We need ideas, concepts, plans, purpose, memory of lecture notes, mathematical equations — in other words, information — in order to complete the paper. Does the stuff of paper and ink contain these ideas? An accidental spillage of ink can leave an interesting pattern of dots, lines, and circles on a piece of paper, but we do not see information there. Nor do we see it when a two year old decides to brighten up the wallpaper with some felt-tip pens! However, when we see writing on a piece of paper, we expect to gain information as we read it.

Why is this so? Unlike the accidental spill or the example of the two year old with felt-tip pens, a person who used his intelligence to put information down was responsible for the writing of the paper. There is no difference between the accidental spillage of ink on paper and the paper with writing on it as far as the materials used. However, information is present on one and not the other. Where does the information come from? Is it the property of the materials, the paper and ink? Many an examination student would wish so! The information is not a product of the paper or ink, but the thinking mind that has so organized these two things. There is intention, purpose, design, and meaning riding on the straight lines, the curves and circles of ink that form the letters.

Take the example of a piece of paper with the words written in ink, "John passed math." We could just as easily have conveyed the information by writing with our finger in the sand. Only one material, sand, is used here and yet the message is the same; the message is not part of the property of the sand. We could pass on the message by talking. This would involve the vibration of a column of air in a particular sequence of patterns in the mouth and throat. The message would be the spoken form of English, but it is not a property of the vibrations nor of the words themselves. These words just happen to code for the meaning in English. We could use sign language to convey the information — a different language, but the same message conveyed. Also, here no material would be involved, just the movement of hands. The information is not in the hands and face; it is transferred in coded form through the instructions for the contraction and relaxation of muscles and face.

I would like to go back to the illustration of the examination student again. If we have written half the examination paper and cannot remember the other key points, no amount of copying and rewording what we have already written will give us more marks from the examiner. The student needs to recall more information from the brain. The same applies to the origin of information that is coded in the genes. There is nothing special about DNA; it is just a collection of molecules as is paper and ink. DNA molecules can be strung out in line, copied, and still not contain information. It needs a thinking mind to design the cells of living things and then to commit that design in coded form to the DNA, so that each organism can function and reproduce itself. Beyond that, to make another organism with new and different structures needs the addition of further coded information. Copying out a recorded part of information will do no more for the plant or animal than it did for that unfortunate examination student halfway through his examination paper.

Failure of Supporting Arguments

During lectures and television presentations and in his book *The Blind Watchmaker* (1986), Dawkins, a leading proponent of evolution, has used computer examples to show the creative power of natural selection in generating new information. One demonstration involves the generation of a phrase on a computer screen from Hamlet's "To be or not to be" (written without the gaps). This is done to supposedly simulate the appearance of a short portion of new genetic code. The correct number of slots is set out and then filled at random with letters from the alphabet. Letters are then randomly re-allocated to the slots until the correct ones appear at each position. In a short time, the correct phrase appears on the screen. Dawkins argues that over a long period of time it is therefore possible for the processes of evolution to generate all the information required to code for the new structures of novel species. He also used computer graphics to demonstrate the development of new animal shapes. He omits just one thing from his discussion: *the information was already in hand in both examples.*

In the first, the target phrase "tobeornottobe" was in the memory of the computer and all that was necessary was a matching exercise. In the second, the design was already present in his own intelligent mind and he was controlling the process. In sharp contrast to his intention, he has provided a powerful demonstration of an intelligent designer at work.

I have found the arguments about the origin of information very useful, but there are many examples quoted where new features are said to have come about, for example, the peppered moth, evolution of tolerance to pollution, antibiotic resistance, and sickle-cell anaemia. In the peppered moth, large numbers of the dark form appeared in the age of heavy industry in the United Kingdom, but small numbers of this form have always existed (Kettlewell, 1958). In the same way, populations of plants include those that survive better in polluted environments because of small differences in the structure of the plant and in its metabolism, as discussed earlier. These variations are inherited in the genes. Planting a mixed bag of seed at a polluted site would mean that the more tolerant individuals would survive and the less tolerant would die, or at best survive to grow as less healthy individuals and produce less seed. This is a clear example of natural selection acting on a pre-existing gene pool, in response to change in environment.

However, this sort of natural selection tells us nothing about the origin of the gene or genes for tolerance, whether it is a mutant form, or part of the variation within the species. It tells us nothing about the origin of that plant species. It is equivalent to the selection of red smarties from a bag of mixed sweets; nothing new has appeared in the genes, no new information. Many other examples of such variation are known: winter or summer flowering in clover, variations between populations of yarrow in a transect across the Sierra Nevada mountain range in central California and between rice populations grown for successive generations at various latitudes in Japan (discussed in Bradshaw and McNeilly, 1981). Now, is this evolution? No, it is not that understood by Darwin or any of the present-day proponents of the theory, such as Dawkins (1986) and Simpson (1967). Why not? Because no new designs, no new organs have appeared. Here we simply have a reworking of what is already present. We could call such a re-working micro-evolution, but this is an unsatisfactory term because no amount of micro-evolution can add up to evolution proper, since nothing new, however "micro," has been formed.

In other examples, changes do occur in the genes of individuals. Spetner (1997), in his book *Not by Chance*, discusses details of changes leading to antibiotic resistance in bacteria, and it would be useful to summarize the points here. One example of resistance to antibiotics that involves changes in the genes is that of the antibiotic streptomycin. The molecule works by interfering with the manufacture of protein within the bacterial cell. This happens when the streptomycin molecule attaches itself to the specific part of the cell where the reaction to form a protein is taking place. This does not stop protein being made, but the streptomycin interferes with the results. The bacterium is now unable to put the right amino acid in the chain at this point; the wrong amino acid is included, and so the wrong protein is made. This wrong product cannot fulfil its task in the bacterium; the cell cannot grow, divide, and multiply, and the infection disappears. When a bacterium becomes resistant to streptomycin, a mutation has occurred in the DNA so that streptomycin can no longer lock on to the site of protein manufacture and interfere with the process. The change could occur at a number of places in the gene, but will always have the same effect. What has actually happened to the bacterium is that there has been a loss of information in the genes. No longer does the DNA contain all the necessary information to make the manufacturing site the correct shape. The bacterium is not able to grow and multiply as effectively as before, but nonetheless has gained resistance to the antibiotic.

Similar changes have occurred in the example of sickle-cell anemia. This is a condition found in areas of the world where malaria is prevalent (Cavalli-Sforza and Bodmer, 1971). The mutation alters the composition of the hemoglobin that carries the oxygen in red blood cells and, as a consequence, the red blood cells change to become sickle-shaped. This means that the malarial parasite is no longer able to live and grow inside the red blood cells, and the individual with this altered gene does not suffer from the malaria. Again, this change has also occurred by a loss of information. The ability to put together the right combination of molecules to enable the red blood cells to function efficiently has been lost. Instead an inferior form is manufactured in its place (Ling, 1992).

These examples provide convincing evidence of changes without information being added to the genes of a living organism and in some cases the loss of information. In a recorded interview, Dawkins was asked to give examples of changes in organisms that have occurred by the addition of new information. He was unable to do so (Keziah, 1997). As Spetner points out, "The failure to observe even one mutation that adds information is more than just a failure to find support for the theory. It is evidence against the theory."

The Probability of a New Species — Possible or Not

Another very powerful argument against evolution comes from the calculations of Spetner (1997) into the chance of one event of evolution occurring: the emergence of a new species. Many authors of books on the evolution controversy have touched on this issue in the past, but in this book Spetner uses numbers taken from the scientific literature as the basis for detailed calculations. He takes estimates of the chance of getting a mutation, the number of replications (births) in each step of the chain towards a new species, and an estimated value of the number of steps necessary to get a new species. He assumes that at each step information is added to the genetic code and that the smallest change possible to the genetic code is advantageous. Both are unproved assumptions of enormous proportions in favor of the theory of evolution, as the author points out, but need to be made for the calculations. Then he estimates the chances that a typically advantageous mutation would occur and spread throughout the population. From this he went on to work out the chance of a new species evolving, assuming that only one potential copying error was of advantage at any one point. The possibility was found to be extremely small, and the chances against were extremely large. No evolutionist shown the detailed calculations has been able to refute them. Suggested alterations to some of the assumptions may increase the chances at some stages, but are totally insufficient to make the theory of evolution an event of acceptable probability.

Irreducibly Complex — It's All or Nothing

Another major challenge to my acceptance of neo-Darwinian evolution came through an awareness of the complexity of living things. At the biochemical level, I know of some of the complexities of metabolism in living things. I could look with amazement at the chart of biochemical pathways in cells even after several years of research work. The chart is the size of a large student poster and is covered with small print showing the various pathways that synthesize the molecules required for the cell to function. Needless to say, the publisher updates it at regular intervals as more is learned of biochemical processes in cells. Biochemical pathways are, however, very different from pathways that lead down the sides of a mountain in various directions; they are more like a network. Most pathways are highly integrated with other pathways, and the levels of certain manufactured products (metabolites) can inhibit or increase the activity of that pathway and often of other pathways, too. Certain products are synthesized that are needed in the pathways to make quite different products. All this forms an intricately balanced web of biochemical processes within the cell. It would be very difficult to introduce a completely new pathway into the network, and this would be the sort of change that would need to occur in an organism that was evolving. More than that, it is very difficult to conceive of the gradual evolution of such a complex system. For any one part to be functional, many other pathways would also have to be fully functional.

Behe (1996) considers that many biochemical systems are the product of intelligent design. His criteria are evidence for "highly specified, irreducible complexity — the ordering of separate, well-fitted components to achieve a function that is beyond any of the components themselves." He uses the example of a mousetrap as a simple analogy. On top of a piece of wood are fixed a number of items.

A metal hammer	will hold down and kill the mouse.
A spring	will allow the metal hammer to move across the trap at speed and do the job quickly and efficiently.
A metal restraining bar	holds the hammer back when the trap is set.
A catch	sufficiently sensitive so that the slight pressure of a mouse sampling the food will release it.

Each one of these parts is essential to the success of the trap. Without the hammer, the mouse would not be caught and could take the food with impunity night after night. Without the spring, the hammer and platform would not be able to act together as a vice to catch the mouse. Without the catch or the metal restraining bar, the trap could not be set for later action when the mouse arrived; it would be more likely to have a go at one of your fingers when you are attempting to set the trap! Without the piece of wood forming the base, the components could not be arranged in the correct position to work with one another. All parts have to be of the correct size, mounted in the correct position, made of appropriate material, and in working order. Otherwise it would be back to the hardware shop for another trap!

If one part of the trap were missing, it would not work just occasionally — it would never do the job at all, or do the wrong job. To apply this principle to living systems, a partly evolved form is not a candidate for natural selection, because it is not yet able to perform the required function at all. Behe then goes on to demonstrate design in the natural world using several examples of irreducible complexity taken from biochemical processes and structures within cells. These examples include the cilium, a sub-cellular structure "which looks like a hair and beats like a whip"; the process of blood clotting, and intra-cellular transport. He also discusses the human eye, making the point that here there are a number of irreducibly complex systems, for example, the retina, the tear ducts, and eyelids. I would agree with Darwin when he wrote of his difficulty in understanding how the eye could have evolved, because he was aware that such a complex organ could not have originated in a few steps. In his words, the idea was "absurd in the highest possible degree" (Darwin, 1859, edited 1959).

Nevertheless, Darwin proposed that beneficial changes leading to the development of the eye accumulated over many generations, each intermediate being useful to its possessor. However, since publication of *The Origin of Species*, much more has been discovered about the structure and function of the eye. Much is known about the physiology and biochemistry of vision itself, and developments in neurosciences have helped us to understand more about the processing of the visual image in the neurological pathways and the brain. Baker (1991a, 1991b, 1992) provides a readable account of the structure and function of the eye and a discussion of the even greater difficulties raised for the theory of evolution.

The Evidence Directs

My main arguments against evolution are well illustrated by the human eye:

- Where would the new information come from to provide the genetic blueprint for this new structure?
- How did the irreducibly complex systems within the eye come about? I would agree with Behe (1996) when he concludes that an intelligent designer is necessary to explain their origin. The changes necessary for the appearance of the eye are more complex than for a new species.
- The probability of this organ evolving by chance is therefore even more remote than those of a new species evolving, which Spetner (1997) estimates to be impossible anyway.

The evidence points to an intelligent designer of the vast array of life, both living and extinct, rather than to unguided mindless evolution. However, some see that evidence from the natural world requires a designer but are content just to accept the possibility of an intelligent force behind the universe. If an intelligent force designed the world, surely we, as intelligent beings, must take this further and find out the nature of this being. The Bible tells me that the intelligent mind behind the universe is a God who is in total control; this excludes the possibility that He acted through evolution. The basis of my own faith is the inerrancy of the biblical account, and this provides my starting point in understanding the scientific evidence — my paradigm, my "presuppositions," if you wish. A short time scale is eminently possible for a world originated by an intelligent designer, although it is not necessarily required. What is no longer needed are the long periods of time to try to explain the origin of chance improvements. Reasoning from the scientific observations and faith in the Bible, I conclude that creation was the result of an intelligent designer, entirely possible within the short period of six days.

Readings

Andrews, E.H. *Christ and the Cosmos.* Welwyn, England: Evangelical Press, 1986.

Baker, S. "Seeing and Believing. The Amazing Process of Human Vision." *Origins: Journal of the Biblical Creation Society,* 4, (10) 9–11, 1991a.

Baker, S. "Seeing and Believing 2. The Amazing Process of Human Vision." *Origins: Journal of the Biblical Creation Society,* 4, (11) 16–18, 1991b.

Baker, S. "Seeing and Believing 3. The Amazing Process of Human Vision." *Origins: Journal of the Biblical Creation Society,* 4, (12) 11–14, 1992.

Behe, Michael J. *Darwin's Black Box. The Biochemical Challenge to Evolution.* New York: Free Press, Simon and Schuster, 1996.

Bell, N.J.B., and C.H. Mudd. "Sulphur Dioxide Resistance in Plants; a Case Study of Lolium Perenne." In *Effects of Air Pollutants on Plants,* ed. T.A. Mansfield. New York: Cambridge University Press, 1976, p. 87–103.

Bradshaw, A.D., and T. McNeilly. *Evolution and Pollution. Studies in Biology, No 130.* London: Edward Arnold, 1981.

Cavalli-Sforza, L.L. and W.F. Bodmer. *The Genetics of Human Populations.* San Francisco, CA: Freeman, 1971.

Darwin, Charles *The Origin of Species.* Edited by J.W. Burrow, Harmondsworth, England: Penguin Books, 1968.

Dawkins, Richard. *The Blind Watchmaker.* London: Penguin Books, 1998 (1986).

Dawkins, R. in *From a Frog to a Prince*. Keziah;Video production available from Answers in Genesis, UK, Australia, USA, 1997.

Heywood,V.H. *Plant Taxonomy. Studies in Biology, No 5*. London: Edward Arnold, 1967.

Horsman, D.A., et al. "Evolution of Sulphur Dioxide Tolerance in Perennial Ryegrass." *Nature*, 276, 493–4, 1978.

Johnson, Phillip E. *Reason in the Balance. The Case against Naturalism in Science, Law and Education*. Westmont, IL: InterVarsity Press, 1995.

Kettlewell, H.B.D. "A Survey of the Frequencies of Biston Betularia (L) (LEP) and its Melanic Forms in Great Britain." *Heredity*, 12, 51–72, 1958.

Ling, J. "Haemoglobin — a Pedagogic Protein." *Origins: Journal of the Biblical Creation Society*, 4, (12) 20–5, 1992.

Simpson, George Gaylord. *The Meaning of Evolution*, revised edition. New Haven, CT:Yale University Press, 1967, p. 344–345.

Spetner, Lee. *Not by Chance*. New York: The Judaica Press, Inc., 1997.

Roberts, T.M., N.M. Darrall and P. Lane. "Effects of Gaseous Air Pollutants on Agriculture and Forestry in the UK." *Advances in Applied Biology*, 9, 2–130, 1983.

Taylor, G.E. "Genetic Analysis of Ecotype Differentiation of an Annual Plant Species, Geranium carolinianum L., in Response to Sulphur Dioxide." *Botanical Gazette*, 136, 362–8, 1978.

Tozer, A.W. *The Knowledge of the Holy*. London: James Clarke, 1961.

Wilder-Smith, A.E. *The Natural Sciences Know Nothing of Evolution*. Green Forest, AR: Master Books, 1981.

Author's note: I would like to thank P. Garner and M. Garton for their helpful comments on an earlier draft of this article.

john m. cimbala

Mechanical Engineering

Dr. Cimbala is professor of mechanical engineering, Pennsylvania State University. He holds a B.S. in aerospace engineering with highest distinction from Pennsylvania State University, an M.S. in aeronautics from the California Institute of Technology, and a Ph.D. in aeronautics from the California Institute of Technology. As well as publishing a number of research papers in the area of fluid dynamics, Dr. Cimbala served as a visiting senior research scientist at the NASA Langley Research Center. He was a pioneer in the development of the Internet for teaching enhancement and, in 1997, received the George W. Atherton Award for Excellence in Teaching at Pennsylvania State University.

I was raised in a Christian home, believing in God and His creation. However, I was taught evolution while attending high school, and began to doubt the authority of the Bible. If evolution is true, I reasoned, the Bible cannot also be true. I eventually rejected the entire Bible and believed that we descended from lower creatures; there was no afterlife and no purpose in life but to enjoy the short time we have on this earth. My college years at Penn State were spent as an atheist, or at best as an agnostic.

Fortunately, and by the grace of God, I began to read articles and listen to tapes about scientific evidence for creation. Over a period of a couple of years, it became apparent to me that the theory of evolution has no legitimate factual evidence, and that scientific data from the fossil record, geology, etc. could be better explained by a recent creation, followed by a global flood. Suddenly I realized that the Bible might actually be true! It wasn't until I could believe the first page of the Bible that I could believe the rest of it. Once I accepted the fact that there is a creator God, it was an easy step for me to accept His plan of salvation through Jesus Christ as well. I became a follower of Christ during my first year of graduate school at Cal Tech.

Since then, I have devoted much time to studying the evidence for creation and a global flood. The more I study, the more convinced I become that there is a loving God, who created this universe and all living things. God revealed some details about His creation in the Book of Genesis, which I now believe literally — six days, a young earth, and a global flood.

There are many pieces of evidence about which I could write; here I choose one: the second law of thermodynamics. A formal definition of the second law of thermodynamics is: "In any closed system, a process proceeds in a direction such that the unavailable energy (the entropy) increases." In other words, in any closed system, the amount of disorder always increases with time. Things progress naturally from order to disorder, or from an available energy state to one where energy is more unavailable. A good example: a hot cup of coffee cools off in an insulated room. The total amount of energy in the room remains the same (which satisfies the first law of thermodynamics). Energy is not lost, it is simply transferred (in the form of heat) from the hot coffee to the cool air, warming up the air slightly. When the coffee is hot, there is available energy because of the temperature difference between the coffee and the air. As the coffee cools down, the available energy is slowly turned to unavailable energy. At last, when the coffee is room temperature, there is no temperature difference between the coffee and the air, i.e., the energy is in an unavailable state. The closed system (consisting of the room and the coffee) has suffered what is technically called a "heat death." The system is "dead" because no further work can be done, since there is no more available energy. The second law says that the reverse cannot happen! Room temperature coffee will not get hot all by itself, because this would require turning unavailable energy into available energy.

Now consider the entire universe as one giant closed system. Stars are hot, just like the cup of coffee, and are cooling down, losing energy into space. The hot stars in cooler space represent a state of available energy, just like the hot coffee in the room. However, the second law of thermodynamics requires that this available energy constantly change to unavailable energy. In another analogy, the entire universe is winding down like a giant wind-up clock, ticking down and losing available energy. Since energy is continually changing from available to unavailable, someone had to give it available energy in the beginning! (In other words, someone had to wind up the clock of the universe at the beginning.) Who or what could have produced energy in an available state in the first place? Only someone or something not bound by the second law of thermodynamics. Only the Creator of the second law of thermodynamics could violate it and create energy in a state of availability in the first place.

As time goes forward (assuming things continue as they are), the available energy in the universe will eventually turn into unavailable energy. At this point, the universe will be said to have suffered a heat death, just like the coffee in the room. The present universe, as we know it, cannot last forever. Furthermore, imagine going backwards in time. Since the energy of the universe is constantly changing from a state of availability to one of less availability, the further back in time one goes, the more available the energy of the universe. Using the clock analogy again, the further back in time, the more wound up the clock. Far enough back in time, the clock was completely wound up. The universe therefore cannot be infinitely old. One can only conclude that the universe had a beginning, and that beginning had to have been caused by someone or something operating outside of the known laws of thermodynamics. Is this scientific proof for the existence of a creator God? I think so. Evolutionary theories of the universe cannot counteract the above arguments for the existence of God.

edward a. boudreaux

Theoretical Chemistry

Professor Boudreaux is professor emeritus of chemistry at the University of New Orleans, Louisiana. He holds a B.S. in chemistry from Loyola University, an M.S. in chemistry and a Ph.D. in chemistry from Tulane University. Professor Boudreaux has spent 29 years in graduate education and research in the area of theoretical and inorganic chemistry and chemical physics, and is the author or co-author of four technical books in the area of inorganic chemistry, as well as numerous scientific papers in peer-reviewed journals and textbooks.

Certainly it must be agreed among rational individuals that for anyone bold enough to admit it, the origins issue is strictly a matter of history. Having been initiated and completed prior to the genesis of man at some time in the past, the events of this origins process are non-repeatable. It matters not whether one believes the mechanism of the process to be via *de fiat* actions of a supernatural intelligence, some naturalistic evolutionary process, or a mixture of the two; the fact remains that the material universe is in a stable state of static equilibrium.

The initial processes responsible for this stasis are not amenable to the methods of scientific testing, because they were unobservable events. Yet, in spite of this, evolutionists claim that a trail of evidences have been imprinted in the fossil record over long periods of geologic time. Furthermore, it is suggested that biological similarities among various levels of living organisms all imply a common ancestral origin. Similarly, cosmologists maintain that some sort of big-bang scenario, initiated from a unique physical singularity undergoing a quantum fluctuation in some 10^{-43} seconds, is the process by which the origin of the entire universe was initiated.

Hence, the geological, biological, and cosmological sciences have been established as *ivory towers*, from which so-called *proofs* of evolution emanate, while the scientist practitioners within these disciplines are the *gurus* who promote, preach, and publish what is regarded as scientific data supporting evolution. But there is not one single instance whereby all the tests essential to the establishment of the scientific validity of evolution have been satisfied. There are hypotheses, grandiose models, suppositions, and inferences, all of which are formulated and reinforced within the collective and self-serving collaborations of the evolutionist gurus. However, none of this amounts to true scientific evidence for evolution.

It was in the 1970s that, to my great surprise, bewilderment, and disgust, I became enlightened to all of what has been stated above. Up until that time I had not given the evolution matter very much thought. On the contrary, I presumed that researchers committed to the study of evolution possessed the same integrity as that expected of any credible scientist. While it is true that I may not have been as thoroughly schooled in those *ivory tower disciplines* of evolution as are the so-called "experts," I was, nonetheless, more than adequately informed as a scientist to be able to read and comprehend various technical publications on evolution. Subsequently, the greatest embarrassment of all was for me to find that there simply was no valid science whatever, in any of these numerous publications touting evolution.

A number of evolutionists openly admit that the coveted fossil record is devastating to the entire scheme of organic evolution, be it neo-Darwinism, punctuated equilibrium, or whatever. It has also been clearly demonstrated that observed similarities between organisms, fossil or living, have absolutely nothing to do with proving evolution per se. Similarly, there is neither a single model nor combination thereof, regarding the evolution of the cosmos, that provides an adequate explanation of all observed cosmological data. In fact, the actual data is frequently in disagreement with the various proposed models.

My own fields of specialization are in the areas of theoretical inorganic chemistry and chemical physics. Both of these areas are reasonably immune to the contaminations of evolution. But, once my interest had been aroused sufficiently to study the evolution literature, I also became aware of unique features among chemical properties of specific elements. These characteristics are clearly a reflection of created design.

Consider the element carbon (C). This is the most unique of all the chemical elements in the Periodic Table. It is a non-metal, having unlimited capacity to participate in every known type of covalent chemical bonding (i.e., pairs of electrons shared between atoms), which unites atoms of the same kind to each other and to other kinds of atoms as well. This feature, called *catenation*, is virtually unlimited for the element carbon alone.

Other elements, such as silicon (Si), nitrogen (N), sulphur (S), phosphorus (P), etc., display some very limited capacities for catenation, which do not even come close to rivalling the catenation ability of C. Without this unique feature, the formation of such essential biomolecules as proteins, DNA, RNA, cellulose, etc., would be impossible. Ironically, in spite of its crucial importance, carbon comprises only 9 to 10 percent by weight of the composition of all living things and only 0.017 percent of the earth's composition. Nonetheless, there is no other element that can replace even one or two C atoms in biomolecules, without destroying the biological integrity of these systems.

Elements such as carbon (C), nitrogen (N), sulphur (S), phosphorus (P), and other non-metals are called representative or main group elements. With the exception of oxygen, atoms of these elements are stable only when even numbers of their electrons unite in pairs; otherwise the presence of "*unpaired*" electrons imparts *chemical instability*. On the other hand, metallic elements such as chromium (Cr), Iron (Fe), nickel (Ni), etc., called transition metals, are among the sub-group elements and do *contain unpaired* electrons, but surprisingly are *chemically very stable*.

The element oxygen (O) exists freely in nature as the gaseous diatomic molecule O_2. There are other representative elements which also occur as free diatomic molecules, e.g., hydrogen (H_2), nitrogen (N_2), fluorine (F_2), and chlorine (Cl_2). However, O_2 *is the only molecule of this type possessing two unpaired electrons*; the others all have paired electrons. In spite of this, O_2 is still chemically stable. This singular notable exception to the electron-pair rule of stability for representative elements has no known explanation. The only other molecule with an electron arrangement exactly that of O_2 is S_2. However, S_2 is a highly unstable molecule, which is the reason that sulphur does not exist in this form. Furthermore, if it were not for the two unpaired electrons in O_2, it would not be capable of binding to the iron (Fe) atoms in hemogloblin, with precisely the amount of energy needed to carry the O_2 into the bloodstream and then release it. Some other molecules such as CO and NO can replace O_2 in binding to hemogloblin, but they completely destroy the hemoglobin function.

Similarly, there are several other transition metals comparable to iron which can replace it in hemoglobin and also bind O_2, but this binding is either too strong or too weak. Thus, there are no non-iron analogues of hemoglobin having the required properties of normal hemoglobin for transporting O_2 in blood metabolism.

The structured portion of hemoglobin which binds iron is called a *porphrin ring*. If this porphrin is translated into another biomolecular environment and the iron atom replaced by magnesium (Mg), chlorophyll, a key component essential to plant metabolism, is the most efficient photoelectric cell known. It is some 80 percent more efficient than any photocells fabricated by man. While calcium (Ca) and some other metals can replace Mg in chlorophyll, the products do not at all duplicate the photoelectric efficiency of true chlorophyll.

Proteins are composed of amino acid molecules chemically bound together by what are called *polypeptide bonds*. The amino acids themselves are carbon hydrogen compounds containing an amine group, i.e, $-NH^2$, $-NHR$, or $-NR^2$ (where R represents one or more carbon hydrogen groups) bonded to a C atom, plus an acid group (-COOH) bonded to the same C atom. Although there are thousands of varieties of amino acids, only *20* are involved in *all* protein structures.

Furthermore, amino acids exist in two structural forms, D and L, which are non-superimposable mirror images of each other. In the absence of any imposed controls, both D and L forms will naturally occur in essentially equal amounts; however, all proteins are made of *only* the L form. By way of contrast, sugars (saccharides), which are carbon–hydrogen–oxygen compounds, have closed ring structures and also exist in both D and L isomeric forms. While there are numerous varieties of sugars, it is only the simplest, 5-membered ring structure called *ribose*, in only its D form, that is present as one of the three fundamental molecular components in the structures of DNA and RNA.

Both DNA (deoxyribonucleic acid) and RNA (ribonucleic acid) are in some respects more complex than proteins, because they contain a greater variety of molecular units forming nucleosides (nucleotide bases, ribose, and phosphate). These nucleosides are all joined together in very specific patterns so as to perform unique and crucial functions. The ribose and phosphate ($-PO_4$) units are bonded together in a regularly alternating sequence, thus producing long chains coiled in a right-handed helix. Each nucleotide is bound to one specific C atom on each ribose unit. In the case of RNA, the structure is a single-stranded *right-handed helix* containing four different nucleotides (adenine, cytosine, guanine, uracil) arranged in very specific repeating sequences throughout the length of the chain. Each type of RNA has a different pattern in the sequencing of the four nucleotides. The DNA structure consists of a *right-handed double helix*, also containing four nucleotides. Three of these are the same as in RNA, but one is different: thymine replaces uracil.

The nucleotides themselves belong to two classes of molecules called *purines* and *pyrimidines*. Adenine and guanine are purines, while cytosine, thymine and uracil are pyrimidines. There are many hundreds of varieties of purines and pyrimidines, but *only these select five* determine the structures and functions of DNA and RNA.

Similarly, ribose is only one of a large number of molecules called *saccharides*. Why only *ribose* and its *D* isomer, but not one or more other saccharides in DNA and RNA? Likewise, why *only phosphate* and not sulfate or silicate, etc? *Only phosphate works.*

These few examples contain clear evidence of complex design imparting tailor-made functions. Such characteristics defy the probability that any random evolutionary process could account for such unique specificity in design.

Admittedly, it may require some general comprehension of chemistry to fully appreciate these chemical evidences of creative design which have been presented. But it is this evidence provided not only from chemistry, but from all other areas of science as well, that convinces me to accept creation by God as the only viable and scientifically reasonable explanation of origins. Of course, science cannot prove either creation or evolution, but it certainly is in agreement with the former and not the latter. Consequently, it should take considerably more faith to believe in evolution rather than divine creation.

Hence, having concluded that creation by the power of an omnipotent God is the only acceptable explanation for the origin of life, I was convinced that the only reliable source of this account must be from the Creator alone. Now the Bible claims to be the written word of God to man. While this documentation was by the hand of man, the information is directly from God. If God actually is who He reveals himself to be, He is perfectly capable of preserving the complete accuracy and integrity of His own word.

God begins the Bible with the revelation of himself as the Creator. The Book of Genesis relates specific details of God's own account of His creation, details which are, for the most part, in complete contradiction to the evolution scenarios. One major contradiction is the length of time for the entire creation process to be completed. All popular evolution models maintain billions of years from the origin of the cosmos, to hundreds of millions of years —

involving death, destruction, and survival of the fittest — for the total completion of macroscopic biological evolution. But the Bible says that all of creation was completed in just *6 days*.

There has been much controversy regarding the interpretation of six biblical days for creation. Many believe that these *days* could be indefinite long periods of time, thus accommodating requirements for the evolution process. However, the most complete and reliable exegesis of the Hebrew word *yom* (day), as it is used in Genesis, is that it can only mean a literal 24-hour period. In fact, the complete context of the Genesis creation account does not even allow for *yom* to be translated as an indefinite length of time.

Finally, I am forced to conclude, as reason dictates, that if the Bible is truly the Word of God (as I am convinced that it is), then it must be accurate in every detail, including the account of creation in *6 literal days*. Science tells me that *evolution is certainly not scientific*, while *creation is not in disagreement with what is truly scientific*. Hence, creation is the more acceptable account of origins. Since creation requires a supernatural, omnipotent Creator, and the Bible is the only convincing source of who this creator God actually is, then the biblical account of creation must be accurate in every detail, including six 24-hour days for completion from beginning to end.

e. theo agard

Medical Physics

Dr. Agard is a former director of medical physics at Flower Hospital Oncology Center, Ohio. He holds a B.S. (hons) first class in physics from the University of London, an M.S. in physics from the Middlesex Hospital Medical School at the University of London, and a Ph.D. in physics from the University of Toronto. In 1993 Dr. Agard was elected to the national board of directors of the Health Physics Society.

My belief in the supernatural creation of this world in six days is summarized largely in the following points: The theory of evolution is not as scientifically sound as many people believe. In particular, the problem of the origin of life is well stated by the question, "Which came first, the chicken or the egg?" Every egg anyone has ever seen was laid by a chicken and every chicken was hatched from an egg. Hence, the first chicken or first egg which appeared on the scene in any other way would be unnatural, to say the least. The natural laws under which scientists work are adequate for explaining how the world functions, but are inadequate to explain its origin, just as the tools which service an automobile are inadequate for its manufacture.

From my reading I understand that the fossil record has failed to produce the intermediate forms of life required by evolution as transitions between the species.

Another problem, as I see it, for the non-creationist is the first law of thermodynamics which affirms the natural process of energy conservation. Energy cannot be created or destroyed by natural processes, but can only be converted from one form to another. Since matter is a form of energy ($E=mc^2$ as stated by Einstein), natural sciences cannot account for the total energy, including matter, in the universe. This law consequently implies a role for the supernatural in the origin of the total energy in the universe.

Furthermore, any effort to validate evolution scientifically must involve extrapolation, since current observations must be used to deduce the course of events which occurred several millenia ago (even thousands or millions of millenia). While extrapolation is a valid scientific procedure, it is pertinent to be aware of its limitations. Where there is a sound scientific basis for its use, confidence in the accuracy of an extrapolated result is dependent on the proximity of the point or region of interest to the region of observations.

It is also important to note that scientific principles and laws that apply under one set of conditions may not necessarily carry over to other circumstances where they are not expected to change. A very good example of this is the failure of Newton's laws of motion to explain observed phenomena for sub-atomic particles. Such limitations of extrapolation are well stated in the following words by G. Tyler Miller in his book *Energetics, Kinetics and Life: An Ecological Approach*:

> We know so little about our tiny portion of the universe and have observed it for such a minute period of

time, relative to cosmic time, that extrapolating this meager knowledge to the entire universe seems highly speculative and perhaps somewhat arrogant.[1]

These issues seriously question the scientific basis of evolution.

Endnote

1 G. Tyler Miller, *Energetics, Kinetics and Life: An Ecological Approach* (Belmont, CA: Wadsworth Pub. Co., 1971), p. 233.

ker c. thomson

Geophysics

Dr. Thomson is a former director of the U.S. Air Force Terrestrial Sciences Laboratory. He holds a B.A. in physics and geology from the University of British Columbia and D.Sc. in geophysics from the Colorado School of Mines. Dr. Thomson served as professor of geophysics at Baylor University and professor of science at Bryan College. He has published numerous technical papers in the area of geophysics and seismology.

Many, if not most, educated people throughout the world believe that life originated from non-life (abiogenesis) by natural processes. Following the laws of physics and chemistry, the concept is that through "natural selection" operating over vast periods of time, fortuitous favorable events happened that brought about successively more complex biological chemicals, which again, either fortuitously or through some undefined inherent property of matter, concatenated, leading upward to protocells, cells, living creatures, and then man himself. "Natural selection" processes are such that biologic or pre-biologic products occurring in any given environmental niche that favor that niche are the ones that propagate and reproduce, and that random changes in either or both the environment and the progeny that are more appropriate for the new conditions will be the ones favored to expand into the future. In a single paragraph, this is the general theory of neo-Darwinian evolution.

The above stands in stark contrast to creationism, which holds that currently observable natural processes are quite inadequate to explain the origin of life or its current, enormous observable complexity and variability. Rather, it postulates that a great creative mind must lie behind the origin of our observable universe and its living creatures — a mind and power vastly greater than anything of which man is capable. The questions of how long the creative process was and when it occurred vary from one creationist to another, but the concept of an original conscious creative act by a Creator who is distinct from His creation is common to all creationist viewpoints considered here.

Both creationists and evolutionists, by and large, concur that the evolutionary scenario outlined in the first paragraph above is highly improbable. It gains whatever credibility it enjoys only through the apparent availability of enormous amounts of time during which the most improbable events might conceivably occur.

It should be apparent that evolution is capable of an immediate scientific test: Is there available a scientifically observable process in nature which on a long-term basis is tending to carry its products upward to higher and higher levels of complexity? Evolution absolutely requires this.

Evolution fails the test. The test procedure is contained within the second law of thermodynamics. This law has turned out to be one of the surest and most fundamental principles in all of science. It is, in fact, used routinely in science to test postulated or existing concepts and machines (for instance perpetual motion machines, or a proposed chemical reaction) for viability. Any process, procedure, or machine which would violate this principle is discarded as impossible. The second law of thermodynamics states that there is a long-range decay process which ultimately and surely grips everything in the universe that we know about. That process produces a breakdown of complexity, not its increase. This is the exact opposite of what evolution requires.

The argument against evolution presented above is so devastating in its scientific impact that, on scientific grounds, evolution would normally be immediately rejected by the scientific community. Unfortunately, for the preservation of truth, evolution is not adhered to on scientific grounds at all. Rather, it is clung to, though flying in the face of reason, with an incredible, fanatical, and irrational religious fervor. It loudly claims scientific support when, in fact, it has none worthy of the name.

If the evolution or creationism discussion were decided by sensible appeals to reason, evolution would long ago have joined the great philosophical foolishnesses of the past, with issues such as how many angels can dance on the head of a pin, or the flat-earth concept.

To bury evolutionary faith, then, it seems necessary to look beyond the general second law argument presented above to the specific details, and to consider and dispose of the quibbles raised by the evolutionary community.

One objection that can be posited to the preceding argument is that the second law deals with long-term results, or equilibrium states, in more chemical language. An evolutionary response then is that evolution must be somehow tucked in between the successive equilibrium states.

Reconsider the implications of the evolutionary theory's requirements for large time spans. Is it not obvious that the second law of thermodynamics is what is most pertinent here? The huge amounts of time available that evolution claims for itself will provide plenty of time for successive equilibrium states to be achieved and the second law of thermodynamics to apply. The fast-moving intermediate states are irrelevant in the long range of time. The long-range end results of each chemical reaction will be what dominates the long ages of evolution. The clear and inescapable statement by the second law will be that the end results must be in a downward direction, not the upward direction evolution requires.

A second quibble to consider is that of "micro vs macro": Could it be if we consider evolution from an atomic or molecular level (micro), rather than from the level of matter at the state where we can feel, see, and touch it (macro), that evolution might be found tucked away among the infinitesimally small (i.e., among the molecules, atoms, or subatomic particles)? This really won't do, however.

As a minor first consideration here, note that we do not feel or see atoms and molecules with our unaided senses or rarely even perceive them at all at the individual atomic-level by any process.

In other words, our knowledge and perceptions at the micro level are obtained through a maze of complex machines which are themselves constructed from a large assortment of assumptions and abstruse theories. (No denial of atomic theory is being made here. Rather, it is simply being put in relative perspective.) On the other hand, the laws of thermodynamics rest on direct observations of matter in the aggregate and require only relatively sure and simple observations for their truth to be evident. In terms of reliability it should be apparent that, in general, results deduced from the second law should weigh in a little higher on the truth scale than results deduced only from atomic or molecular considerations. (Note, however, that the second law is not confined solely to aggregate matter, but applies at the micro level also.)

Regardless of the considerations in the preceding paragraph, when the actual chemical reactions of life are considered, especially those that might be involved at its inception, we find that the reactions are balky and require high concentrations of the reactants in order to proceed at all. Obviously then, this consideration results in levying a requirement for aggregate amounts of matter. This places us precisely back in situations uncontestably dominated by the second law. Again, the second law points to lower levels of complexity, not higher.

Another quibble about application of the second law is contained in the claim that the second law of thermodynamics applies only in closed systems. This is nonsense of a high order. Surely all of us are familiar with the everyday expression of this law in open systems. (The humorous popular version of the second law is Murphy's Law: "Whatever can go wrong will go wrong.") Metals corrode, machines break down, our bodies deteriorate, and we die. Constant maintenance and planning against contingencies are required if life is to be sustained for even a transitory period, such as the lifetime of the individual. Ultimately, the second law takes over, and our bodies return to dust and our automobiles to the junkyard. By the application of our minds, we can resist the demands of the second law temporarily. General evolution collapses around this concept, however, because at the initiation of the evolutionary process in antiquity, there was no mind available to construct purposive "machines" to temporarily obviate the second law's demands. The idea that the second law can be confined to closed systems is a piece of confusion on the part of the proponent of such a concept.

As an aside, note also an important implication for evolution implied in the last paragraph. The second law tells us clearly that life could never get started by the activities of matter and energy unaided by outside intelligence. If life could never get started, surely we have an incredible waste of intellectual talent going on around us as many minds try to follow the pathways of evolution upwards from something that never started in the first place!

Now let us come back to the question of closed systems. Consider an experiment to see if the second law is true. It will be necessary to create a closed system to do so, a system protected from any outside confusing inputs. In this way it will be possible to see what is happening in the system, independent of outside events. When this is done, it is indeed found that inside the system, the trend is downward to disorganization, as the second law requires. What happens then in an open system is that at any point we see the sum of all the different downward trends acting there.

To believe that the second law applies only in closed systems is to confuse the experimental necessity for a closed system to test for the existence of the second law, with the actual actions of the second law evident in the open systems in which we live.

There is another quibble levied against the anti-evolutionary arguments developed here. It has to do with the word "randomness." Refer to the very first paragraph defining evolution. Some evolutionists will quarrel with words like "randomness" or "fortuitous," but others will agree with this definition.

There are, then, two schools of evolutionary thought. Consider first the group who believe that evolution is due to the random concatenation of available materials and the laws of physics and chemistry.

This concept can be readily treated by the mathematical laws of probability. Several writers have done this. Probably the best known is Fred Hoyle. The procedure is to estimate probabilities at each individual step of a postulated evolutionary path and concatenate these to arrive at the probability of finding an evolutionary product at any point along that path. Before proceeding very far along the path, probabilities drop to values so low that the proper word to describe such happenings is impossible. Hoyle put it roughly like this: The probability that life arose by random processes is equivalent to believing that a tornado striking a junkyard would reassemble the trash and leave a completed, assembled, and functioning Boeing 707 there.

Then there is the evolutionary group who think that randomness is only a minor or non-existent aspect of evolution. Their perspective is that evolution is the inevitable outcome of the laws of physics and chemistry. This idea is even easier to test than the randomness concept. We simply note that one of the surest generalizations in all of physics and chemistry is the second law of thermodynamics which, as we have already shown, completely devastates any idea that matter unaided by mind or outside involvement will proceed to higher levels of organization.

Now we come to the evolutionists' quibble that the second law was different in the past from now. This is simply an adult wish fulfilment on the part of the evolutionist espousing such notions. Unless he assumes what he is trying to prove, he is left at this point with no reliable evidence whatever to support his thesis. Science relies on measurements. Measurements we make now oppose evolution totally. To point for support to conditions in the distant past, where they can't be measured, puts the evolutionists in the same intellectual camp as those who believe in the tooth fairy.

Despite the arguments against evolution presented above and particularly in the last paragraph, the evolutionist clinging to his faith may say "Well, we are here, aren't we?" One may point out to him that he has just finished engaging in circular reasoning. That is, he has obviously attempted to support evolution by assuming that evolution is true and is what has led to his human existence and presence here.

When the circularity of his reasoning is pointed out to him, the evolutionist may then grope for evidence in the fossil record. But again he is trotting out another batch of circular reasoning. This is so because evolution is used to interpret the fossil record, so it cannot be used to justify evolution. To do so puts the proponent in the intellectual booby hatch. Whatever the explanation for the fossil record may be, it cannot be one that in effect denies the second law of thermodynamics.

In fact, the most obvious feature of the fossil record is not upward synthesis but rather death and decay. We find strong evidence for the steady loss of species within the fossil record. This is more in consonance with the second law of thermodynamics than with the upward growth posited by evolution.

Not all creationists hold to six-day creationism. This writer is of the opinion that the scriptural evidence somewhat favors the six-day position. The scientific evidence for a long age rests primarily on the selection of evidence favorable to the long-age position rather than to the evaluation of all available evidence. The subject of time in this context requires a separate article to deal properly with the issue.

I hope that the above article has whetted the appetite of the reader to dig deeper into the evolution-creation controversy. I have given an opinion on the controversy through the dictates of the second law. The earnest reader needs to track back through to the original sources.

john r. baumgardner

Geophysics

Dr. Baumgardner is a technical staff member in the theoretical division of Los Alamos National Laboratory. He holds a B.S. in electrical engineering from Texas Tech University, an M.S. in electrical engineering from Princeton University, and an M.S. and Ph.D. in geophysics and space physics from UCLA. Dr. Baumgardner is the chief developer of the TERRA code, a 3-D finite element program for modelling the earth's mantle and lithosphere. His current research is in the areas of planetary mantle dynamics and the development of efficient hydrodynamic methods for supercomputers.

I live in the town of Los Alamos, located in the mountains of northern New Mexico. It is the home of the Los Alamos National Laboratory which, with approximately 10,000 employees, is one of the larger scientific research facilities in the United States. In recent years I have debated the origins issue with a number of fellow scientists. Some of these debates have been in the form of letters to the editor in our local newspaper.[1] What follows are some of the important issues as I see them.

Can Random Molecular Interactions Create Life?

Many evolutionists are persuaded that the 15 billion years they assume for the age of the cosmos is an abundance of time for random interactions of atoms and molecules to generate life. A simple arithmetic lesson reveals this to be no more than an irrational fantasy.

This arithmetic lesson is similar to calculating the odds of winning the lottery. The number of possible lottery combinations corresponds to the total number of protein structures (of an appropriate size range) that are possible to assemble from standard building blocks. The winning tickets correspond to the tiny sets of such proteins with the correct special properties from which a living organism, say a simple bacterium, can be successfully built. The maximum number of lottery tickets a person can buy corresponds to the maximum number of protein molecules that could have ever existed in the history of the cosmos.

Let us first establish a reasonable upper limit on the number of molecules that could ever have been formed anywhere in the universe during its entire history. Taking 10^{80} as a generous estimate for the total number of atoms in the cosmos,[2] 10^{12} for a generous upper bound for the average number of interatomic interactions per second per atom, and 10^{18} seconds (roughly 30 billion years) as an upper bound for the age of the universe, we get 10^{110} as a very generous upper limit on the total number of interatomic interactions which could have ever occurred during the long cosmic history the evolutionist imagines. Now if we make the extremely generous assumption that each interatomic interaction always produces a unique molecule, then we conclude that no more than 10^{110} unique molecules could have ever existed in the universe during its entire history.

Now let us contemplate what is involved in demanding that a purely random process find a minimal set of about 1,000 protein molecules needed for the most primitive form of life. To simplify the problem dramatically, suppose somehow we already have found

999 of the 1,000 different proteins required and we need only to search for that final magic sequence of amino acids which gives us that last special protein. Let us restrict our consideration to the specific set of 20 amino acids found in living systems and ignore the hundred or so that are not. Let us also ignore the fact that only those with left-handed symmetry appear in life proteins. Let us also ignore the incredibly unfavorable chemical reaction kinetics involved in forming long peptide chains in any sort of plausible non-living chemical environment.

Let us merely focus on the task of obtaining a suitable sequence of amino acids that yields a 3D protein structure with some minimal degree of essential functionality. Various theoretical and experimental evidence indicates that in some average sense about half of the amino acid sites must be specified exactly.[3] For a relatively short protein consisting of a chain of 200 amino acids, the number of random trials needed for a reasonable likelihood of hitting a useful sequence is then in the order of 20^{100} (100 amino acid sites with 20 possible candidates at each site), or about 10^{130} trials. *This is a hundred billion billion times the upper bound we computed for the total number of molecules ever to exist in the history of the cosmos!!* No random process could *ever* hope to find even one such protein structure, much less the full set of roughly 1,000 needed in the simplest forms of life. It is therefore sheer irrationality for a person to believe random chemical interactions could ever identify a viable set of functional proteins out of the truly staggering number of candidate possibilities.

In the face of such stunningly unfavorable odds, how could any scientist with any sense of honesty appeal to chance interactions as the explanation for the complexity we observe in living systems? To do so, with conscious awareness of these numbers, in my opinion represents a serious breach of scientific integrity. This line of argument applies, of course, not only to the issue of biogenesis but also to the issue of how a new gene/protein might arise in any sort of macroevolution process.

One retired Los Alamos National Laboratory fellow, a chemist, wanted to quibble that this argument was flawed because I did not account for details of chemical reaction kinetics. My intention was deliberately to choose a reaction rate so gigantic (one million million reactions per atom per second on average) that all such considerations would become utterly irrelevant. How could a reasonable person trained in chemistry or physics imagine there could be a way to assemble polypeptides in the order of hundreds of amino acid units in length, to allow them to fold into their three-dimensional structures, and then to express their unique properties, all within a small fraction of one picosecond!? Prior metaphysical commitments forced the chemist in question to such irrationality.

Another scientist, a physicist at Sandia National Laboratories, asserted that I had misapplied the rules of probability in my analysis. If my example were correct, he suggested, it "would turn the scientific world upside-down." I responded that the science community has been confronted with this basic argument in the past but has simply engaged in mass denial. Fred Hoyle, the eminent British cosmologist, published similar calculations two decades ago.[4] Most scientists just put their hands over their ears and refused to listen.

In reality this analysis is so simple and direct it does not require any special intelligence, ingenuity, or advanced science education to understand or even originate. In my case, all I did was to estimate a generous upper bound on the maximum number of chemical reactions — of any kind — that could have ever occurred in the entire history of the cosmos and then compare this number with the number of trials needed to find a single life protein with a minimal level of functionality from among the possible candidates. I showed the latter number was orders and orders larger than the former. I assumed only that the likely candidates were equally so. My argument was just that plain. I did not misapply the laws of probability. I applied them as physicists normally do in their everyday work.

Just How Do Coded Language Structures Arise?

One of the most dramatic discoveries in biology in the 20th century is that living organisms are realizations of coded language structures. All the detailed chemical and structural complexity associated with the metabolism, repair, specialized function, and reproduction of each living cell is a realization of the coded algorithms stored in its DNA. A paramount issue, therefore, is how do such extremely large language structures arise?

The origin of such structures is, of course, the central issue of the origin-of-life question. The simplest bacteria have genomes consisting of roughly a million codons. (Each codon, or genetic word, consists of three letters from the four-letter genetic alphabet.) Do coded algorithms which are a million words in length arise spontaneously by any known naturalistic process? Is there anything in the laws of physics that suggests how such structures might arise in a spontaneous fashion? The honest answer is simple. What we presently understand from thermodynamics and information theory argues persuasively that they do not and cannot!

Language involves a symbolic code, a vocabulary, and a set of grammatical rules to relay or record thought. Many of us spend most of our waking hours generating, processing, or disseminating linguistic data. Seldom do we reflect on the fact that language structures are clear manifestations of non-material reality.

This conclusion may be reached by observing that the linguistic information itself is independent of its material carrier. The meaning or message does not depend on whether it is represented as sound waves in the air or as ink patterns on paper or as alignment of magnetic domains on a floppy disk or as voltage patterns in a transistor network. The message that a person has won the $100,000,000 lottery is the same whether that person receives the information by someone speaking at his door or by telephone or by mail or on television or over the Internet.

Indeed, Einstein pointed to the nature and origin of symbolic information as one of the profound questions about the world as we know it.[5] He could identify no means by which matter could bestow meaning to symbols. The clear implication is that symbolic information, or language, represents a category of reality *distinct* from matter and energy. Linguists today, therefore, speak of this gap between matter and meaning-bearing symbol sets as the "Einstein gulf."[6] Today in this information age there is no debate that linguistic information is objectively real. With only a moment's reflection we can conclude that its reality is qualitatively different from the matter/energy substrate on which the linguistic information rides.

From whence, then, does linguistic information originate? In our human experience we immediately connect the language we create and process with our minds. But what is the ultimate nature of the human mind? If something as real as linguistic information has existence independent of matter and energy, from causal considerations it is not unreasonable to suspect that an entity capable of originating linguistic information is also ultimately non-material in its essential nature.

An immediate conclusion of these observations concerning linguistic information is that materialism, which has long been the dominant philosophical perspective in scientific circles, with its foundational presupposition that there is no non-material reality, is simply and plainly false. It is amazing that its falsification is so trivial.

The implications are immediate for the issue of evolution. The evolutionary assumption that the exceedingly complex linguistic structures which comprise the construction blueprints and operating manuals for all the complicated chemical nanomachinery and sophisticated feedback control mechanisms in even the simplest living organism — that these structures must have a materialistic explanation — is *fundamentally wrong*. But how, then, does one account for symbolic language as the crucial ingredient from which all living organisms develop and function and manifest such amazing capabilities? The answer should be obvious: an intelligent Creator is unmistakably required. But what about macroevolution? Could physical processes in the realm of matter and energy at least modify an existing genetic language structure to yield another with some truly novel capability, as the evolutionists so desperately want to believe?

On this question Professor Murray Eden, a specialist in information theory and formal languages at the Massachusetts Institute of Technology, pointed out several years ago that random perturbations of formal language structures simply do not accomplish such magical feats. He said, "No currently existing formal language can tolerate random changes in the symbol sequence which expresses its sentences. Meaning is almost invariably destroyed. Any changes must be syntactically lawful ones. I would conjecture that what one might call 'genetic grammaticality' has a deterministic explanation and does not owe its stability to selection pressure acting on random variation."[7]

In a word, then, the answer is no. Random changes in the letters of the genetic alphabet have no more ability to produce useful new protein structures than could the generation of random strings of amino acids discussed in the earlier section. This is the glaring and fatal deficiency in any materialist mechanism for macroevolution. Life depends on complex non-material language structures for its detailed specification. Material processes are utterly impotent to create such structures or to modify them to specify some novel function. If the task of creating the roughly 1,000 genes needed to specify the cellular machinery in a bacterium is unthinkable within a materialist framework, consider how much more unthinkable for the materialist is the task of obtaining the roughly 100,000 genes required to specify a mammal!

Despite all the millions of pages of evolutionist publications — from journal articles to textbooks to popular magazine stories — which assume and imply that material processes are entirely adequate to accomplish macroevolutionary miracles, there is in reality no rational basis for such belief. It is utter fantasy. Coded language structures are non-material in nature and absolutely require a non-material explanation.

But What about the Geological/Fossil Record?

Just as there has been glaring scientific fraud in things biological for the past century, there has been a similar fraud in things geological. The error, in a word, is uniformitarianism. This outlook assumes and asserts that the earth's past can be correctly understood purely in terms of present-day processes acting at more or less present-day rates. Just as materialist biologists have erroneously assumed that material processes can give rise to life in all its diversity, materialist geologists have assumed that the present can fully account for the earth's past. In so doing, they have been forced to ignore and suppress abundant contrary evidence that the planet has suffered major catastrophe on a global scale.

Only in the past two decades has the silence concerning global catastrophism in the geological record begun to be broken. Only in the last 10–15 years has the reality of global mass extinction events in the record become widely known outside the paleontology community. Only in about the last 10 years have there been efforts to account for such global extinction in terms of high energy phenomena such as asteroid impacts. But the huge horizontal extent of Paleozoic and Mesozoic sedimentary formations and their internal evidence of high energy transport represents stunning testimony for global catastrophic processes far beyond anything yet considered in the geological literature. Field evidence indicates catastrophic processes were responsible for most, if not all, of this portion of the geological record. The proposition that present-day geological processes are representative of those which produced the Paleozoic and Mesozoic formations is utter folly.

What is the alternative to this uniformitarian perspective? It is that a catastrophe, driven by processes in the earth's interior, progressively but quickly resurfaced the planet. An event of this type has recently been documented as having occurred on the earth's sister planet Venus.[8] This startling conclusion is based on high-resolution mapping performed by the *Magellan* spacecraft in the early 1990s which revealed the vast majority of craters on Venus today to be in pristine condition and only 2.5 percent embayed by lava, while an episode of intense volcanism prior to the formation of the present craters has erased all earlier ones from the face of the planet. Since this resurfacing, volcanic and tectonic activity has been minimal.

There is pervasive evidence for a similar catastrophe on our planet, driven by runaway subduction of the pre-catastrophe ocean floor into the earth's interior.[9] That such a process is theoretically possible has been at least acknowledged in the geophysics literature for almost 30 years.[10] A major consequence of this sort of event is progressive flooding of the continents and rapid mass extinction of all but a few percent of the species of life. The destruction of ecological habitats began with marine environments and progressively enveloped the terrestrial environments as well.

Evidence for such intense global catastrophism is apparent throughout the Paleozoic, Mesozoic, and much of the Cenozoic portions of the geological record. Most biologists are aware of the abrupt appearance of most of the animal phyla in the lower Cambrian rocks. But most are unaware that the Precambrian-Cambrian boundary also represents a nearly global stratigraphic unconformity marked by intense catastrophism. In the Grand Canyon, as one example, the Tapeats Sandstone immediately above this boundary contains hydraulically transported boulders tens of feet in diameter.[11]

That the catastrophe was global in extent is clear from the extreme horizontal extent and continuity of the continental sedimentary deposits. That there was a single large catastrophe and not many smaller ones with long gaps in between is implied by the lack of erosional channels, soil horizons, and dissolution structures at the interfaces between successive strata. The excellent exposures of the Paleozoic record in the Grand Canyon provide superb examples of this vertical continuity with little or no physical evidence of time gaps between strata. Especially significant in this regard are the contacts between the Kaibab and Toroweap Formations, the Coconino and Hermit Formations, the Hermit and Esplanade Formations, and the Supai and Redwall Formations.[12]

The ubiquitous presence of crossbeds in sandstones, and even limestones, in Paleozoic, Mesozoic, and even Cenozoic rocks is strong testimony for high energy water transport of these sediments. Studies of sandstones exposed in the Grand Canyon reveal crossbeds produced by high velocity water currents that generated sand waves tens of meters in height.[13] The crossbedded Coconino sandstone exposed in the Grand Canyon continues across Arizona and New Mexico into Texas, Oklahoma, Colorado, and Kansas. It covers more than 200,000 square miles and has an estimated volume of 10,000 cubic miles. The crossbeds dip to the south and indicate that the sand came from the north. When one looks for a possible source for this sand to the north, none is readily apparent. A very distant source seems to be required.

The scale of the water catastrophe implied by such formations boggles the mind. Yet numerical calculation demonstrates that when significant areas of the continental surface are flooded, strong water currents with velocities of tens of meters per second spontaneously arise.[14] Such currents are analogous to planetary waves in the atmosphere and are driven by the earth's rotation.

This sort of dramatic global-scale catastrophism documented in the Paleozoic, Mesozoic, and much of the Cenozoic sediments implies a distinctively different interpretation of the associated fossil record. Instead of representing an evolutionary sequence, the record reveals a successive destruction of ecological habitat in a global tectonic and hydrologic catastrophe. This understanding readily explains why Darwinian intermediate types are systematically absent from the geological record — the fossil record documents a brief and intense global destruction of life and not a long evolutionary history! The types of plants and animals preserved as fossils were the forms of life that existed on the earth prior to the catastrophe. The long span of time and the intermediate forms of life that the evolutionist imagines in his mind are simply illusions. And the strong observational evidence for this catastrophe absolutely demands a radically revised time scale relative to that assumed by evolutionists.

But How Is Geological Time to Be Reckoned?

With the discovery of radioactivity about a century ago, uniformitarian scientists have assumed they have a reliable and quantitative means for measuring absolute time on scales of billions of years. This is because a number of unstable isotopes exist with half-lives in the billions of year range. Confidence in these methods has been very high for several reasons. The nuclear energy levels involved in radioactive decay are so much greater than the electronic energy levels associated with ordinary temperature, pressure, and chemistry that variations in the latter can have negligible effects on the former.

Furthermore, it has been assumed that the laws of nature are time invariant and that the decay rates we measure today have been constant since the beginning of the cosmos — a view, of course, dictated by materialist and uniformitarian belief. The confidence in radiometric methods among materialist scientists has been so absolute that all other methods for estimating the age of geological materials and geological events have been relegated to an inferior status and deemed unreliable when they disagree with radiometric techniques.

Most people, therefore, including most scientists, are not aware of the systematic and glaring conflict between radiometric methods and non-radiometric methods for dating or constraining the age of geological events. Yet this conflict is so stark and so consistent that there is more than sufficient reason, in my opinion, to aggressively challenge the validity of radiometric methods.

One clear example of this conflict concerns the retention of helium produced by nuclear decay of uranium in small zircon crystals commonly found in granite. Uranium tends to selectively concentrate in zircons in a solidifying magma because the large spaces in the zircon crystal lattice more readily accommodate the large uranium ions. Uranium is unstable and eventually transforms, through a chain of nuclear decay steps, into lead. In the process, eight atoms of helium are produced for every initial atom of U-238. But helium is a very small atom and is also a noble gas with little tendency to react chemically with other species. Helium, therefore, tends to migrate readily through a crystal lattice.

The conflict for radiometric methods is that zircons in Precambrian granite display huge helium concentrations.[15] When the amounts of uranium, lead, and helium are determined experimentally, one finds amounts of lead and uranium consistent with more than a billion years of nuclear decay at presently measured rates. Amazingly, most of the radiogenic helium from this decay process is also still present within these crystals, that are typically only a few micrometers across. However, based on experimentally measured helium diffusion rates, the zircon helium content implies a time span of only a few thousand years since the majority of the nuclear decay occurred.

So which physical process is more trustworthy — the diffusion of a noble gas in a crystalline lattice or the radioactive decay of an unstable isotype? Both processes can be investigated today in great detail in the laboratory. Both the rate of helium diffusion in a given crystalline lattice and the rate decay of uranium to lead can be determined with high degrees of precision. But these two physical processes yield wildly disparate estimates for the age of the same granite rock. Where is the logical or procedural error? The most reasonable conclusion in my view is that it lies in the step of extrapolating as constant presently measured rates of nuclear decay into the remote past. If this is the error, then radiometric methods based on presently measured rates simply do not and cannot provide correct estimates for geologic age.

But just how strong is the case that radiometric methods are indeed so incorrect? There are dozens of physical processes which, like helium diffusion, yield age estimate orders of a magnitude smaller than the radiometric techniques. Many of these are geological or geophysical in nature and are therefore subject to the question of whether presently observed rates can legitimately be extrapolated into the indefinite past.

However, even if we make that suspect assumption and consider the current rate of sodium increase in the oceans versus the present ocean sodium content, or the current rate of sediment accumulation into the ocean basins versus the current ocean sediment volume, or the current net rate of loss of continental rock (primarily by erosion) versus the current volume of continental crust, or the present rate of uplift of the Himalayan mountains (accounting for erosion) versus their present height, we infer time estimates drastically at odds with the radiometric time scale.[16] These time estimates are further reduced dramatically if we do not make the uniformitarian assumption but account for the global catastrophism described earlier.

There are other processes which are not as easy to express in quantitative terms, such as the degradation of protein in a geological environment, that also point to a much shorter time scale for the geological record. It is now well established that unmineralized dinosaur bone still containing recognizable bone protein exists in many locations around the world.[17] From my own firsthand experience with such material, it is inconceivable that bone containing such well-preserved protein could possibly have survived for more than a few thousand years in the geological settings in which they are found.

I therefore believe the case is strong from a scientific standpoint to reject radiometric methods as a valid means for dating geological materials. What then can be used in their place? As a Christian, I am persuaded the Bible is a reliable source of information. The Bible speaks of a worldwide cataclysm in the Genesis flood, which destroyed all air-breathing life on the planet apart from the animals and humans God preserved alive in the ark. The correspondence between the global catastrophe in the geological record and the flood described in Genesis is much too obvious for me not to conclude that these events must be one and the same.

With this crucial linkage between the biblical record and the geological record, a straightforward reading of the earlier chapters of Genesis is a next logical step. The conclusion is that the creation of the cosmos, the earth, plants, animals, as well as man and woman by God took place, just as it is described, only a few thousand years ago, with no need for qualification or apology.

But What about Light from Distant Stars?

An entirely legitimate question, then, is how we could possibly see stars millions and billions of light years away if the earth is so young. Part of the reason scientists like myself can have confidence that good science will vindicate a face-value understanding of the Bible is because we believe we have at least an outline of the correct answer to this important question.[18]

This answer draws upon important clues from the Bible, while applying standard general relativity. The result is a cosmological model that differs from the standard big-bang models in two essential respects. First, it does not assume the so-called cosmological principle and, second, it invokes inflation at a different point in cosmological history.

The cosmological principle is the assumption that the cosmos has no edge or boundary or center and, in a broad-brush sense, is the same in every place and in every direction. This assumption concerning the geometry of the cosmos has allowed cosmologists to obtain relatively simple solutions of Einstein's equations of general relativity. Such solutions form the basis of all big-bang models. But there is growing observational evidence that this assumption is simply not true. A recent article in the journal *Nature*, for example, describes a fractal analysis of galaxy distribution to large distances in the cosmos that contradicts this crucial big-bang assumption.[19]

If, instead, the cosmos has a center, then its early history is *radically* different from that of all big-bang models. Its beginning would be that of a massive black hole containing its entire mass. Such a mass distribution has a whopping gradient in gravitational potential which profoundly affects the local physics, including the speed of clocks. Clocks near the center would run much more slowly, or even be stopped, during the earliest portion of cosmic history.[20] Since the heavens on a large scale are isotropic from the vantage point of the earth, the earth must be near the center of such a cosmos. Light from the outer edge of such a cosmos reaches the center in a very brief time as measured by clocks in the vicinity of the earth.

In regard to the timing of cosmic inflation, this alternative cosmology has inflation *after* stars and galaxies form. It is noteworthy that recently two astrophysics groups studying high-redshift type Ia supernovae both concluded that cosmic expansion is greater now than when these stars exploded. The article in the June 1998 issue of *Physics Today* describes these "astonishing" results which "have caused quite a stir" in the astrophysics community.[21] The story amazingly ascribes the cause to "some ethereal agency."

Indeed, the Bible repeatedly speaks of God stretching out the heavens: "O LORD my God, You are very great . . . stretching out heaven as a curtain (Ps. 104:1–2); "Thus says God the LORD, who created the heavens and stretched them out" (Isa. 42:5); "I, the LORD, am the maker of all things, stretching out the heavens by myself" (Isa. 44:24); "It is I who made the earth, and created man upon it. I stretched out the heavens with my hands, and I ordained all their host" (Isa. 45:12).

As a Christian who is also a professional scientist, I exult in the reality that "in six days the LORD made the heavens and the earth" (Exod. 20:11). May He forever be praised.

Notes

1 A collection of these letters is available on the World Wide Web at http://www.nnm.com/lacf.

2 C.W. Allen, *Astrophysical Quantities*, 3rd ed. (London: University of London, Athlone Press, 1973), p. 293; M. Fukugita, C.J. Hogan, and P.J.E. Peebles, "The Cosmic Baryon Budget," *Astrophysical Journal*, 503 (1998), 518–30.

3 H.P. Yockey, "A Calculation of the Probability of Spontaneous Biogenesis by Information Theory," *Journal of Theoretical Biology*, 67 (1978) 377–398; (Hubert P. Yockey) *Information Theory and Molecular Biology* (Cambridge, UK: Cambridge University Press, 1992).

4 Fred Hoyle and Chandra Wickramasinghe, *Evolution From Space* (London: J.M. Dent, 1981).

5 A. Einstein, "Remarks on Bertrand Russell's Theory of Knowledge," in *The Philosophy of Bertrand Russell,* P.A. Schilpp, editor (New York: Tudor Pub, 1944), p. 290.

6 John W. Oller Jr., *Language and Experience: Classic Pragmatism* (Lanham, MD: University Press of America, 1989), p. 25.

7 M. Eden, "Inadequacies of Neo-Darwinian Evolution as a Scientific Theory," in P.S. Moorhead and M.M. Kaplan, eds., *Mathematical Challenges to the Neo-Darwinian Interpretation of Evolution* (Philadelphia, PA: Wistar Institute Press, 1967), p. 11.

8 R.G. Strom, G.G. Schaber, and D.D. Dawson, "The Global Resurfacing of Venus," *Journal of Geophysical Research,* 99, 1994, 10899–926.

9 R.E. Walsh, editor, *Proceedings of the Third International Conference on Creationism, Technical Symposium Sessions,* "Catastrophic Plate Tectonics: A Global Flood Model of Earth History," by S.A. Austin, J.R. Baumgardner, D.R. Humphreys, A.A. Snelling, L. Vardiman, and K.P. Wise, p. 609–621; "Computer Modeling of the Large-Scale Tectonics Associated with the Genesis Flood," by J.R. Baumgardner, p. 49–62; "Runaway Subduction as the Driving Mechanism for the Genesis Flood," p. 63–75, (Pittsburgh, PA: Creation Science Fellowship, Inc., 1994).

10 O.L. Anderson and P.C. Perkins, "Runaway Temperatures in the Asthenosphere Resulting from Viscous Heating," *Journal of Geophysical Research,* 79, 1974, 2136–2138.

11 S.A. Austin, editor, *Grand Canyon: Monument to Catastrophe,* "Interpreting Strata of the Grand Canyon," by S.A. Austin (El Cajon, CA: Institute for Creation Research, 1994), p. 46–47.

12 Ibid., p. 42–51.

13 Ibid., p. 32–36.

14 R.E. Walsh, editor, *Proceedings of the Third International Conference on Creationism, Technical Symposium Sessions,* "Patterns of Ocean Circulation Over the Continents During Noah's Flood," by J.R. Baumgardner and D.W. Barnette (Pittsburgh, PA: Creation Science Fellowship, Inc., 1994), 77–86.

15 R.V. Gentry, G.L. Glish, and E.H. McBay, "Differential Helium Retention in Zircons: Implications for Nuclear Waste Containment," *Geophysical Research Letters,* 9, 1982, 1129–1130.

16 R.E. Walsh and C.L. Brooks, editors, *Proceedings of the Second International Conference on Creationism, Vol. II,* "The Sea's Missing Salt: A Dilemma for Evolutionists," by S.A. Austin and D.R. Humphreys (Pittsburgh, PA: Creation Science Fellowship, Inc., 1990), p. 17–33.

17 G. Muyzer, P. Sandberg, M.H.J. Knapen, C. Vermeer, M. Collins, and P. Westbroek, "Preservation of the Bone Protein Osteocalcin in Dinosaurs," *Geology,* 20, 1992, 871–874.

18 D. Russell Humphreys, *Starlight and Time* (Green Forest, AR: Master Books, 1994).

19 P. Coles, "An Unprincipled Universe?" *Nature,* 391, 1998, 120–121.

20 D.R. Humphreys, "New Vistas of Space-Time Rebut the Critics," *Creation Ex Nihilo Technical Journal,* 12, 1998, 195–212.

21 B. Schwarzschild, "Very Distant Supernovae Suggest That the Cosmic Expansion Is Speeding Up," *Physics Today,* 51, 1998, 17–19.

arthur jones

Biology

Dr. Jones is a science and education consultant. He has a B.S. (hons) from the University of Birmingham in biology; an M.Ed. from Bristol University and a Ph.D. in biology from the University of Birmingham. Dr. Jones has taught science and religion courses at London and Bristol Universities. He presently works for the Christian Schools' Trust as their research consultant for curriculum development. He is a member of the Institute of Biology, London.

It is commonly claimed by secular scientists that creationism is a "science stopper." The contention is that to ascribe anything (e.g., the origin of living organisms) to the direct action of God is to cut off all scientific inquiry. This seems such simple common sense that it has been very persuasive. Nevertheless, it is not difficult to show that the argument is fallacious.

A number of general points can be made. First, the argument is based on ignorance of all the different ways in which Christian faith can enter into science and of how fruitful these have been. After all, many of the great scientists of the past were committed Christians and many of those were consciously exploring the implications of their Christian faith for science. Second, whereas the direct action of God may cut off one type of explanation, others will remain and may even be enhanced. To say that God created the different kinds of animals and plants certainly cuts off explanation in terms of evolutionary continuity. However, it leaves wide open scientific investigation of every other pattern of relationship (ecological, developmental, etc.) between these kinds. Scientists have been so indoctrinated in the belief that all patterns can only be explained historically in terms of the happenstances of Darwinian evolution that many wouldn't even know how to look for explanations in other terms. Third, there is abundant documentation of the fact that evolutionary naturalism has often stopped scientific research. To take just one example, the evolutionary assumption that certain organs or features are vestigial has often long delayed the (fruitful) research into their functions.

More specifically, one can appeal to experience and this is where this essay becomes a personal testimony to the scientific fruitfulness of a commitment to creation.

During my undergraduate days when my "heretical" views became known, my professor (Otto Lowenstein, Professor of Zoology) made a point of telling me that no creationist would be allowed to do research in his department! However, he did allow me to do research. From the pressure that was put on me, I can only assume that it was thought that I could be convinced of the error of my ways. If that was the intention, then it badly backfired. Many a visiting scholar was brought into my laboratory to convince me, from their area of expertise, that evolution was indisputably true. Of course, hardly knowing their field, I never had an answer at the time, but after they had gone I would look up the relevant research and carefully analyze it. I always found that the evolutionist case was much weaker than it had seemed and that alternative creationist interpretations were available which were just as or more convincing. My position was further strengthened by the results of my own research.

I had decided to tackle the issue of the identity and nature of the created kinds. This was in response to a common evolutionist challenge that always seemed to me to be a reasonable one. If there are created kinds then they should be identifiable. I wanted to investigate the processes of variation within a kind, and gain some handle on the limits to that variation. I needed to be able to keep and breed large numbers of species. My background was in vertebrate studies, so that meant fish. My supervisor was a fan of the cichlid aquarium fish, so that was quickly settled! Those years of research were fascinating. For all the diversity of species, I found the cichlids to be an unmistakably natural group, a created kind. The more I worked with these fish the clearer my recognition of "cichlidness" became and the more distinct they seemed from all the "similar" fishes I studied. Conversations at conferences and literature searches confirmed that this was the common experience of experts in every area of systematic biology. Distinct kinds really are there and the experts know it to be so. Developmental studies then showed that the enormous cichlid diversity (over 1,000 "species") was actually produced by the endless permutation of a relatively small number of character states: 4 colors, ten or so basic pigment patterns and so on. The same characters (or character patterns) appeared "randomly" all over the cichlid distribution. The patterns of variation were "modular" or "mosaic"; evolutionary lines of descent were nowhere to be found. This kind of adaptive variation can occur quite rapidly (since it involves only what was already there) and some instances of cichlid "radiation" (in geologically "recent" lakes) were indeed dateable (by evolutionists) to within time spans of no more than a few thousand years. On a wider canvas, fossils provided no comfort to evolutionists. All fish, living and fossil, belong to distinct kinds; "links" are decidedly missing. Incidentally, creationists have no reason to be committed to any particular classification scheme, nor to any particular taxa above the kind level. "Orders," "classes," and "phyla" must not be allowed to become hallowed by tradition. They may be correctly identified (higher taxa *are* real), but there again they may not. Some "missing links" have been artifacts of bad classification systems. Morphology (and now biochemistry) have dominated classification, but ecology may yet prove to be a better guide.

My fish were supposedly strictly freshwater, but were found in the tropical fresh waters of three continents — from the Americas through Africa to Asia. I hypothesized that all, or at least most, fish kinds that survived the Flood must be able to survive both sea water and fresh, and much mixing of the two. After the post-Flood diversification within the kinds we should still find that, in marine kinds, there are some species that can tolerate much fresher water and, in freshwater kinds, some species that can tolerate much saltier water. With my cichlids I found that this was indeed the case. I was able to keep some species in pure sea water for more than two years with no harmful effects — they lived and reproduced normally. Literature searches again revealed that this was a common pattern throughout the fish classes.

I was also looking at heredity and already becoming skeptical of the dogma that "DNA is all" (so linked to reductionistic and evolutionary schemes). I discovered there is substantial evidence that there is more to heredity than genes and genic processes.

Indeed, it is clear that the whole cell system is a minimum unit of organism heredity. Genic processes have much to do with variation within kinds, but probably little to do with the distinction of kinds. Genes are best regarded as triggers in complex developmental systems rather than as creators or causes of organic structures. In this regard I found that there had been a vibrant creationist research program in developmental biology before Darwin that has been partly taken up again by the modern "structuralist" biologists (e.g., Stuart Kauffman and Brian Goodwin). Not surprisingly, the latter evolutionists are anti-Darwinian and anti-Dawkins. However, their work can readily be interpreted in creationist terms. It may, of course, ultimately prove wrong (our science is always approximate and liable to error), but it at least makes the point that creationism is not a science stopper. In my view, evolutionary explanations turn out to be fatally inconsistent.

Readings

"A Creationist Critique of Homology," *Creation Research Society Quarterly,* 19(3), 1982, p. 166–75 and 20(2), 1983, p. 122.

Developmental Studies and Speciation in Cichlid Fish. Ph.D. thesis, Department of Zoology and Comparative Physiology, Birmingham University, United Kingdom, 1972, Diss S2 B72.

"The Genetic Integrity of the "Kinds" (Baramin) — A Working Hypothesis," *Creation Research Society Quarterly,* 19(1), 1982, p. 13–18.

religion and origins

george f. howe

Botany

Dr. Howe is professor, Division of Natural Sciences and Mathematics, the Masters College, Newhall, California. He holds a B.S. in botany from Wheaton College, an M.S. in botany and a Ph.D. in botany from Ohio State University, where he was a Charles F. Kettering fellow. He also completed post-doctoral studies in botany at Washington State University; in desert biology at Arizona State University; and in radiation biology at Cornell University. As well as publishing technical papers and books in the area of botany, he has published numerous papers in the area of creation versus mega-evolution, and philosophy of science. He served as president of the Creation Research Society from 1977 to 1983.

In 1953, I enrolled as a graduate student in the botany department of Ohio State University. My time at OSU (1953–1959) was filled with research in plant physiology, botany coursework, meetings at church and Intervarsity Christian Fellowship, and my marriage in 1955. As a result, there was little time left for evaluating origins theories. While never adopting theistic evolutionism, I continued to orient my view of fossils around the day–age interpretations, assuming that God's miraculous acts of creation were somehow interspersed throughout eons of geologic time.

One day, in an advanced plant physiology class, C.A. Swanson (a respected authority on the translocation of sugars inside flowering plants) was finishing a stunning lecture on DNA and its detailed genetic code — a subject that was new and exhilarating in 1955. Upon realizing that DNA carries precise information regarding most aspects of plant life, I asked Swanson how the original DNA came to possess these intricate instructions. With a knowing smile on his face, C.A. Swanson wisely replied, "Howe, that is a question science cannot answer!"

Many profitable conversations occurred with fellow graduate students at the coffee shop. On one such occasion, I discussed origins philosophies with Bill (a liberal Christian, who espoused wholesale theistic evolutionism) and Ken (a committed atheist, who put no stock in divine intervention). Each of us defended our respective convictions and just before we had to leave, Ken (the atheist who stoutly disagreed with me) summarized our discussion as follows: "George, both your system and mine are philosophically coherent and clear-cut. The middle position of Bill, however, is worthless and hopelessly confusing!"

When graduate studies were nearing an end in 1959, I applied to several colleges for positions teaching botany. Pursuant to each application, the O.S.U. placement office sent my file (including transcripts of grades and various reference letters) to each college. I also contacted my old friend and advisor, the ebullient John Leedy at Wheaton College, Illinois, where I had been an undergraduate student. He informed me that there was a full-time opening to teach in the biology department at Westmont College, Santa Barbara, California, a school that was known back then as the "Wheaton of the West." After visiting our home in Columbus, Ohio, Roger Voskuyl, president of Westmont, sent me a contract to teach there.

For two reasons I promptly signed that document and mailed it back: (1) there had been no firm offers from any of the other colleges; and (2) I felt somewhat obligated to the Lord to spend at least one year teaching in a Christian college in return for the academic and spiritual blessings that an education at a Christian college had afforded me. Only a few days after the contract was mailed back to Westmont, a college of education in the state of Washington sent me a telegram containing an apology for a mix-up, and an invitation to teach for them at a salary that would have been $1,200 more annually than the Westmont offer! Instead of mailing *my* file to the Washington college, the Ohio State University office had inadvertently sent to Washington the job file of a certain George *Earl* Howe, a different OSU grad who had earned his advanced degree in some other field, such as business! Puzzling over this anomaly, the biology people in Washington had delayed processing my application. By the time the error had been rectified and an offer sent, I had, of course, accepted the other job. It appeared to me that this peculiar turn of events was a sign from God for me to go to Westmont. The Washington offer was rejected, and the position at Westmont lasted for nine years, not just one.

In terms of the work God had ahead for me, this little glitch was no mistake at all, but an instance of divine serendipity. At Westmont I encountered academic freedom, as well as productive contacts with students and other faculty. There were opportunities to correspond and even visit with such renowned creationists as John Whitcomb Jr. and Walter Lammerts. It was an environment which allowed me to mature as a Christian teacher and to re-evaluate my own ideas about the fossil record. In spite of a very full teaching schedule, there was time for me to attempt to untie the Gordian knot: how to handle geology and Genesis at once.

Teaching an origins course forced me to delve into the literature of both creation and evolution and to study the various approaches conservative Bible scholars were making to the events in Genesis chapter 1. The textbook I selected on evolution, *Evolution: Process and Product*, was by E.O. Dodson, an outstanding evolutionary geneticist from Canada. Twenty years later, Dodson patiently carried out an eight-year correspondence about origins with me, which gave rise to our co-authored book *Creation or Evolution: Correspondence on the Current Conflict.*[1]

In that first origins class and in other science courses, I presented two or three approaches to the timing of creation events, and then I recommended that students make their choice. In some of those classes, there was a gifted individual named Art Hubbard. Whenever I presented various long-age creation theories involving deviant interpretations of Genesis, Art would cordially object and assert that the real meaning of the passage was being violated by such tactics. Another student who promoted a recent creation in my first classes was David Nicholas, who later became president of Shasta Bible College.

In 1960 my department chairman, mentor, and friend, Robert Frost, encouraged me to read Flood geology books by the self-taught geologist, George McCready Price. I believe that one ought not to categorically reject the writings of people who lack a formal education in science. It must be remembered that Lyell was a lawyer (not a geologist) and Charles Darwin was a theologian. Bob Frost also lent me a copy of *The New Diluvialism*, a fascinating book in which the author, Harold Clark, accounted for the different assemblages of fossils in successively higher strata as the consequence of pre-Flood ecological life zones. These biomes, he proposed, were sequentially inundated and fossilized while the Flood waters rose and churned across the early land masses. This book showed me that there are viable alternatives to uniformitarianism in explaining the biostratigraphic "law of floral and faunal succession" — explanations that do not involve lengthy and unlikely periods of gradual sedimentation.

A few years after that, a landmark paper appeared in *Scientific American* magazine entitled "Crises in the History of Life" by Norman Newell, a secular geologist.[2] In this paper Newell marshalled plenty of evidence to show that fossils had been deposited by catastrophic (not gradual) means. Yet the author still clung to the overall uniformitarian framework by speculating that many catastrophes (not just one) must have occurred across earth's elongated history. This view came to be known as "catastrophic uniformitarianism," a binomial that is clearly an oxymoron. Readings from Price, Clark, and even Newell compelled me to broaden my horizons and to think about geological catastrophism as a likely corollary of the Noahic deluge.

Concerning Bible interpretation, a monumental essay was penned by Raymond Surburg, "In the Beginning God Created," in *Darwin, Evolution, and Creation*, in which this Hebrew scholar asserted that whenever the Bible word "day" (*yom* in Hebrew) is accompanied by the definite number like "first" day, "second" day, etc., it invariably means a real day, not some long age.[3] This exegetical truth took root and began to undermine my speculations about age-long "days" in Genesis chapter 1. By his insistence on six real days of creation, Surburg jerked the rug from underneath the plethora of alternate readings for the creation time scale. This book likewise contained some anti-evolutionary chapters by eminent creation scientists, who later became my esteemed fellow board members in the Creation Research Society: Paul Zimmerman, John Klotz, and Wilbert Rusch Sr.

While I have listed notable authors who promoted young-earth creationism in the early 1960s, I have saved the most prominent for last. Although it was published early in 1961, *The Genesis Flood*, by Henry Morris and John C. Whitcomb Jr., did not find its way into my reading schedule until some months later, when my brother Fredrick, a distinguished theologian, began pressing me to study it. Between those two covers, Morris and Whitcomb had packed a vast array of data that fit squarely with young-earth catastrophism.[4] *The Genesis Flood* was and still is controversial among Christian apologists.

Another worker who prodded me toward approaching a young-earth position was Bolton Davidheiser, a brilliant and uncompromising professor who had taught biology at Westmont before my time there. After hearing me review a book at a 1959 meeting of the American Scientific Affiliation in Los Angeles, Davidheiser corresponded with me about my neutrality concerning the issue of time in Genesis. In his own direct and guileless manner, he helped in the clarification of my origins stance.

By 1963 my path had crossed with that of Walter Lammerts, a creation scientist who had already become known as the "Father of Modern Rose Breeding" because of his success in producing such exceedingly popular roses as "Charlotte Armstrong" and "Queen Elizabeth." In 1964 Walter was the first president of the Creation Research Society. Although he knew of my lingering doubts about a young earth, he nevertheless allowed me to become a CRS member.

At my invitation, Lammerts presented a Westmont creation seminar which was well attended by students, faculty, and off-campus visitors. He encouraged me to pursue my study of germination rates in seeds after weeks of soaking in ocean waters, as a means to understand how plants might have survived during and after the Flood. Lammerts likewise helped kindle my interest in performing various other creation research projects years later at Los Angeles Baptist College (now The Masters College) in Newhall, California.

Many of Lammerts' horticultural colleagues believed in gradual evolution, involving long spans of time. But as a creationist Lammerts assumed that whatever variation is possible will occur in the present and rapidly. It was to this underlying supposition that he attributed his achievements in plant breeding. His evolution-minded friends felt there was little chance of effecting any immediate change. Ironically, it was Lammerts, the creationist, who proceeded to find those changes and to use them in developing new roses!

Lammerts' circle of personal friends always included some "long-agers" and even a few hard-core macroevolutionists, with whom he carried on spirited but friendly dialogues. Herein I believe is an important lesson for creationists: whenever possible, let us take an irenic approach to our adversaries.

During 1964 a threshold in my thinking was gradually crossed. Up to that year it had seemed to me that there was ample scientific evidence which demanded long ages. I imagined that such phenomena as C-14 decay, U-238 dating, the formation of coal, and the genesis of oil bore undeniable testimony to a vast prehistory for the earth. After crossing a mental "continental divide," however, it became increasingly apparent to me that there is nothing in empirical science that compels anyone to embrace billions or even millions of years.

The U-238 method and other radiochemical "clocks" are based on unprovable assumptions, which in some instances have actually been falsified. There is no rock or any other object, for example, that says, "I am 40 million years old; use me as a calibration sample."

C-14 dating has even led to truncating previous estimates for the elapsed time since the onset of the Ice Age. The disequilibrium between the measured rate of C-14 decay and the rate of its atmospheric production support an age of less than 10,000 years for the earth's atmosphere. And so it goes. There is not even one scientific fact that furnishes an unequivocal demonstration of great antiquity. All the data find favorable alternative explanations within a recent creation position.

My foremost question changed from, "How can we interpret Scripture to accommodate the enormous ages known from science?" to "Is there any feature about any dating method that actually satisfies all the ordinary criteria of real science?"

As the end of this age and the Final Judgment draw near, believers everywhere are constrained to reaffirm the literal truths God has revealed about origins. Some day we must all answer Christ's haunting query individually, "When the Son of Man cometh, shall He find faith on the earth?" (Luke 18:8).

Endnotes

1 Edward O. Dodson and George F. Howe, *Creation or Evolution: Correspondence on the Current Conflict* (Ottawa, Canada: University of Ottawa Press, 1990).

2 Norman Newell, "Crises in the History of Life," *Scientific American* magazine, vol. 208, number 2, 1963, p. 76–92.

3 Paul Zimmerman, editor, *Darwin, Evolution, and Creation,* "In the Beginning God Created," by Raymond Surburg (St. Louis, MO: Concordia Publishing House, 1959), p. 36–81.

4 Henry M. Morris and John C. Whitcomb Jr., *The Genesis Flood* (Phillipsburg, NJ: Presbyterian and Reformed, 1960).

a.j. monty white

Physical Chemistry

Dr. White is student advisor, dean of students office, at the University of Cardiff, in the United Kingdom. He holds a B.S. with honors, a Ph.D. in the field of gas kinetics from the University College of Wales, Aberystwyth, and has completed a two-year post-doctoral fellowship at the same University. Dr. White subsequently served in a number of university administrative posts. Over the years he has written several books and numerous articles relating to creation-evolution, and science and the Bible, as well as making several appearances on British television and radio programs dealing with these issues.

My parents brought me up to be an atheist, but as a result of discussions with Christians during my first year at university, I came to the conclusion that there was a God, that the Bible could be trusted as both a history book and a book of prophecy, and also that Christianity was a miraculous life-transforming religion. My conversion experience came some months later and I became a Christian.

The following October (1964) I began to study geology at university. The first geology lecture I attended was given by Professor Alan Wood, the head of department. He gave a talk about the evolution of life on earth — the usual story about how inorganic chemicals on the earth's prebiotic surface joined up to produce organic molecules and how these organic molecules formed themselves into self-replicating organisms, which then evolved into all the extinct and living life-forms on the earth. Professor Wood was at pains to point out that the human species was not the end product of evolution, and he then speculated on the future evolution of humankind. Toward the end of his lecture, he suggested that in a few hundred million years, whatever was the most advanced creature on the earth at that time would find fossilized remains of 20th century humans and say, or by means of telepathic communication with one another, declare, "How primitive!"

I left the lecture thinking a great deal about what Professor Wood had said. How could I reconcile it with what the Bible taught in Genesis about the creation and the early history of the earth? I decided to ask my Christian friends about the creation/evolution question. I was, however, mildly surprised at their response, for they all told me to believe in evolution and to interpret the early chapters of Genesis accordingly. Such a belief is called *theistic evolution* — in other words, that evolution occurred and that God controlled the processes. The implication of this belief is that the early chapters of Genesis are not interpreted as history, but in terms of myths, allegories, legends, and parables. As a result of talking with my Christian friends, I came to accept theistic evolution and believed it for a few years.

I really enjoyed studying geology and within two years had advanced to degree level. However, I continued to major in chemistry and obtained an honors degree in that subject in 1967 and then began research for my doctorate in the field of gas kinetics. During this time I married and shortly afterwards my wife challenged my theistic evolutionary views by asking me to explain the Scripture found in 1 Corinthians 15:22: "As in Adam all die, even so in Christ all will be made alive."

I realized that I was being asked to answer the fundamental question "Who was Adam?" I remember thinking that if I believed in a literal Adam, I would also have to believe in a literal Eve, a literal Garden of Eden, and a literal six-day creation. If I did this, I would have to commit intellectual suicide, for at that time, I knew *no one* who believed creation. Everyone I knew believed evolution. Every book I read, even those written by Christians, taught evolution. What was I to do?

The question of who Adam was really bugged me. In order to try to answer this question, I read the books in the New Testament to see what was the attitude of its characters (including the Lord Jesus Christ) towards the early chapters of Genesis. I soon realized that in the New Testament all of the events that are recorded in the first chapters of the Bible — the creation, Adam, Eve, the fall, Noah, the flood, and so on — are accepted as being literal and historical. There is absolutely nothing in the New Testament about their being mythical, allegorical, legendary, or even evolutionary.

I realized that if I, too, were to be of this same persuasion, then I would have to stop believing in evolution. The question I now asked myself was, "Is it possible, *intellectually*, to reject evolution?" Over the next two years, I came to the conclusion that it was possible not only to reject the idea of evolution but also to accept the historicity of the early chapters of Genesis without committing intellectual suicide. I did not reach this conclusion hastily. I was extremely busy pursuing my research: first in gas kinetics, for which I was awarded my Ph.D. in 1970, then in the study of the electrical and optical properties of organic semiconductors. However, I made time to pursue three main areas concerning the creation/evolution question: chemical evolution, the fossil record, and dating methods. I did this by reading my old geology lecture notes and by reading evolutionary text-books. At the time, I was totally unaware of any other creationist and I did not know of the existence of any anti-evolution/pro-creation book, article or organization. It may therefore come as a surprise to realize that I became a creationist as a result of reading about evolution!

Let me share some of the reasons that persuaded me to become a creationist. The first area is chemical evolution. I was, and still am, amazed at the naivety of the statements made by chemical evolutionists. They purport to have proven that life originated by chance on a prebiotic earth and they point to the results of their laboratory experiments in support of such conclusions. Yet their experiments are designed *not* by chance, but by their own intellect! What in fact they are saying is something like this, "If I can synthesize life here in my laboratory, then I will have proven that no intelligence was needed to create life in the beginning and I will also have proven that it originated by chance!"

In the famous Miller experiment conducted in 1953, a mixture of amino acids was produced by passing an electric discharge through a mixture of ammonia, hydrogen, methane, and water vapor. Since that time, various mixtures of amino acids, sugars, and nucleic acid bases have been produced in similar experiments. As these chemicals are the building blocks of living systems, it is argued that such experiments prove beyond doubt that life was produced by chance on the earth. Yet these experiments prove *nothing* about the origin of life for a variety of reasons.

The first, which has already been mentioned, is because such experiments have been designed by intelligent scientists; they have nothing at all to do with chance. Another reason is that in Miller's experiment, for example, amino acids were produced only because they were removed from the experiment as soon as they were formed.

Had they been left in the apparatus, then they would have been destroyed by the same electrical discharge that caused them to be synthesized. Furthermore, the amino acids that are produced in all such experiments are in the right-handed as well as the left-handed forms, whereas living systems contain only left-handed amino acids. Additionally, had oxygen been present in the mixture of gases, the amino acids would not have formed in such experiments. This point is extremely important because the evidence from geology indicates that the earth's atmosphere has always contained oxygen. Hence, the mixture of gases in such experiments does not mimic the composition of the earth's atmosphere. This means that the experiments have absolutely nothing at all to do with what may or may not have happened on the so-called prebiotic earth.

The second area at which I looked was the fossil record — that is, the remains of life-forms that are trapped in the sedimentary rocks. I soon realized that the fossil record does not show the gradual evolution of one life-form into another as predicted and demanded by evolution. The missing links are called that because they are truly missing — none has ever been found. There are gaps in the fossil record at all the major breaks: fish to amphibian, amphibians to reptiles, reptiles to birds, and reptiles to mammals. Furthermore, no fossil remains of any creature linking humans to ape-like ancestors have ever been discovered; half-ape/half-human creatures are figments of the imagination of the artists who draw them for the books in which they appear. I was, and still am, disturbed to read about the famous Piltdown forgery, when a deliberate hoax was perpetrated in order to make part of a modern skull and the jaw bone of an orangutan appear to be the fossilized remains of a half-ape/half-human creature. If the evolutionists have the evidence for the evolution of apes into humans, why fake it?

The other scientific area at which I looked was that of dating. How do we *know* that a rock is such and such an age? This is the crucial question. As a chemist I could see that the accuracy of any dating methods relied on a number of assumptions, some of which are unprovable and others unknowable. For example, in order to determine the age of a rock by radiometric dating, three things must be known:

- the present concentrations of the parent and daughter elements in the rock;
- the original concentrations of parent and daughter elements in that rock; and
- the rate of decay of the parent into the daughter element.

Now in most cases it is possible to measure the amounts of parent and daughter elements in the rock. However, it is not always possible to know the original concentrations. Sometimes it is *assumed* that there was no daughter element present when the rock was formed, but there is no way of telling this. It is an assumption. Although the present rate of decay of parent into daughter can usually be measured accurately, there is no way of knowing that this rate does not change throughout time. Again, it is an *assumption* that the present rate has remained unchanged in the past, as there is no way of telling.

Of course, the proof of the accuracy of the different dating methods should be that different methods give the same age for the same rock sample. However, as I searched the literature I became aware of articles in which it was reported that different methods gave different ages for the *same* rock. In these papers the authors spent a great deal of space discussing why there were discrepancies and why the age should be determined from the fossil content of the rock or from the fossils in the adjoining rocks. But there is circular reasoning here:

- The age of the rock is determined from the age of a fossil, the age of which in turn is determined by evolution;
- The proof of evolution is the age of the rocks in which the fossil is found.

In other words, I saw that the basis for dating rocks is evolution and the only proof of evolution is the ages of the rocks in which the fossils are found. The assumption of evolution is, therefore, the main evidence for evolution.

During this time I began to realize that the idea of evolution was at best a hypothesis and that it had not been proven. I became convinced (and still am convinced) that people believe in evolution because they choose to do so. It has nothing at all to do with evidence. Evolution is not a fact, as so many bigots maintain. There is not a shred of evidence for the evolution of life on earth.

At the same time that I found I could reject evolution and not commit intellectual suicide, I began to realize that I could also accept a literal creation and still not commit intellectual suicide. First of all, I realized that it made sense to believe that in the beginning God created, as this did not violate the laws of thermodynamics. I noted that modern-day observations, as well as the evidence of the fossil record, indicate that both plants and animals reproduced after their own kind as stated in Genesis chapter 1.

I also realized that there was no simple explanation for the evolution of the information content which is found in living systems. Contemplating the amount of information in living systems has caused two professors at my own university (Professor Chandra Wickramasinghe and Professor Sir Fred Hoyle) to make the famous analogy that if you believe the information content in living systems to be the result of chance, then you believe that a tornado can go through a junk yard and assemble a Jumbo Jet!

d.b. gower

Biochemistry

Professor Gower is emeritus professor of steroid biochemistry at the University of London, United Kingdom. He holds a B.S. in chemistry from the University of London, a Ph.D. in biochemistry from the University of London and was awarded a D.Sc. from the University of London for his research into the biochemical mechanisms for the control of steroid hormone formation. Professor Gower is a fellow of the Royal Society of Chemistry, a fellow of the Institute of Biology and a chartered chemist.

I was not always a creationist, that is, one who believes in the Genesis account of our origins. I was brought up to attend a church where the creation of heaven and earth by God was considered as a fact and any doubt, or even discussion, was thought of as strange. Later on, as I studied chemistry and, especially, biology, I found that there were more and more questions which needed to be answered. By this time, at the age of 15 or 16 years, I was a convinced Christian and firmly believed that the Bible was the Word of God, but the questions remained and I had to be content with the verse in Hebrews 11:3:

> By faith we understand that the universe was formed by God's command.

Time went on and I studied chemistry (with physics, mathematics, and biology) for my first degree. Then, some years after completing my Ph.D. in biochemistry, literature concerning dating methods and other matters relating to the accuracy of the Genesis account of creation began to be published. I believe that it was about this time, in the mid-1960s, that my ideas of the greatness of God were transformed. No longer was He a "pocket" God who did things as I could imagine from my "human viewpoint," but He had staggeringly great power, far beyond anything I could possibly comprehend. I began to realize that the Bible is entirely consistent on this point as, for example, in Isaiah 40:25:

> To whom will you compare me? or who is my equal?
> says the Holy One.

If God is so great, then there is nothing He could not do. This realization of the almighty power of God having come to me, I began to study the "creation-type" literature available at that time. During the past three decades, a great deal of work has been done and published in the field of "creation research." This has stimulated me to criticize evolutionary theory in three areas which are of particular interest to me:

1. My chemical knowledge has allowed me to understand the criticisms of isotopic dating methods for rock samples and to realize that there are enormous problems with the interpretation of the data. Consequently, my own view is that rocks are nowhere near as old as they are alleged to be.

2. From the biochemical point of view, the idea that

amino acids, sugars, etc., some of the vital "building blocks" for proteins and deoxyribonucleic acid (DNA), could be formed simply by interaction of electrical discharges with a primitive reducing-type atmosphere, can be criticized in so many ways and at so many levels.

3. My own studies in numerous biochemical control mechanisms, especially in the control of steroid hormone formation (for which I was awarded the higher doctorate, DSc) convince me that all these processes are ordered precisely. This order and the extraordinary complexity are entirely consistent, in my own opinion, with the existence of a Creator, who himself must be capable of creating with such design.

Such complexity is also being found in virtually every other branch of science in general, and is especially evident in the field of nature. Far from pointing towards formation by the chance processes of evolution, this clearly speaks to me of an Almighty Creator.

walter j. veith

Zoology

Dr. Walter J. Veith is professor and chair of the Department of Zoology at the University of Western Cape, South Africa. He holds a B.S. (hons) cum laude and an M.S. in zoology from the University of Stellenbosch, and a Ph.D. in zoology from the University of Cape Town. He is the author of *The Genesis Conflict: Putting the Pieces Together.*[1]

To most scientists in the world today, the theory of evolution is no longer just a theory but is regarded as a fact. There are differences of opinion regarding the tempo, mode, and mechanisms of evolution, but the basic concepts of the theory have become an established paradigm. Even in the religious world, the old animosities between science and religion have been largely forgotten and are shrugged off as unfortunate history based on ignorance. The educational systems of the world propagate evolution by natural selection as the only feasible theory of origin, to the exclusion of all others, and alternative models are regarded with skepticism.

Natural selection in itself is not a scientific principle, as it is based on circular reasoning. By natural selection, less fit organisms are eliminated and the fitter organisms survive to propagate the species. Organisms thus survive the process because they are fitter, and they are fitter because they survive. Also, the process operates by elimination, not addition. In order for the *fitter* to survive, there must have been a *less fit* that did not survive.

The evidence for evolution is based largely on the fossil record and interspecific, as well as intraspecific, genetic, biochemical, and morphological homologies. In addition, geological interpretation and radiometric dating provide the rationale for the long ages required for the evolutionary events to have taken place. However, each of these parameters is open to alternative explanations which are, in my opinion, equally plausible and also happen to be in harmony with the biblical account. Evolutionary scientists argue that creationism is not science, as it is based on a preconceived ideology, which excludes it from the realms of science. However, if the facts fit the biblical paradigm, cannot it then be argued that the creation account could be right, or would "right" be excluded on the grounds of having been preconceived?

In my own life I have been confronted with this dilemma and have become convinced that the alternative view of origin by design is worthy of support. For most of my academic career, I was a committed evolutionist and presented the theory of evolution to my students as an established fact. My university training and subsequent scientific endeavors had exposed me exclusively to the evolutionary paradigm and this had molded my thinking. It may well be asked: why the change of heart? In my religious experience I came to accept the Word of God as the most trustworthy book I have ever read. This Word has power to change lives, to lift people up and to give hope. It makes one willing to listen, to compare notes; it challenges one to test its trustworthiness. "Come let us reason together" (Isa. 1:18), says the Word. My change of view regarding evolution was not instantaneous, not emotional, but the result of a long and often hard road in search of truth. I now believe that the available facts support the concept of origin by design.

1 *The Genesis Conflict* (Amazing Discoveries: Delta, BC, Canada, 1997).

danny r. faulkner

Astronomy

Dr. Faulkner is professor of astronomy and physics at the University of South Carolina, Lancaster. He holds a B.S. in mathematics from Bob Jones University, an M.S. in physics from Clemson University, and an M.A. and Ph.D. both in astronomy from Indiana University. Dr. Faulkner's primary research interest is stellar astronomy and, in particular, binary stars. He has published 38 technical papers in the area of astronomy research.

Most people have the impression that scientists are methodically logical people who harbor no preconceptions and thus reach rational conclusions unencumbered by preconceptions. As with most stereotypes, this is almost entirely incorrect. Scientists are people, complete with all the foibles and lapses in judgment that are common to man. Probably the least appreciated biasing factor among scientists is the starting assumptions that we make. We all make assumptions, whether we realize it or not. Contrary to popular opinion, presuppositions are not necessarily bad. In fact, it is impossible to have no presuppositions. Self-recognition of our starting assumptions allows us to acknowledge our biases and in some cases adjust for them. A tremendous problem arises when we are not aware of our assumptions, because then we think that we have no bias.

Much of science today is based upon the assumption that the physical world is the only reality, though this has escaped the notice of most people. This has not always been the case. When science as we know it began to develop more than three centuries ago, scientists came to realize that the world follows certain rules. Sir Isaac Newton and many of his contemporaries believed that these rules were God-ordained, and that the rules were divinely imposed at the time of creation. Today most scientists assume that physical laws merely exist and that they can be extrapolated into the past to tell us how creation happened. In other words, God is irrelevant to the question of origins. This does not mean that most scientists are atheists, for I have found that most are not. Unfortunately, this does mean that for all practical purposes much of science has become an atheistic enterprise. Sadly, the god of most scientists is at best the one of the deists and at worst entirely ad hoc.

So what kinds of assumptions do I make? I assume that there is a Creator (I cannot fathom the world otherwise). I assume that He is interested and involved in the world. I assume that He has revealed himself to mankind through the Bible. Interestingly, the Bible never attempts to prove God's existence or that the Bible is God's unique revelation — it merely assumes these propositions to be true. Given these assumptions, the biblical account of creation must be true. Genesis tells us that creation was accomplished in six days. The six days is just one of the many aspects of the biblical account of creation that is at variance with what much of modern science says about the origin of the world. Note that my quarrel is not with all of science, but merely the assumption that science alone can give us ultimate answers to question of origins.

Were the six days of creation literal days? How old is the world? The answers to these two questions are related. The best exegesis of the creation account of Genesis 1 is that the days were literal (roughly 24-hour) days. Many Christians attempt to find ways to read these days as long periods of time, but I am convinced that these attempts start with the assumption (from science) that the world is very old. This is eisogesis, not exegesis. The chronologies of the Old Testament give us a pretty complete history of mankind, and allow us to roughly date the period of time since the creation week at about 6,000 years.

This is a radical idea, and many people are astonished to find that there are scientists who take this idea very seriously. It is the job of creation scientists, such as myself, to study and interpret the world with this presupposition. Is there evidence of recent creation in the world around us? I think that there is. Keep in mind that some indications of recent origin act as an upper limit. That is, they give a maximum age, but the actual age could be less than the maximum. All this tells us is that the world could be at most a certain age, but no older.

As an example, consider the earth-moon system. Most people assume that the moon has been orbiting the earth since about the time the two bodies formed. To most scientists, the time of formation for either body would have been about 4.5 billion years ago; for recent creationists it was about 6,000 years ago. Over a century ago George Darwin, the astronomer son of the famous Charles Darwin, discovered that the moon is slowly spiraling away from the earth. The cause of this effect is the tidal interaction of the earth and moon, which also causes the earth's rotation rate (the day) to slowly increase. We cannot theoretically predict the rate of tidal evolution, because it depends upon the complex interplay of the ocean tides with the continental shelves. However, we can measure the current rate. Each year the moon moves about 4 cm farther from the earth, and the day is increasing at a rate of 0.0016 seconds per century. These are very modest changes, but over time they accumulate. More interesting, the rate of tidal evolution is a very steep function of the earth-moon distance, so in the past when the moon was much closer to the earth the rate to change would have been far greater than today. Fixing the modern rate and extrapolating the theory into the past, we find that the moon would have been in contact with the earth as recently as 1.3 billion years ago, about one-third the supposed age of the earth-moon system. About a billion years ago the moon would have been so close to the earth to cause monstrously high tides. No one believes that this was the case.

Does this mean that the earth-moon system is only 6,000 years old? No, but this is consistent with a 6,000 year old earth-moon system. That is, this information does not eliminate the possibility that the earth-moon system is 6,000 years old, as it does for a 4.5 billion year old system. How do those who believe that the earth and moon are billions of years old respond to this? They assert that we live in a time of unusually fast tidal interaction, and that in the past the tidal interaction was far less. This is a possibility, but how does it stand up to scrutiny? Let us assume that the world is billions of years old and that rock layers have been laid down over time pretty much as scientists claim. There have been several studies of fine layers of sedimentary rock that supposedly show daily high and low tides. This establishes a relationship between the lengths of the day and the month, which are all that are needed to track tidal evolution. These studies span over a half billion years and show that the current rate has been prevalent during this time. This means that by the evolutionists' own data the current rate of tidal evolution is not unusually large, and that there must have been some large event a little more than a billion years ago. This is not a problem for the recent creationist, but it is for those who believe that the earth and moon are more than a billion years old.

Similar evidence comes from the sun. We believe that the sun gets its energy from the thermonuclear fusion of hydrogen into helium in its core. According to the theory, the sun has enough nuclear fuel to power itself for about 10 billion years. If the sun is 4.5 billion years old, then it has exhausted about half of its potential lifetime. During those 4.5 billion years the sun would not have remained static — the sun must have gradually changed. The conversion of hydrogen into helium in the solar core would have altered the core's composition, which would have resulted in the sun's core slowly shrinking and increasing in temperature. This would have increased the nuclear fusion rate and hence brightened the sun. Calculation shows that the sun ought to be about 40 percent brighter today than when it allegedly formed 4.5 billion years ago and that the sun ought to be 30 percent brighter today than when life supposedly appeared on the earth 3.5 billion years ago. With all the concern today with global warming that some fear will happen if we increase the retention of solar energy only slightly, one must wonder what effect that gradual solar warming would have had. If there had been no change in the terrestrial atmosphere over billions of years, there would have been a 16–18 C increase in the average earth temperature. Since the current average earth temperature is about 15 C, the early earth ought to have had an average temperature below freezing. No one believes that this is the case. Most assume that the average terrestrial temperature has not changed much, if at all, during earth history.

How do we explain this early faint sun paradox? Evolutionists, who believe that the earth and sun are billions of years old, must assume that the atmosphere of the early earth had much more greenhouse gases than our current atmosphere. As the sun gradually brightened, the earth's atmosphere gradually evolved so that it had less greenhouse gases to counter the increase in the sun's luminosity. How two completely unrelated processes could have evolved in exactly compensating ways for billions of years is amazing. I find it more reasonable to assume that the earth was created only a few thousand years ago with pretty much the atmospheric composition that it now has and that the sun has not brightened appreciably since its formation a few thousand years ago.

Comets are extremely fragile things. Comets may be lost by collisions with planets, as was witnessed in 1994 when a comet smashed into Jupiter. Another catastrophic loss of comets is by gravitational forces of planets that kick comets out of the solar system. This has been observed a number of times. Perhaps more often comets just wear out. A comet's coma and tail are composed of dust and gas that are dislodged from the tiny comet nucleus as the comet nears the sun once each orbit. As a comet nucleus loses material each orbit, there is less material available in each successive orbit. Since comets gradually wear out, we can estimate an upper limit upon the length of time that comets can orbit the sun. Even with the most generous of assumptions, there should be no comets left after a few tens of millions of years. This is far less than the assumed 4.5 billion-year-old age of the solar system. This would seem to rule out the possibility of a solar system that is billions of years old, but not one that is only thousands of years old.

Of course, astronomers have long been aware of this problem and have devised a solution. Short period comets are said to originate in the Kuiper belt, a collection of comet nuclei orbiting the sun beyond the orbit of Neptune, while long period comets come from the Oort cloud, a swarm of comet nuclei orbiting much farther out. Gravitational perturbations are suggested to rob comet nuclei of energy and cause them to fall into the inner solar system to replace older comets as the older comets die. Thus, there has been a nearly steady state of comets for billions of years. Starting in the 1990s many large objects have been discovered orbiting where the Kuiper belt is supposed to be. Most astronomers assume that these are larger members of the Kuiper belt. However, these objects are orders of magnitude larger than any comet nuclei ever seen. This raises questions as to if these actually are comet nuclei. Far more problematic is the Oort cloud. No Oort cloud object has ever been detected, and given the great distance of the hypothetical Oort cloud, none likely ever will. With no evidence and no realistic possibility of evidence, the Oort cloud hardly constitutes a scientific concept.

Do not think that creationists have all the answers. There are many perplexing problems that we must study within our starting assumptions. The greatest is the light travel time problem. Simply put, the universe appears to be billions of light years in size, so how can we see distant objects if the universe is only a few thousand years old? A number of solutions have been proposed, but I do not find any of them to be entirely satisfactory. My primary interest is stellar astronomy, the study of stars. Creation scientists have spent very little time discussing exactly what our creation model has to say about stars. I look forward to this work.

edmond w. holroyd

Meteorology

Dr. Holroyd is research physical scientist for the U.S. Bureau of Reclamation, Denver, Colorado. He holds a B.S. in astrophysics from the University of Rochester, and a Ph.D. in atmospheric science from the University of New York at Albany. Dr. Holroyd has specialized in cloud physics and weather modification and remote sensing research for more than 30 years.

The biblical account presents a creation in which each thing was fully functional when it was made. The first trees did not come from seeds. The first mammals did not come from embryos. Adam was not an infant on his first day. All things appeared as if they had been in existence before their day of creation. That is "the appearance of age." In today's culture, our entertainment industry is continually giving us productions in which the action starts at some point and continues through to the end of the program. There is an apparent prior "history" that occurred before the opening scenes. We readily accept this "appearance of age" in our movies and television programs and plays. We make no claims that the playwright or producer is deceiving us. Similarly, I believe we should be able to accept a creation with the appearance of age without calling God a liar. He told us how He did it all. So there is no deception. We just do not have all of the details that we might like, as with a movie mystery.

Astronomical Indications

The starry heavens, when considered along with the speed of light, certainly appear to have had a history longer than a few thousand years. We can now readily sense the immense distances by the many hours it takes to send radio messages to our outer planet space probes, such as the Voyagers, and back. We can directly measure distances to the nearest stars in terms of light years by measuring how much they move back and forth against the background sky as the earth orbits the sun. We can calibrate various classes of stars as having an intrinsic brightness, and then estimate their distances from how much their apparent brightness has faded with distance. Even within our own Milky Way Galaxy and our local group of galaxies, this quickly brings us to apparent elapsed times for star light to travel to us much greater than the elapsed time in the biblical account of creation. This part of the universe is still the region in which our interpretations are guided by standard, not relativistic, physics. We young-earth advocates have an apparent problem, therefore.

Over a decade ago, there was a supernova in the Magellanic Clouds, small satellite galaxies to our own at an apparent distance of about 150,000 light years. Did that star actually explode that many years ago? Or did God, only a few thousand years ago, make a self-consistent field of electromagnetic waves (including light) that has only recently given us the appearance of an exploding star? Here is another example in which there is an appearance of age. Scientifically it appears that the star was that old when it exploded, just as Adam looked as if he were many years old on the seventh day. To be biblical, we have to be in awe of our God, who can orchestrate the entire heavens in such great detail!

The Hubble telescope is now showing galaxies incredibly far away. The distances are based upon an expanding-universe theory, where spectral shifts are interpreted as red shifts of recessional speed. The series of assumptions gives apparent distances of up to about 10 billion light-years. We may want to question the assumptions. We may want to consider that the red shifts might instead be from a solidly rotating cosmos. Tangential, not just radial, velocities can cause red shifts, but we have no way of measuring tangential velocities for distant galaxies. We may want to consider the "white hole" expansion of the universe proposed by Humphreys as a step towards explaining the apparent old universe in light of a biblically young earth and starry heavens. The Bible certainly teaches that God "stretched out the heavens" (Ps. 104:2 and at least eight other passages in Isaiah, Jeremiah, and Zechariah). Perhaps the red shift is the signature of this stretching out of the universe. Ultimately, "the heavens declare the glory of God" (Ps. 19:1). We still have much to learn about them, and so the clash of time scales will be with us for a long time in the future.

However, there is an interesting phenomenon among the stars that gives a time scale in agreement with that in the Bible. By watching other galaxies of similar composition to our own, we know about how often there are supernovae, such as about every 25 years in a galaxy like our own. We do not see that many explosions in our Milky Way because dust obscures our local view. Furthermore, we can measure the general rate of expansion of the nebula remnants of the explosions. We can calculate that we should be able to detect those nebulae for millions of years before they diffuse and blend into the background. Our radio telescopes can see through the dust with ease and detect many more supernova remnants than we can see at optical wavelengths. How many supernova remnants are out there in our own galaxy? There are only enough for about 7,000, not millions of, years of explosions. Here is an important discrepancy that has been known for decades. We need to pursue this topic.

Getting back to our own solar system, I have greatly enjoyed the images of the outer planets and their moons that have been sent back to us by the space probes. They show a fantastic variety out there that was never predicted by any of the theories of solar system evolution. The only major prediction that came true was of the magnetic moments of Uranus and Neptune, proclaimed in advance by Humphries, a creationist, based upon arguments with biblical connections. For the rest of the discoveries, it is as if God created that variety out there just to keep us humble. We have a long way to go to understand how God made the creation, and the God-less theories will always be proven wrong in the end.

It is similarly interesting that scientists are now accepting semi-global-scale flooding on Mars, where there is no longer any surface water. They can now see a relatively recent global resurfacing of Venus by flooding with lava. Jupiter's large moon known as Europa is totally flooded right now with a surface layer of cracking water-ice, with indications of a liquid ocean below. Yet most scientists are reluctant to admit that the earth might also have had global flooding in the recent past, even though the earth is still over 70 percent flooded, and most of the continental areas are covered with vast sheets of water-laid sediments. These phenomena relate to the Genesis flood rather than the six-day creation, but support the acceptability of the early chapters of Genesis.

Geological Indications

Most creationist work in the interpretation of the geology of the earth relates to the Flood event, with its global resurfacing by catastrophic means. The polonium radiohaloes caused by alpha decay of radioactive isotopes are one of the few phenomena that have been addressed which seem to point back to creation week. The presence of 218Po haloes in biotite, for example, appear to be a signature placed in the rocks about three minutes after creation. (Some might interpret that as three minutes after activation of the process of decay, such as the second law of thermodynamics.) The heat from volcanic emplacement, the traditional interpretation for growing biotite crystals, would erase the haloes within hours, as proved by laboratory observations.

Most of the justification for vast geologic ages comes from radiometric dating. We are told that certain rocks are millions to billions of years old. There are self-consistent regional patterns of dates, suggesting the trustworthiness of the findings. Such "dates" are inconsistent with the biblical time scale of only thousands of years. This is an area in which further study is important and progressing. For now we have numerous examples in which radiometric dating gives the wrong answers, such as ⅓ to 3 million years for Mount St. Helens lava, historically dated at about 20 years old. Potassium-argon dating, upon which most of the geologic column and especially hominid fossils are dated, is particularly prone to "excessive argon" which gives inflated ages.

It appears that one or more of the basic assumptions for radiometric dating are violated in the usual measurements. The first assumption is that the amounts of "mother" and "daughter" isotopes are known at "time-zero," with the daughter amounts assumed to be zero. Yet the rocks might be put in place with a non-zero daughter/mother ratio, invalidating the assumption. Secondly, there may be leaching into or out of the rock of the various mother and daughter elements, invalidating the assumption of a "closed system." Dating cannot be accurate if the radiometric clocks are being reset. The third assumption is that the rate of decay has been constant throughout geologic history. However, we have only measured that rate for about a century. While it seems risky to extrapolate such rates by up to eight orders of magnitude, for now it appears that the third assumption is generally valid. What we do know with generally great accuracy are the present ratios of mother and daughter isotopes and the present decay rates. To my knowledge, creationist scientists do not yet have a good replacement theory of radioactivity, and so such important work must continue.

There are numerous indicators of age that give dates much less than the radiometric clocks. The amount of helium in the atmosphere is more consistent with the biblical time scale than with millions and billions of years. The amount of salt in the oceans is much less than would be deposited during the supposed vast geologic ages. Present erosion rates would level even the Himalaya Mountains to sea level in roughly ten million years. Therefore, it is absurd, for example, to have the present Rocky Mountains of North America standing high above sea level for over 50 million years with so many of the peaks being in relatively youthful erosion states today.

The creationist scientists do not yet have any commonly accepted criterion for separating those rocks that date from the creation week from those laid down by the Genesis Flood. Neither is there general agreement on which rocks are post-Flood, though there are numerous strong proposals.

In considering the flood phenomena, I believe we must identify one or more mechanisms for the rapid destruction of hard crystalline rocks. Simple inundation by water is inadequate, because rocks can be submerged for ages without significant deterioration, as proved by underwater archaeological sites. The process of cavitation of water requires high speed (more than 30 m/s) and shallow (less than 10 meters deep) water, but it can destroy hard steel. Direct hydraulic pressures of high speed water are more probable destructive agents.

Somehow, we need to properly account for the levelling of great mountain ranges within a small fraction of a year.

It is my view that there is also need to address the continuity of matter during the Flood. The sediment material came from somewhere. We need to identify the sources and account for the volumes of the sediments that were laid down. Deposition rates seem slow under today's conditions. Yet the preservation of fossils indicates that the rates were much greater when the enclosing sediments were laid down. The topography of the erosion and deposition surfaces of the past seem to be different from what we observe at today's surfaces. Past surfaces seem flatter over greater areas, which would be consistent with global resurfacing during the Flood. Much more could be addressed with respect to Flood studies, but this series of articles is particularly about creation week.

Archaeological Indications

We do not have normal archaeological artifacts that relate to creation week. However, new discoveries keep arising that verify the truthfulness of the history given in the Bible.

I have all of the coin types mentioned in the Bible, confirming that such denominations were real. I have numerous coins bearing the names of rulers mentioned in the Bible. So we know that they really lived. Furthermore, over 80 percent of the settlements mentioned in the Book of Acts minted coins at some time, and we can read those city names on their coins, verifying their previous existence. The historical part of the Bible is therefore trustworthy.

If we have found the Bible to be truthful in what we can independently check, we have a reason to trust it when it talks repeatedly about origins. When God says in the Bible that He made the universe in six days, I believe Him.

robert h. eckel

Medical Research

Dr. Eckel is professor of medicine, and of physiology and biophysics, and program director, General Clinical Research Center, at the University of Colorado Health Sciences Center. He holds a B.S. cum laude in bacteriology, University of Cincinnati, and an M.D. from the University of Cincinnati College of Medicine. Dr. Eckel has published more than 80 research papers, 17 book chapters and received 20 research awards. He is a reviewer for 50 medical journals, a member of the American Society for Clinical Investigation and The Association of American Physicians, and chairman, Nutrition Committee, American Heart Association.

Several years ago I was contacted by a high school student who had chosen to allow his precocious knowledge of and commitment to creation science to take on the local board of education. The issue before him was how the science of the origins of life on earth was being taught (and not taught) in the classroom. As a scientist and professing six-day creationist and member of the technical advisory board of the Institute for Creation Research, I was presumably in a position to provide academic wisdom about the issue before him. Yet, I was amazed that the scientific acumen he had already assimilated was incredibly advanced for a 16 year old, leaving me with little to add but a bit of advice.

The positions of concern and criticism that this young man had taken were that biologic origins were being taught as fact, not theory. This was true for both textbook and teacher. The student's response by faith was that the origins of life were not a consequence of evolution, but a result of the sovereign and undeniable will of God. Although his position and defense of the Bible were clear, I perceived more than an effort to open the minds of the world around him; there was also an evangelistic hope that the message of creation might ultimately prove to be a vehicle to seed and reap lost souls.

The advice to follow may have been anything but profound, but represented a position as a scientist and six-day creationist believer that rests only in part on the evidence available. Creation in six days is not an intellectual argument to be won by in-depth and repetitive examinations of the scientific evidence available. The same data are available to both evolutionists and creationists. The issue scientifically is a single experiment, never to be repeated, with two basic theories to be considered. And in the case of the origins of life on earth, the hypothesis has followed the experiment rather than preceded it.

Evolutionists claim that biologic life began as atoms in a primordial soup. Subsequently molecules, organelles, cells, and ultimately multicellular organisms would develop over billions of years. Numerous lines of evidence from the fossil record, based mostly on isotopic dating, are repeatedly used to support this position. Nevertheless, the same fossil record has been used by six-day creationists; however, because of perceived flaws in the use of isotopic dating to determine the timing of events, six-day creationists use fossils to support a young earth.

In science, hypotheses typically are developed a priori and are examined subsequently by the use of scientific methods previously validated and accepted by most, if not all, experts in the given field of endeavor. With the assumption that the experimental design is appropriate to address the hypothesis to be tested, a series of observations is gathered to either support or refute the hypothesis. In most areas of science, observations are made at least several times by a single scientist, which are then repeated and confirmed by other scientists prior to accepting the "truth" of the hypothesis being tested. Moreover, it is often difficult, if not impossible, to substantiate conclusions by retrospective examination of data. For "origins" where at best the data are insufficient, this is particularly true. Thus, with evolution/creation, a scientific impasse exists which historically, presently, or forever has, does, and will create uncertainty in interpretation. How then should this student have proceeded?

The unbelieving world does not heed the things of the Lord, nor was it intended for them to do so because they are spiritually perceived (1 Cor. 1:18–29). Therefore, any argument to support a six-day creation (or any other view of creation for that matter) that is presented on the basis of faith is perceived flawed and labelled as religion, not science, by evolutionists. Thus, the position of the apologist needs to be scientific and sufficiently well developed academically so that the interchange of information can be implemented in the world's terms. After the discussion begins, it is important to establish the position that the origins of life on earth was an "experiment" carried out only once in history, never to be repeated, and the proof of either position will never be substantiated.

When examining the evidence available for either assertion, it becomes important to evaluate critically the precision and scientific accuracy of the methods used in the analysis. Here the evolutionists' acceptance of the tools utilized becomes questionable. Isotopic dating makes many assumptions that will remain unproven, for example, the linearity of isotopic decay over time. Yet, when experiments are carried out in their own laboratories, all scientists (evolutionists and six-day creationists alike) require a standard of validation for the methods used that are proven or at least well defended scientifically. It is amazing to consider how incomplete evolutionists have been in applying scientific rigor to the methods they have used to retrospectively analyze data that deals with "origins." This is nothing but an act of blind faith on their behalf. Nevertheless, six-day creationist believers must remain objective in their approach to the data.

In the end, this student's objection to the method utilized by the local school system to educate about "origins" reached a public forum in the county in which he resided. Although support for both positions was articulated by citizens, the majority of professionals who spoke up claimed evolution to be a fact. Thus, it was no surprise that the final decision was to continue as before, with the creationist position left out of the classroom. Nevertheless, the issue of "origins" is not a battle for us to win, but the life of the Lord Jesus Christ to be seen (Phil. 1:21). A well-informed, spirit-led believer is in the best position for this to occur.

jack cuozzo

Orthodontics

Dr. Cuozzo is a research orthodontist and head of the orthodontic section, Mountainside Hospital, Montclair, New Jersey. He majored in biology at Georgetown University, and has a D.D.S. from the University of Pennsylvania and an M.S. in oral biology from Loyola University, Chicago, Illinois. Dr. Cuozzo took the first cephalometric (orthodontic) radiographs of the Neanderthal fossils in France and subsequently in many other countries. He has published a number of articles related to origins from a biblical perspective, and a book, *Buried Alive*.[1] He was a member of the American Association of Orthodontists for more than 30 years.

While studying with Francis Schaeffer in the summer of 1977, I acquired the term "true truth." Dr. Schaeffer coined this term because of the lack of respect the word *truth* commands in our day. He said it was not a tautology but a necessity. The absolutes, including those in the first chapters of Genesis, are not up for election. They are not running in any ballot, except in the imaginary constructs in men's minds. I knew this well because I had quite a few of these mental images floating around in my own mind in 1975. It was in that year that the truth set me free from my sin and began to set me free from these mental images concerning the beginning of mankind.

I understood these facts incompletely in 1975, but nevertheless bent my knees, bowed my head, and gave Jesus my heart. It was then that the battle for my whole mind began. The evolutionary ideas from my past began pressing into my being. It seemed as if my entire scientific educational background rose up and challenged my literal acceptance of the Genesis account of creation and the Fall. This will surely happen to anyone who has swallowed large doses of modern science and reads the Bible the way it was written. Thus, the war for my whole mind began, and I don't think I was the first or will be the last to travel this road. The peaceful biblical rendition of man's origin stood in direct contrast to the millions of years of bloodshed and violence that would have characterized a world in the throes of evolution. My dilemma was real, and my faith was being threatened. Were there millions of years of bloodshed in the Garden of Eden before sin? The Bible makes this point very clear: the answer is *no*, because there were six mornings and six evenings, while everything was "very good."

Nevertheless, I continued questioning my faith in a literal interpretation of Genesis. So, in 1979, after two years of study in paleoanthropology and the Bible, and with the help and encouragement of Wilton M. Krogman, Ph.D., I embarked on a study of fossil man in Europe. (Dr. Krogman was the forensic anthropologist who identified Hitler's remains in Berlin at the close of WW II.) My first destination in 1979 was Paris, France, the home of many Neanderthal fossils. We were loaned a sophisticated x-ray machine and an apartment. Fortunately, the assistant director of the Musée de l'Homme allowed me to work with those precious Neanderthal remains. His parents were rescued by American soldiers after the invasion of Normandy. He said he owed Americans a favor and I was the recipient of that favor. Nineteen years and many museums later, I still express shock at what I found. There have been efforts by many paleoanthropologists to "adjust" the fossils to tell of the glory of evolution rather than the glory of God.

I found that the Neanderthals lived longer lives than we do today and that their children had later maturation times than modern children.[2] It also seems very likely that they were people who inhabited Europe and the Near East much later than previously supposed and not 200 thousand to 30 thousand years ago. Through anatomical studies and a series of standardized radiographs similar to the ones utilized by orthodontists across the world, I have been able to calculate the Neanderthal life span in southwestern France to between 250 and 300 years. I was also able to uncover some misconstructions of the bones which prevented a good scientific interpretation of these remains.[3] This information can be found in my book entitled *Buried Alive*.[4] Most people know that the Bible speaks of the early men in our history who lived hundreds of years. With or without my research, that would be true. However, it is my hope that knowing the remains of such people actually exist will help our educated generation love God more with their minds and overcome the challenges to their faith. I have found that the Bible is accurate when it describes time, and historical or scientific facts. This is why I believe in a literal six-day creation.

Endnotes
  1 Jack Cuozzo, *Buried Alive* (Green Forest, AR: Master Books, Inc., 1998).
  2 Jack Cuozzo, "Earlier Orthondontic Intervention: A View from Prehistory," *Journal of New Jersey Dental Association*, Vol 58, No. 4, Autumn 1987.
  3 Jack Cuozzo, "Neanderthal Children's Fossils: Reconstruction and Interpretation Distorted by Assumptions," *Creation Ex Nihilo*, 8: (part 2) 1994, p. 166–178.
  4 Cuozzo, *Buried Alive*.

andrew snelling

Geology

Dr. Snelling is the former editor of *Creation Ex Nihilo Technical Journal* in Australia. He holds a B.S. (hons) with first class honors in geology from the University of New South Wales and a Ph.D. in geology from the University of Sydney. Dr. Snelling has worked for more than 15 years in the area of creation research, first with Answers in Genesis in Australia, and now with the Institute for Creation Research in the United States. He is the author of a number of technical papers dealing with origins issues and, in particular, radioactive dating problems.

So, why do I believe in the biblical account of creation by God over six literal days as the origin of life on earth, followed later by a year-long global geological catastrophe that totally renovated the earth's surface, as described in the biblical account of Noah's flood? The reason is that the Bible clearly teaches a literal six-day creation and a global flood, not only in the opening chapters of the Book of Genesis, but also throughout the Old and New Testaments, including being confirmed by Jesus Christ himself. No matter how clever we scientists are in our research, we can only study all the evidence today (as it exists today) and then extrapolate backwards into the past. In doing so we have to make assumptions, and we can never be absolutely certain that our assumptions are correct and, therefore, our interpretation of what happened in the past is correct. On the other hand, the Bible claims over 3,000 times to be the Word of the transcendent, personal God, who has always existed, who is all knowing, and is totally truthful.

Furthermore, when we compare the biblical account of the origin of life and of the global Flood with the evolutionary view of millions of years of billions of creatures living and dying through countless geological ages, it should be immediately obvious to any thinking person that there are irreconcilable contradictions. Indeed, if the evolutionary view of the evidence is true, then God could not have created the world in six literal days initially with no death by bloodshed, and all people and air-breathing, land-dwelling animals cannot be descended from the eight people and all the air-breathing, land-dwelling animals that were aboard the ark that Noah built at God's command. Thus, the early chapters of the Book of Genesis are full of error and can be rejected, as can all the references to God creating and to Noah's flood throughout many other books in the Old and New Testaments. This means also that God was telling Moses and the children of Israel a lie when He gave them the Ten Commandments and commanded them to observe a seven-day week, just as He had observed a literal seven-day creation week himself, which would mean He was guilty already of contravening His own ninth commandment. Furthermore, Jesus Christ himself must have also lied when He referred to God creating and to the days of Noah, the ark, and the Flood, so therefore He cannot be what He claimed to be ("the way, the truth and the life") or the "Son of God."

It follows then that having made one's decision about the reliability and truthfulness of these events as recorded in the Bible, ultimately by God himself as claimed, there is no reason why the truthfulness of the Bible cannot be tested historically and scientifically. That is not to say that the Bible is a textbook of science and history, but rather that if it is truth, then whenever it touches on matters of history and science, these should be verifiable by the normal means of scientific and historical investigations. To put it another way, if what we read in the Bible is true, then the evidence in the world that God created, and then judged by a global catastrophic flood, should be consistent with what the Bible records about those events. And so it is. I am convinced, as are many other scientists, that the evidence overwhelmingly supports these claims that the Bible makes about the origin of life and the history of the earth.

For example, as a geologist I encounter many fossils in the rock layers exposed at the earth's surface, being the remains of animals and plants that once lived on the earth but now are dead, buried, and preserved in the rocks. Like the biologists who study the living creatures, I can still see among the preserved remains of the dead creatures the evidence of God's creative handiwork. Indeed, if life was created by a transcendent personal God, rather than the impersonal random mechanisms of evolution, then creatures, alive or dead, should show evidence of being designed by a designer. And they do.

Evidence of Design

Perhaps my favorite example is that of the trilobites, arthropods (invertebrates with jointed legs) that are extinct and only found as fossils worldwide. They occur among the earliest fossils in the so-called Cambrian rocks, and are the lowermost multi-cellular fossils with hard parts found in the Grand Canyon, for example. Often regarded as primitive creatures, their anatomy reveals that they are, perhaps, the most complex of all invertebrate creatures. They are thought to have been marine creatures, because their fossils are commonly found with the remains of creatures that still live in the oceans today. Furthermore, they appear to have had a set of gills associated with every leg. The animal's shell is usually divisible into three sections or lobes — the head, thorax, and tail. Hence, the animal's name (*tri* for three, and *lobite* for the lobes). Because of their jointed legs and antennae, the trilobites are classified with lobsters, crabs, scorpions, spiders, and insects. The legs require them to have had complex muscle systems, and because of their similarity to modern arthropods, trilobites are thought to have had a circulation system, including a heart. They also had a very complex nervous system, as indicated by antennae, which probably had a sensory function, and the presence of eyes on many species.

Indeed, some scientists believe that the aggregate (schizochroal) eyes of some trilobites were the most sophisticated optical systems ever utilized by any organism. The schizochroal eye is a compound eye, made up of many single lenses, each specifically designed to correct for spherical aberration, thus allowing the trilobites to see an undistorted image under water. The elegant physical design of trilobite eyes also employs Fermat's principle, Abbe's sine law, Snell's laws of refraction, and compensates for the optics of birefringent crystals. Such a vision system has all the evidence of being constructed by an exceedingly brilliant designer!

The trilobite's extraordinary complexity hardly warrants the creature being called "primitive," but herein lies the dilemma for evolutionists. There are no possible evolutionary ancestors to the trilobites in the rock layers beneath where the trilobites are found, for example, in the Grand Canyon. In fact, the trilobites appear in the geological record suddenly, fully-formed and complexly integrated creatures with the most sophisticated optical systems ever utilized by any organism, without any hint or trace of an ancestor in the many rock layers beneath. There is absolutely no clue as to how the amazing complexity of trilobites arose, and thus they quite clearly argue for design and *fiat* creation, just as we would predict from the biblical account in Genesis.

Evidence of the Flood

As a geologist I am also interested in the biblical account of earth history, particularly the record of the year-long global catastrophic Flood in the days of Noah that must have totally reshaped the entire surface of the globe. In fact, based upon the biblical description of the Flood event, it is logical to predict that it would leave behind billions of dead animals and plants buried in sediments eroded and deposited by the moving flood waters, that would all end up being fossils in rock layers laid down by water all over the globe. And that's exactly what we find — layers of water-deposited sedimentary rocks containing fossils all over the earth.

There is impressive evidence that fossil deposits and rock strata were formed catastrophically. There are also many indications that there were not millions of years, or even thousands, between various rock units. The rock sequence in the Grand Canyon is a case in point. Not only can it be shown that each of the rock units exposed in the walls of the canyon must have formed very rapidly under catastrophic watery conditions, but there are not significant time gaps between the various rock layers. Thus, the total time involved to put in place some 4,000 feet (1,200 meters) thickness of rock strata is well within the time constraints the Bible stipulates for the flood event.

What is also spectacular about the Grand Canyon area in

northern Arizona is the scale and magnitude of the rock units and the awesomeness of the canyon itself. One can physically walk up and down the sequence of rock units that go back before the Flood, and then right through the Flood event up until post-Flood times. While the sequence is not complete, there are few places where such a complete sequence is so fully exposed and so much evidence for the Flood and its catastrophic nature.

No geologist denies that the oceans once covered the land, since rocks containing marine fossils may be found at elevations above sea level today anywhere from one to five miles (1.6 to 8 km). That the ocean waters should have covered the land is exactly what one would expect to happen during a global flood, while earth movements concurrent with the retreating flood waters would be expected to leave strata with marine fossils now perched high and dry at considerable elevations, just as we observe, for example, in the Himalayas.

In Australia, without doubt, one of the most impressive areas demonstrating catastrophic deposition during the Flood is Ayers Rock (or Uluru). The scale of the sandstone beds that have been upturned to form the rock gives clear testimony to the scale of deposition in the Flood. The mineral grains making up the sandstone are a witness to the cataclysmic speed of the deposition process and the young age of this awesome desert landform.

Research

Research has always been an important component of my responsibilities, and in recent years it has been possible to increase the research effort through collaborative work, and through focusing on investigating the radioactive dating methods by collecting samples and having laboratory work done ourselves. In this way the evidence that is being comprehensively gathered and systematized is proving to be totally consistent with the biblical record of creation in six days and a global catastrophic Flood.

There are three important international collaborative projects. First is the Flood model project with U.S. creationists Drs. Steve Austin, John Baumgardner, Russ Humphreys, Larry Vardiman, and Kurt Wise. We are trying to build a comprehensive understanding of the geological data from a biblical perspective of earth history centred on what happened during the Flood, and before and after, up until the present day. We have suggested that catastrophic plate tectonics may provide a suitable mechanism for earth movements and tectonic activity, continental "sprint" (rather than "drift"), and patterns of sedimentation and volcanic activity during the Flood event. So we presented a preliminary paper on the topic at the Third International Conference on Creationism in Pittsburgh in 1994. Our model still has problems to overcome, but we remain confident it will prove to be workable and unifying.

In a separate but related project, Dr. Kurt Wise and I, with technical computer support from Donna Richardson, and help from others with data collection, are developing a global geological database using sophisticated software that has been largely donated to us for this purpose. This project involves recording all the known geological data on every area across the globe — a mammoth and daunting task. The database will enable us to look at global geological patterns for different rock types, fossils, radiometric "dates," indication in the rocks of former water current directions, and much more. By looking at the bigger picture, we hope to get a better understanding of what happened during the Flood. After all, the Flood was a global event; therefore we would expect to find global patterns of sedimentation, volcanic activity, mineral deposits, etc. Though a long-term project, this is strategic because it will allow us to make important pronouncements based on hard data.

In a sub-project, we have teamed up with astronomer Dr. Danny Faulkner to look at the patterns of impact and explosive volcanic cratering with the passage of the geological record on the earth, compared with that of the moon and our closest planetary neighbors, Venus and Mars. There is a distinct possibility that such impacts and explosions triggered cycles of catastrophic sedimentation during the Flood, volcanic activity in conjunction with plate movements, and more.

A third international collaborative project is focused on the radioactive dating methods. Though easily discredited because of the basic flaws in the methods and the anomalous results, patterns of "dates" that are consistent with the evolutionary time scale are still a major challenge to the biblical account of earth history. It would be a powerful advance to be able to explain the "good" data accepted by the evolutionists and the anomalous data they reject, in terms other than "ages." So I am working with Drs. Steve Austin, John Baumgardner, Eugene Chaffin, Don DeYoung, Russ Humphreys, and Larry Vardiman on the RATE (Radioisotopes and the Age of The Earth) research project. Thus far, two possibilities have emerged — radioactive decay rates may have been very rapid at the time of creation and/or the Flood, and/or the "ages" represent patterns connected to the primordial geochemical make-up of the earth's interior, particularly the mantle, and to processes of recycling of rocks during the Flood.

Linked into my participation in the RATE project are an increasing number of case studies in which particular geological units are targeted for sampling and laboratory work, in order to test possible geochemical explanations for the radioisotopic ratios in the rocks. So far these case studies involve samples from Australia, New Zealand, the United Kingdom, the Grand Canyon, and elsewhere in the USA. Initial results are proving to be significantly helpful in our quest. For example, anomalous "ages" of up to 3.5 million years have been found for 1954 lava flows at Mt. Ngauruhoe on the North Island of New Zealand, and it has been demonstrated that these have been caused by excess radiogenic argon that has come from the mantle source area for these lavas and been trapped in the lavas when they cooled. Furthermore, a survey of the literature confirms that this argon gas may reflect the primordial argon concentration in the earth's mantle and not have been derived from radioactive decay, even though it is indistinguishable from argon so produced. This, in turn, means that in the case of ancient lava flows where we do not know their true age, we cannot be sure that the argon gas measured in the rocks comes from radioactive decay of potassium, and thus the measured argon gas cannot be a true reflection of "age," contrary to the principles involved in the potassium-argon and argon-argon radioactive dating methods. This work was reported in a paper delivered to the Fourth International Conference on Creationism in Pittsburgh in 1998 and won the Technical Excellence Award.

Other research projects have likewise been targeted at specific geological issues that for a long time have seemingly been at odds with the biblical record of earth history, and which have been baffling to solve. Two such issues are the metamorphic changes in rocks over large regions of the earth's crust due to elevated temperatures and pressures, and the emplacement and cooling within the earth's crust of large bodies of molten rock such as granites. Both of these geological processes have been regarded conventionally as taking millions of years and so have been persistently cited by those antagonistic to the biblical time scale for the creation of life and of earth history. However, papers in the *Creation Ex Nihilo Technical Journal* and presented at the Third International Conference on Creationism, both in 1994, have shown how the regional metamorphic changes only require low to moderate temperatures over a short time scale in the presence of hydrothermal waters and reflect the compositional zonations of the original sediments and constituent minerals. The latter paper won the Technical Excellence Award at that conference.

Likewise, it now has been demonstrated in a paper presented at the Fourth International Conference on Creationism in 1998 that the intrusion and cooling of large bodies of granitic magma only require hundreds to a few thousand years, the expulsion of contained magmatic water inducing fracturing and concurrent rapid convective heat loss via its mixing and circulation with ground water. Research into these and other geological issues thus continues to verify the accuracy of the biblical account of the history of the earth and of life.

Conclusion

I believe in the creation of life by God in six literal days, and in God's destruction of life and the earth by a year-long cataclysmic global Flood, for two reasons — first, and foremost, because the Bible clearly records these events as real, literal history, and second, because the scientific evidence, correctly understood, is totally consistent with this biblical account. As a geologist I continue to find scientific investigation of God's world very satisfying and exhilarating, because I always discover that ultimately the evidence in God's world agrees with what I read in God's Word.

stephen taylor

Electrical Engineering

Dr. Taylor is senior lecturer in electrical engineering at the University of Liverpool. He holds a B.S. in electrical engineering and electronics from the Imperial College of Science and Technology, University of London, United Kingdom, and an M.Eng. and a Ph.D. in electrical engineering from the University of Liverpool. Dr. Taylor has written over 80 scientific articles, and is a reviewer for the journals *IEE Electronic Letters*, *Solid State Electronics*, *Journal of Applied Physics* and *Applied Physics Letters*.

The purpose of this article is to state reasons for my belief as a scientist and engineer in an eternal, all-powerful, all-wise Creator God, a God who can be known and trusted, One who has spoken in the Bible to reveal His will and ultimately, through His Son the Lord Jesus Christ, to reveal His person. I would also like to highlight some of the problems scientifically with the naturalistic (evolutionary) view of origins and say why, in my opinion, the scientific facts support the biblical framework rather than the evolutionary belief system.

A Design Demands a Designer

On the table in front of me is a reproduction of a beautiful landscape painting of a country scene, dating from about 1770, by Paul

Sandby. In the foreground, the artist has captured the sunlight falling on a tree in a meadow. Nearby there is a horse and some children, and in the background, we see a river making its way past green hill and dale toward the sea. Far in the distance, gray clouds give way to a light blue sky. You ask me how the painting came to be. If I were to insist to you that suddenly and for no apparent reason, oil paints began to arrive upon a canvas, in such a way and in just such proportions that the result was a work of art, you would think me to be mad. It is an impossible scenario. My difficulties in convincing you would be made worse if I were unable to give an explanation for the existence of the canvas and the paints in the first place!

Evolutionary naturalism is asking us to believe in just such a scenario: a picture without a painter, art without an artist. Let us remember, also, that however good it is, the painting is only a dead, two-dimensional representation of a far more wonderful three-dimensional living reality: the landscape itself, trees, horses, children, sky, sun, and clouds! How wrong and how foolish to praise the work of a human hand and eye yet deny the work of the divine artist who put all things in place and gave existence and skill to that same human hand and eye!

Not only does a design imply a designer, a design says something about its designer. As we consider the vastness of deep space, the intricacies of the human brain, the powerful forces holding the nucleus of each atom together, we may conclude that God is indeed immense, great in intelligence and in power. If God is thus, why shouldn't creation take six 24-hour days? He could have done it in six hours or six seconds if He had chosen to. Such a God can do whatever He chooses, whenever He likes, consistent with His own nature.

A Man Who Claimed to Be God

The second and perhaps most convincing reason for Christian belief in general and in a literal six-day creation in particular is the Lord Jesus Christ. Approaching the second millennium He is still the central figure of human history. Every newspaper, computer, and coin bearing today's date reminds us that it was He who split time in two: A.D. and B.C. He never wrote a book or a song, yet millions of books and some of the world's greatest music have been written about Him. He never erected a monument yet tens of thousands of buildings have been erected in His honor. He never led an army or drew a sword, yet by His love down through the years, He has conquered the hearts of millions. Some of His enemies, on meeting Him, were changed into men who gave their lives for Him. His example and teachings have been the greatest influence for the good of mankind. Universities, schools, hospitals, orphanages, charities, and social reforms have been founded and progressed in His name as in the name of no other person.

His life story is told to us in the eyewitness accounts of the writers of the New Testament. These men were present when Jesus healed the blind, fed the hungry, calmed the storm, walked on water, and raised men from the dead. They heard Him speak, watched Him live, saw Him die, and walked, talked, and dined with Him after He had risen from the dead, as He predicted that He would. He did and claimed things about himself that only God can do or should claim. Jesus spoke of God as His Father, and said, "I and the Father are one" (John 10:30); and, "He who has seen me has seen the Father" (John 14:9).

Now it is important to realize that the Lord Jesus Christ believed in the early chapters of Genesis as historical fact. Indeed, such was His high view of Old Testament Scripture that He called it the

"Word of God," and that God's Word "was truth," affirming that "scripture cannot be broken' (John 10:35, 17:17). That the Lord Jesus Christ believed in Adam and Eve, Cain and Abel, Noah and a worldwide cataclysmic Flood is evident from such passages as Matthew 19:4, 23:35, and 24:37–39. In Mark 10:6 Jesus said, "But from the beginning of the creation God made them male and female." In these words of Jesus, we find that He teaches that Adam and Eve were created at the "beginning of creation," not millions of years after the beginning! This also implies that God had prepared a world for them shortly beforehand. Everywhere we find that the Bible is consistent with the view of a literal six-day, recent creation. This has been the almost universal teaching of the Christian Church until the last hundred years or so.

The Testimony of Others

Many of the world's greatest scientists have been convinced, Bible-believing Christians. In my own discipline of electrical engineering, one has only to think of names like Michael Faraday, James Joule, Lord Kelvin, and James Clerk Maxwell (who wrote against evolution) to see that this is true. The Creation Research Society currently has a membership of 650 scientists, each one holding a master's degree or above in a recognized field of science. In a recent article Dr. Russell Humphreys, physicist at Sandia National Laboratories, New Mexico, estimates that there are around 10,000 practicing professional scientists in the USA alone who openly believe in a six-day recent creation.[1]

Personal Experience

I became a Christian at the age of 16 by seeking forgiveness for my sins and committing my life to the Lord Jesus Christ in a simple prayer. Although aware of the apparent contradiction between science and the Bible, the fact that Jesus believed in the Genesis account as historically true was enough to convince me as a young Christian that I should also! The disciple is not above His Lord. Many years later, I am more than ever convinced not only of the truth of the Christian gospel, but also of the *harmony* between the biblical revelation and true science.

It is extremely important to realize that, contrary to what we are often told, there is no proven fact of science that can be shown to contradict the biblical account. When scientific theories appear to contradict, it is important to examine the evidence for and interpretation behind such ideas. Scientists are subject to error and bias, as the history of science shows. In the closing section of this article, I would like to examine briefly some of the severe *scientific* problems inherent in the evolutionary model of origins.

What Went Bang and How?

According to the "big-bang" theory, the universe began about 10 to 20 billion years ago as an inconceivably small volume of space and matter/energy which has been expanding ever since. However, we are entitled to ask the question: *what* went bang? In simple terms, "Nothing can't go bang." A related question is: When did natural laws governing the physical world come into being? Are we to believe that these laws also are the product of chance? Professor Werner Gitt has recently reviewed the big-bang theory and notes that, "Many discoveries in recent years with improved instruments and improved observational methods have repeatedly shaken this theory."[2]

How Did Life Originate?

Evolution has the fundamental problem of explaining how life came from non-life. In his book *Evolution, a Theory in Crisis*, molecular biologist Dr. Michael Denton claims that his subject lends no support to the theory of evolution. He points out that there is no such thing as a simple cell. He asks the following question: "Is it really credible that random processes could have constructed a reality, the smallest element of which — a functional gene or protein — is complex beyond our own creative capacities, a reality which is the very antithesis of chance, which excels in every sense anything produced by the intelligence of man?"[3]

Professor Sir Fred Hoyle, the former Cambridge astronomer, gave the following analogy to illustrate the difficulty of life originating by chance: "Imagine 10^{50} blind persons each with a scrambled Rubik's cube and try to conceive of them simultaneously arriving at the solved form. You then have the chance of arriving by random shuffling (random variation) of just one of the many biopolymers upon which life depends . . . nonsense of a high order."[4]

Dr. Michael Behe, associate professor of biochemistry at Lehigh University, similarly argues for intelligent design as an obvious logical explanation for the intricacy of the biochemical machines found in all living things. He gives examples of biological systems such as blood-clotting that are "irreducibly complex," requiring all the parts to function. In such systems no direct, gradual route leads to their production, since if one part is missing, the whole system is useless.[5]

Where Did the New Information Come From?

Large-scale amoeba-to-man evolution requires massive increases in genetic information over time. Evolution is said to proceed by the processes of natural selection (the survival of the fittest) and/or mutation. However the *key* question for both of these processes is: Where does the new information come from? For a reptile to become a bird, it must have the extra information necessary for wings and feathers, etc. Natural selection is easily observable, but it cannot of itself create the new information, since there is no upward development in the genetic complexity of the organism. Another alleged source of new information is mutations. For large-scale evolution, mutations *must* on average add information. In a recent book, biophysicist Dr. Lee Spetner shows with detailed probabilistic analysis that this is completely precluded. He examines the classic textbook cases of mutations cited in favor of neo-Darwinian evolution and shows conclusively that, without exception, they are all *losses* of information. There is no such thing as a mutation that adds information.[6] Spetner is well qualified to make these calculations. As a former fellow of Johns Hopkins University he is a specialist in communications and information theory.

The case against evolution is summed up by Berkeley University law professor Philip Johnson, who makes the following points: (1) evolution is grounded not on scientific fact, but on a philosophical belief called naturalism; (2) the belief that a large body of empirical evidence supports evolution is an illusion; (3) evolution is itself a religion; (4) if evolution were a scientific hypothesis based on a rigorous study of the evidence, it would have been abandoned long ago.[7]

In this article we have looked at the clear statement of Scripture and discussed reasons for accepting it at its face value. We have looked at an alternative theory of origins embodied in evolution theory and the scientific difficulties it faces, difficulties which are increasing with time. From these considerations and others I, for one, have no hesitation in rejecting the evolutionary hypothesis of origins and affirming the biblical alternative that "in six days the Lord made heaven and earth, the sea, and all that is in them" (Exod. 20:11).

Endnotes

1 *Creation ex nihilo,* 20(1) 1997, p. 37.

2 *Creation ex nihilo,* 20(3) 1998, p. 42.

3 Michael Denton, *Evolution, A Theory in Crisis* (Bethesda, MD: Adler and Adler, 1985).

4 *Nature,* 294, 1981, p. 105.

5 Michael J. Behe, *Darwin's Black Box* (New York: Free Press, 1996).

6 Lee Spetner, *Not by Chance: Shattering the Modern Theory of Evolution* (Brooklyn, NY: Judaica, 1997).

7 Phillip E. Johnson, *Darwin on Trial* (Washington, DC: Regnery Gateway, 1991).

john morris

Geological Engineering

Dr. Morris is president of the Institute for Creation Research. He holds a B.S. in civil engineering from Virginia Tech, an M.S. in geological engineering and a Ph.D. in geological engineering from the University of Oklahoma. He is a member of the American Association of Petroleum Geologists and the Society of Petroleum Engineers. He is the author of several books in the area of origins and the Bible.

There are two categories of evidence which I keep coming back to as confirmation of creation: (1) that of the incredible design and order in living systems, and (2) the separateness of the basic body styles of plants and animals in the fossil record.

Regarding design, even the smallest single-celled organism, the kind which evolutionists say are similar to those which evolved spontaneously from non-living chemicals, is complex beyond our own ability to understand, let alone recreate. Scientists are just now beginning to understand how the cell works, which genes accomplish which functions, etc., but have no clue as to how these systems may have originated by natural processes. Even the simplest cell is more complex than a super-computer, and yet evolutionists attribute much greater design to chance in the name of science when it relates to the origin and evolution of life.

The cell has been compared, not just to a super-computer, but to a thriving metropolis full of industries, buildings, and factories, each containing super-computers, all functioning together to make this metropolis function. The ability of a cell to carry out its variety of functions, to repair itself when damaged, and to reproduce off-spring of like complexity is beyond the ability of any item created by human ingenuity. Obviously, living systems bear the stamp of God's creative activity and could not be the result of chance pro-cesses.

While the study of living systems gives us evidence in the present that life could not have arisen by chance, a study of the fossil record gives us an indication as to what that life was like in the past. Once again we see unthinkable complexity and variety, but we find no evidence at all of evolutionary origins. If evolution has occurred, it must have involved innumerable "in-between" forms between the various plant and animal types. Yet, the fossil record contains no such intermediate forms, and evolutionists are left scrambling to explain how animals could have descended from supposed com-mon ancestors without leaving any fossil trace.

The fossil record shows (1) that life forms manifest little or no change during their history, (2) that most fossil types are virtually identical to their living descendants, (3) that fossil types appear in the fossil record without ancestral lineages, and (4) that fossil organ-isms either became extinct or have survived into the present. This is exactly what should be present if creation has occurred. The fossil record, while vaguely compatible with evolutionary stories, clearly favors the creationist interpretation.

The real key, however, for resolving the creation/evolution con-troversy is in a study of the age of the earth. Evolution demands long periods of time, but if the earth is much younger, as the Bible teaches, then evolution is even more foolish. Obviously, since scientists are limited to a study of present evidence, they cannot go back in time and observe past processes. What we study are the results of past processes.

As a geologist, I am convinced that the surface of the earth appears to have been shaped and remolded in the past by an incredibly dynamic watery cataclysm. The biblical flood provides the key. If such a flood happened, as the Bible says it happened, then it would have accomplished great geologic work. It would have eroded material from one location and deposited it in another, and in those muddy sediments would be animals and plants which had died in that flood. Over time, those sediments would have hardened into sedimentary rock, and the dead things would have hardened into fossils. Thus, from a flood geology perspective, the rocks and fossils are the results of the flood of Noah's day.

Yet, evolutionists consider the fossils to be the evidence of evolutionary transition, and they consider the rock units to contain evidence of millions and billions of years. I feel they are misinterpreting that evidence, wrongly using it in support of evolution and an old earth. Without the rock and fossil records, there is no evidence worthy of the name to be used by evolution and old-earth concepts. Thus, the flood of Noah's day is the bottom line issue.

Locked in the present, wondering about unobserved history, scientists are not without tools. The proper technique to use in evaluating competing models of earth history is for advocates to formulate their models as best as possible, and then make "predictions" about the evidence. These are not predictions about the future, but predictions about the nature of the evidence. If the biblical flood really happened as the Bible describes, then we would expect the geologic results of that flood to show their cataclysmic origin, the result of processes operating on rates and intensities far beyond those operating in the present, and they would be operating on a regional scale. My evolutionary colleagues advocate slow and gradual processes having been responsible for the geologic units while operating on a local scale. Having formulated the two competing models, we can go to the evidence and see which set of predictions best fits.

As creationists have been maintaining for decades and as even secular geologists are starting to admit, we see much evidence for catastrophe in the rock record. From turbidities to tempestites to evidence of hurricane activity, etc., etc., catastrophism is becoming the rule in geology. Furthermore, by plotting the areal extent of these deposits, we can see that the products of these cataclysmic events in the past were operating on a regional or continental scale with hints toward global continuity. While we didn't see the events taking place, the results of those events are supportive of the biblical doctrine of a global cataclysmic flood and not at all supportive of standard evolutionary ideas. If indeed these rocks and fossils are the result of a global flood, then there is no evidence for evolution, nor for an old earth.

Questions sometimes arise which I can't immediately answer on a scientific basis, but whenever they do arise, I go back to the rocks and fossils and remind myself that the flood of Noah's day is their obviously ultimate cause. Moreover, while I don't understand all the details, I am confident that the secular model of slow and gradual processes is not capable of explaining the broad features of the evidence of the past.

My real confidence in creation and young earth ultimately comes, of course, from Scripture. Fewer doctrines are taught with such clarity in Scripture as recent creation and global flood. The word "day" in Genesis 1 and Exodus 20:11, etc., can only mean a solar day. The fact that God created the various plant and animal types "after their kind," as repeated ten times in Genesis 1, absolutely prohibits them having descended with modification from previously existing kinds. The continual repetition of global terms in the Flood context erases any possibility of a local Flood. Of course, Jesus accepted creation, the Flood, and the young earth as did the other New Testament writers, most particularly Peter and Paul.

As a Christian and as a scientist, my confidence in God's Word is confirmed every time I look at the scientific evidence, and every time I look at the scientific evidence, my understanding of God's Word is enhanced. Truly God's Word and God's world are both accurate self-authenticating and mutually reinforcing records of the unobserved past.

elaine kennedy

Geology

Dr. Kennedy is a research scientist at the Geoscience Research Institute in the United States. She holds a B.S. in geology from Phillips University, a B.S. in teaching sciences from Phillips University, an M.S. in geology from Loma Linda University and a Ph.D. in geology from the University of Southern California. Dr. Kennedy's current research involves a study of an unusual occurrence of dinosaur eggshell fragments in a storm surge deposit in Patagonia, Argentina.

As a geologist, I do not find much evidence for the existence of a *fiat* creation. I just have not found any geologic data that convinces me that God spoke and "it was." So it probably seems strange to some that I believe God created this world in six literal days. After all, scientists base their conclusions on cold, hard facts; they trust their five senses to be the primary source of absolute truth. Unfortunately, the truth about earth history is not so easily discerned. Processes that deposited most of the rock layers cannot be duplicated in the laboratory because the events were too large and complex to be modelled. Geologists use modern analogues to explain a large number of ancient deposits, but many unique deposits cannot be explained by the processes occurring today. These enigmatic units raise many questions related to earth history, and multiple hypotheses have been proposed to resolve the issues, including some that are consistent with the biblical account of our world.

As a Christian, I find abundant evidence for the existence of a Creator and the greatest evidence is found in my personal relationship with Jesus Christ. This is my experience and it is from this platform of faith that I look at the geologic data. From this vantage point, I see evidence that is consistent with the worldwide Flood as it is described in Genesis. The reality of this event resolves for me many areas of conflict between the interpretations of the geologic community and the biblical account of creation. The key to this resolution is the differentiation between data and the current geological interpretations.

It took me several years to learn how to differentiate between data and interpretation. This is such an elementary idea that one would think identifying data would be easy; however, so much of the information we receive is merely the researchers' interpretations without data or alternative views, and even scientists often use interpretations and conclusions to bolster arguments rather than going back to the data for support for ideas. For example, dates cited for the ages of various rocks and fossils are not data. Dates are not directly measured but consist of calculations based on assumptions describing very complex systems. The actual data used by the chronologists is the distribution of the radioactive isotopes in crystals or rocks. Factors that control these distributions are very complex and poorly understood. Those of us who believe in a short chronology and a six-day creation do not have an adequate explanation for radiometric dates; however, we do know that much research needs to be done and we know multiple interpretations of the distributions concerning the processes involved are possible. Despite this possibility, dates are often used to refute biblical chronologies as though no questions or arguments oppose these conclusions.

When interpreting scientific data, I use the same techniques and approaches as my colleagues, but my assumptions come from my biblical paradigm. I often recognize conflicts; indeed, the geologic literature reminds me daily that conflict exists, and many aspects of the geologic record are difficult to explain to the satisfaction of my colleagues or myself. This does not mean that they are correct and I am wrong, but rather that much research needs to be done. This attitude seems an impossible bias to some, but I find my faith leaves me open to alternatives, while I continually question the interpretations in my work because of my science.

Most of the data in the geologic record can be interpreted to support either a long (millions of years) or a short (a few thousand years) history for life on earth. Some data is better explained from the long-age perspective and other data fits better in a short period. Once I realized that the data alone does not mandate either belief system, I found spiritual resolution between the conflicting interpretations of science and the ideas presented in Scripture. I believe that our Creator revealed to us in the Bible an honest and accurate account of our origins and weekly I rejoice in the memorial of that six-day event. Spiritual peace concerning these issues is important for all Christians working in science, but it is not one that comes easily.

Although I have been a Christian since I was seven years of age, it was not until I was in the midst of my geologic education that I decided to include my geologic assumptions within a biblical world view. In effect, I realized that I consider God's revelation more valid than human reason, because I experience His recreative power in my life daily.

colin w. mitchell

Geography

Dr. Mitchell is a former international consultant in the development of arid lands based in the United Kingdom. He holds credits from Harvard University, an M.A. with honors in geography from Oxford University, an M.C.D. (master of civic design) from the University of Liverpool and a Ph.D. in desert terrain geography from Cambridge University. Dr. Mitchell has acted as a specialist consultant to 16 countries, including long term assignments with Iraq, Sudan, Pakistan, Morocco, and the United Nations Food and Agriculture Organization's appraisal of Ethiopia's national land use planning policy.

I was born in London and in my childhood attended a local church. My beliefs changed to that of an agnostic in my teens, which was reinforced during service in the RAF. After this I went to university to read geography. I became a Christian as a result of joining the Oxford Inter-Collegiate Christian Union.

Like so many others, I found it difficult to harmonize the evolutionary ideas in which I had been educated with the basis of the Christian faith that I had learned. The questions were particularly obtrusive since studying for a degree in geography involves a substantial component of geology. I read books which sought to harmonize the two, but found that the more my faith became biblically based the more difficult the task became. The most critical problem centered around the creation/evolution question and specifically the six days of Genesis 1. It was clear that there was no way that either the sequence of events or the chronology could be made to accord with current scientific theories of origins. It was not just a question of interpretation. One or the other explanation (or indeed both) had to be wrong. Choice was necessary, and on this choice hung much of one's life orientation. If the choice had been solely intellectual, it would have been harder because the arguments for and against a young earth both appeared strong, but I was impressed both by conscience and through the lessons of history that the answer must start with ethical principles. Our whole Western culture and civilization were based on the Bible above any other source of wisdom. This appeared to be the reason for its moral worth and the basis for its global influence.

Critique of the Scientific Case

The scientific arguments for an old earth appear strong. How reliable are they? How secure is the idea that there is an uninterrupted creative sequence from the big bang through the formation of the solar system, the solidification of the earth, the spontaneous generation of life, and the evolution of plants, animals, and humans to end in the world around us today? Is this scheme impregnable? By no means. It has fatal gaps and inconsistencies. A few questions can reveal this. Who or what provided the material for the big bang? Why did it not implode rather than explode? How could it coagulate into stars and how could these generate planets? How could life appear spontaneously? How could one kind of living creature change into another when the fossil record shows no evidence of such changes? How could intelligence and mind develop in the face of the second law of thermodynamics which denies such possibilities? None of these questions can be satisfactorily answered.

There are also questions over chronology. Modern calculations of the age of the earth are based on measurements which assume a uniformitarian evolution. They calculate present rates of sediment deposition, radioactive decay, and presumed organic evolution and extrapolate these backwards. All must accept considerable margins of error. These often differ widely in their results, and can give contradictory answers within a single method. Radiogenic dating is today regarded as the most reliable. But if we rely on this we are dependent on a number of unprovable assumptions. These include such matters as the original ratio of parent and daughter isotopes, the constancy of decay rates, the occurrence of apparently parentless isotopes with very short half-lives and the possibilities of neutron flux and of the migration of chemically mobile atoms.

Conclusions

The debate between belief in a literal six-day creation and an old earth has far-reaching consequences. The Bible teaches creationism throughout, starting with the first chapters of Genesis. The Adam and Eve story is cogent for man's whole religious problem. Adam's relationship to his Creator, by identifying divine authority and law, gives a framework for all aspects of life. By elevating conscience above material interest, the story provides the basic rationale for free social, economic, and political institutions. Adam's responsibility for the natural world provides a model for the environmental challenges of today.

But it goes further than this. The creation/evolution debate is marginal to a greater one: about our understanding of the supernatural. This is because our view of origins profoundly affects our understanding of who God is and how He deals with the world. It determines our view of His nature. The principle of atonement was first introduced in the Garden of Eden. This provides inspiration and moral guidance for human conduct. Through this, it influences our approach to science, the arts, education, and theology. Adam's relationship with his family and the world around him is a guide to all religious and social relations. His relation with Eve symbolizes that between Christ and the church and even those within the Trinity. The evolution theory, by denying the historicity of the creation story, is quite destructive of these insights.

Therefore, our response to the idea of a six-day creation governs our vision of the cosmos, and beyond this, of our ultimate destiny. The impossibility of harmonizing today's scientific world view with Scripture leaves a stark alternative. This is between seeing the world as having no meaning and human life as having evolved from primitive beginnings through upward struggle with a view of the future which at best provides some material and cultural advancement for the race, at worst to its destruction, and in either case to oblivion for the individual. On the other hand, all nature can be seen as part of a benevolent divine plan. Our life, both here and hereafter, can depend on our answer.

stanley a. mumma

Architectural Engineering

Dr. Mumma is professor of architectural engineering at the Pennsylvania State University. He holds a B.S. in mechanical engineering from the University of Cincinnati and an M.S. and Ph.D. in mechanical engineering from the University of Illinois. Dr. Mumma, who is also director of the Building Thermal Mechanical Systems Laboratory at Pennsylvania State University, specializes in the optimization of building mechanical components, the applications of solar and alternate energy, and new mechanical technologies research.

How have I, a mechanical engineer with nearly 30 years of industrial and university teaching and research experience, come to the conclusion that the world and all that is seen was created in 6 literal 24 hour days? My academic areas of research are related to building energy utilization and indoor air quality control. The research, which is not devoted to the study of origins, is founded on the fundamental, observable, and reliable principles of the thermal sciences. Therefore, what follows will not link my research activities to my conclusions concerning origins. I bring a research engineer's mind to bear on the things I read and observe around me. Engineers quite often need confidence in the literal accuracy of the Genesis account, while people educated in many other disciplines are quite satisfied to take it as allegory.

I consider the six literal 24-hour days creation model to be foundational to my world view. However, I have not always held this position. In 1978, as a tenured full professor, I embarked upon a journey through the Bible, devoting 15 to 20 minutes per day to study prior to breakfast. The journey was undertaken so that I, an "educated person," would not be ignorant of the contents of the best-selling book of all time. My study was supplemented by a host of additional resources, the most significant of which was Henry Morris's book *Many Infallible Proofs*.[1] I found this book, written by a fellow university engineering professor, to be reliable, scholarly, and well supported with references. Prior to the year-long journey through the Bible, neither origins nor the Creator seemed at all relevant to me. Afterwards, I came to understand a great deal about myself and the human condition. I learned that not a single archaeological find contradicted any of the historical content of the Bible, but rather authenticated it. While it was not a book of science, the Bible spoke accurately concerning many scientific phenomena or processes in the areas of hydrology, geology, astronomy, meteorology, biology, and physics. However, I still had doubts about the reliability of the Book of Genesis. Therefore, it was necessary for me to explore in detail the two views of origins: evolution and biblical creation, including a global flood. Since there were no human eyewitnesses to record the beginning, a legal historical proof was impossible. Furthermore, current scientific laboratory procedures could not be used to authenticate the beginning of either model. So, I was left with only one alternative: undertake a study to determine how well the artifacts that can be observed today fit each model. Some of the convincing evidence that I found demonstrating that the evolution model fails, and the young earth creation/ global flood model fits include:

- comets disintegrate too quickly
- not enough mud on the sea floor
- not enough sodium in the sea
- earth's magnetic field is decaying too fast
- many strata are too tightly bent
- injected sandstone shortens geologic "ages"
- fossil radioactivity shortens geologic "ages" to a few years
- helium in the wrong places
- not enough Stone Age skeletons
- the big bang fails to provide an explanation of where all the information around us and in us comes from
- the time it would take the moon to recede from the earth to its present position, and the lack of a significant layer of dust and meteorite debris on the moon after 4,600,000,000 years.

My conclusion is that the Bible is true and reliable, including its description of origins in the Book of Genesis. The reliability of the six literal 24-hour days creation model is important to me because no person whose mind works similar to mine would accept any of the Bible if the very first part were wrong. Without the Bible, I believe, one cannot find true and reliable answers to life's most critical questions.

Endnotes
1 Henry M. Morris, *Many Infallible Proofs* (Green Forest, AR: Master Books, Inc., 1974).

evan jamieson

Hydrometallurgy

Dr. Jamieson is a research chemist for Alcoa World Alumina, Australia. He holds a B.App.S. (post graduate degree) in applied chemistry from Curtin University and a Ph.D. in hydrometallurgy from Murdoch University. He has also served as a consultant scientist and research scientist for several companies in the areas of ceramics, battery cell design, and mineral processing.

I can't remember a time when I did not believe in God or Jesus Christ as a personal Savior. The creation/evolution debate was quite different, however.

The subject used to be a "non-issue" for the church I attended. If anything, the predominant belief was the "gap theory," but not much was said about the issue at all. This and my strong interest in science led to the inevitable combination of both theories, and another "theistic evolutionist" or "progressive creationist" was born. However, while studying for my Tertiary Admittance Exam (years 11 and 12), I couldn't help but notice the religious passion that teachers put into their discussions on the theory of evolution. In fact when I raised some scientific inconsistencies (e.g., polystrate fossils, young earth ages for non-radioactive dating methods, and complications for Miller's "chemicals of life" experiment), often there was an angry reaction and feeble, if any, explanations. I once asked how sedimentary rocks were dated and was told by "indicator fossils." When I followed with "how were indicator fossils dated," I was told, "by the rock formations they are found in." Try as I might, the teacher could not see that this was circular reasoning!

The lack of credible answers made me quite skeptical of the theory of evolution. After all, it wasn't an obscure theory; it was basically accepted worldwide and had been studied for many years. Simple and obvious questions should have been given simple and obvious answers — so where were they? About the same time I was noticing inconsistencies between the Bible and the theory of evolution. Some examples include:

1. How could a God of love declare everything as "very good" (Gen. 1:31) if He had created man by such a cruel and callous method as evolution?
2. The Bible clearly teaches that from man's sin came death (Rom. 5:12; 1 Cor. 15:21). Evolution teaches that by death came man.
3. Jesus appears to accept Genesis literally and clearly quotes from it (Matt. 19:4).

By the time I went to university, I was a budding creationist. I was expecting to encounter serious scientific argument from the "enlightened ones," but what I found was more of the same. One lecturer told me that man was evolving because we are smarter than our ancestors were. He went on to say that we would all grow larger ears (for learning) and would one day lose our toes because we all wore shoes. Now the irrelevance of this was astounding and I pointed this out. Accumulated knowledge does not prove increased intelligence (it is a product of cooperation), and even people without ear lobes can hear, and therefore learn (i.e., small ears are not an indication of stupidity). As for your toes, lose them and you have enormous problems adjusting your balance, no matter what type of shoe you wear (it was part of the old and refuted vestigial organ debate).[1]

Well, instead of a rational debate, I was bombarded with highly emotive statements that included "people who do not believe the theory of evolution as fact have no right to be studying science." His reasoning was that non-evolutionists lacked rational thinking!

As the years have passed, there were many questions posed regarding the validity of creation. However, these have always been answered to my satisfaction and have strengthened my foundations.

I believe that the Bible is a book of tested or reasonable faith. It declares there is a coming final judgment of the human soul unless there is a repentance of sin. Christians have faith that Jesus can, will, and has forgiven our sin, if we trust in Him (John 3:16–18, 5:24, 20:23; Rom. 10:9; 1 John 5:13).

If God is God, then what He has said must be true. I believe that if we test it, our reasonable faith will be strengthened (1 Pet. 3:15).

Endnotes

1 Jerry Bergman and George Howe, *"Vestigial Organs" Are Fully Functional* (Terre Haute, IN: Creation Research Society Books, 1990).

larry vardiman

Meteorology

Dr. Vardiman is professor, Department of Astro-Geophysics, Institute for Creation Research, in the United States. He holds a B.S. in physics from the University of Missouri, a B.S. in meteorology from St. Louis University and an M.S. and Ph.D. in atmospheric science from Colorado State University. He is a member of the American Meteorological Society and has authored numerous research papers in the area of cloud physics and meteorology.

I reject the theory of evolution because it is based on several faulty premises which are clearly contradicted by observation. Evolution implies chaos and meaninglessness. Creation implies order and value.

The natural world contains incredible evidence for design. Every system is regulated by laws which can be described verbally or through mathematical relationships. The DNA molecule is an example of built-in sources of information which regulate life processes and the inheritance of genetic traits. The law of gravitation is an example of how the Creator orders natural processes. Natural laws and built-in information imply a designer who created the systems and processes. Evolution cannot explain the presence of such design.

Evolutionary theory states that the earth and all life began as a gas several billion years ago and through random processes became more complex with time. Man is the final result of billions and billions of chance mutations of genetic material as the earth aged. Yet, the second law of thermodynamics describes a natural process which causes ordered systems to degenerate into disorder. The second law is undisputed by all reputable scientists and contradicts the basic premise of evolution.

The fossil record is considered to be the primary evidence for evolution, yet it does not demonstrate a complete chain of life from simple life forms to complex. Many gaps are present which should not occur if evolution proceeded smoothly from one species to another. In fact, these discontinuities are recognized by a major part of the evolutionary community when they adopt the "hopeful monster mechanism."

The most telling argument for me in rejecting evolution, however, is the meaninglessness and lack of value it signifies. If evolution occurred, then my existence is not a special event in the Creator's plan. Yet, the Bible says I am special; I was created for a purpose.

geoff downes

Forestry Research

Dr. Downes is senior research scientist with the Commonwealth Scientific and Industrial Research Organisation (CSIRO), Division of Forestry and Forest Products, in Australia. He holds a B.S. (hons) first class from Monash University, a Ph.D. in tree physiology from the University of Melbourne, and spent a year as a post-doctoral fellow at the University of Aberdeen, Scotland. At CSIRO, Dr. Downes researches climatic and environmental effects on wood formation.

I received the last four years of my secondary education at a leading church school in Melbourne, Australia. In year 11, I took a course entitled Biblical Studies. It was a small class taught by our school chaplain, and started with a study of Genesis. We were taught, without equivocation, that Genesis was a mythical account and did not represent real history. I was surprised but, as I had not really considered the issue in any depth, not particularly shocked. Unlike most of my classmates, I was a Christian at the time, having been made to confront the reality of God and His claim over my life when I was 13, as God brought me to that point of personal decision and commitment.

In 1980 I commenced a science degree at Monash University. Almost immediately the discomfort with my theistic evolutionary understanding began to make itself felt. Looking back, I would describe myself as a reluctant theistic evolutionist — a "theistic evolutionist" because that was how I had been trained; "reluctant" because it seemed so inconsistent to accept the Bible where it taught the simple Christian gospel, but reject that part on which the whole Christian position was founded. I knew that if I were challenged about my faith, this inability to confidently affirm the historical truth of the Bible would ultimately undermine my own faith. I would be found to be inconsistent in my belief. If I couldn't believe the first book, what was my basis for believing the rest? In several discussions I had with others at this time, I came to the conclusion that it was not an effective form of evangelism to try to defend the Christian faith by argument. Essentially what I wanted was a world view that was as consistent as possible with the world around me. I suppose that is the ultimate aim of any philosophy. The problem was that I had not been trained to think biblically. Although I had attended a church school, been involved in the church for most of my life, and attended Sunday school, I still had not been taught to think from a Christian world view.

In May 1980 I was sitting in a physical chemistry lecture. The lecturer was expounding the law of entropy. I can still remember the impact on me as what he was saying sank in. He was teaching us that the universe as a whole was proceeding from a more ordered state to a less ordered state. The laws of nature, in a closed system, always behaved this way. Naturally, I extrapolated back in time to the point when the universe began, the time of maximum order. I reasoned that if, in a closed system, the natural laws always increased the entropy of the whole, then *ipso facto*, unknown natural or supernatural laws were required to increase order.

What that lecture did was show me that at some points scientists are forced to be inconsistent. That is, they don't know everything and are sometimes forced to hold theories in tension against the scientific evidence if they are going to hold to their belief systems. This lecturer was teaching us that natural law cannot explain how the universe as a whole can increase in order. Therefore, science cannot explain how this order originated. However, he also (I assumed) believed in evolution. I had never been taught that there were aspects of evolution that scientists could not explain. I thought that if I held to a belief in special creation, as explained in Genesis, then I was holding to a faith position, whereas scientists had evidence to support their view. This lecture helped me to realize that if scientists can't explain all the evidence for evolution, perhaps I don't need to have all the answers for a creationist position either.

Up until that day, my thinking was totally humanistic in that it started with the presupposition that I had the ability to reason things out logically. I had accepted the evolutionary world view and, consequently, its presuppositions. That world view rejected any role of revelation as a foundation for making sense of the world around me.

That day I stepped outside of my evolutionary, long-age mindset, started going to other lectures, and endeavored to evaluate the evidence from both viewpoints. What I found was that the overwhelming majority of the scientific evidence we were taught bore no direct relation to either creation or evolution. The evidence that was presented within an evolutionary framework could equally well be reinterpreted within a creationist framework. As a result of that lecture, I chose to become a young-earth creationist. I chose to accept the Bible as the basis for all my thinking, and understand Genesis in the plain sense in which it was written. I could not explain all the things that I observed in nature within that framework, and I still cannot. But I knew that, if these lecturers could be inconsistent in the sense that they were not able to make the evolutionary framework fit the evidence at every point, then I could also hold in "tension" those areas of science that I could not explain within a creationist framework. My understanding of the creationist perspective became steadily stronger in its ability to accommodate and explain the real scientific evidence.

In 1984 I commenced a Ph.D. degree in tree physiology. Increasingly, I wonder at how anyone can look at the complexity of a living organism and believe that it arose by natural processes. The whole of the biological sciences leads to the conclusion that a Creator was necessary. That anyone can claim that science supports an evolutionary view decries belief. The complexity of not just living organisms but the communities within which they exist cannot be explained satisfactorily without the conclusion that there is a Creator.

Often I hear the argument that science cannot allow the presupposition or conclusion that a Creator exists. The moment you do, you supposedly step outside the realm of science. This is not so.

A large part of my research effort in forestry is trying to separate cause and effect. The vascular cambium is not a tissue that is readily amenable to traditional reductionist approaches in attempting to understand how it functions. Often our data sets contain artifacts that arise simply because we are measuring or observing a tree or forest. One of the fundamental activities we have to undertake when analyzing data is to try to determine where the data is influenced by our measurements and not by processes that occur naturally. That is, we are looking for "events" that cannot be attributed to nature but result from our "intelligent" involvement. The whole area of forensic science is focused on this aspect.

Consider finding a dead body in the park. Did the person die from natural causes, or was some other factor involved? If you find a knife in the back, then it is logical to assume that some outside intelligence was involved. However, if you start by assuming that the death occurred from natural causes, then you can never arrive at the correct conclusion. It is not a question of science, but the foundational assumptions you take to the data.

Over the past 15 years of research experience, my views have only become stronger. I have come to realize that evolution is a religious view founded on the assumption that we can discern truth by using the abilities of our mind to reason and think logically through the evidence perceived by our five senses. However, if we pursue that reasoning, we ultimately arrive at the conclusion that we have no logical basis for believing that we can reason logically. We cannot prove that our thought processes are not just random chemical reactions occurring within our brains. We cannot prove ultimately that we exist. Descartes was wrong when he said, "I think, therefore I am." The decision to trust our ability to reason is a faith step. The theory of evolution is founded on this step of faith. However, even to be able to begin to have confidence in my ability to reason, I have to start with a revelation from the One who made me.

As C.S. Lewis stated, "I grew up believing in this (evolution) Myth and I have felt — I still feel — its almost perfect grandeur. Let no one say we are an unimaginative age: neither the Greeks nor the Norsemen ever invented a better story. But the Myth asks me to believe that reason is simply the unforeseen and unintended by-product of a mindless process at one stage of its endless and aimless becoming. The content of the Myth thus knocks from under me the only ground on which I could possibly believe the Myth to be true. If my own mind is a product of the irrational, how shall I trust my mind when it tells me about evolution?"[1]

Endnotes
1 C.S. Lewis, *Christian Reflections* (Grand Rapids, MI: Wm. B. Eerdmans Pub. Co., 1975), p. 89.

wayne frair

Biology

43

Professor Frair is professor emeritus of biology at The King's College, Tuxedo, New York. He holds an A.B. in zoology from Houghton College, New York, a B.S. in zoology from Wheaton College, Illinois, an M.A. in embryology from the University of Massachusetts, and a Ph.D. in biochemical taxonomy from Rutgers, The State University, New Jersey. He is the author of a number of research papers on turtles and also on creation-evolution topics, including the book *A Case for Creation*.[1] He was a witness for the defense at the famous 1981 creation versus evolution trial in Little Rock, Arkansas. Professor Frair is a fellow of the American Association for the Advancement of Science and, for the years 1986 to 1993, served as president of the Creation Research Society.

My interest in Bible-science issues was amplified after I became a Christian in January 1945, while I was in the U.S. Navy during the Second World War. My personal journey into the mysteries of the origin of life began in 1946 when I was out of the navy and taking classes at the University of Massachusetts in Amherst. We were fed a diet of evolution, but I wondered if there were not other defendable positions.

In my junior year I transferred to a Christian institution (Houghton College) where I continued with a major in zoology and minors in chemistry and Bible. Here, my major professor, Dr.

George Moreland, was a Bible-believing creationist, and I grew in knowledge under his tutelage. After completing a B.A. degree, I entered Wheaton College in Illinois, where I completed a B.S. degree with honors in zoology. Here I probed more into the Bible, theology, and several fields of science while working with professors who were creationists.

For one year I taught science at Ben Lippen, a Christian middle and high school. Then I returned to the University of Massachusetts and completed an M.A. degree in embryology, writing a research thesis on the effects of 8-azaguanine (the first anti-cancer drug) during a chick's embryology.[2] My advisor, Dr. Gilbert Woodside, was chairman of the Department of Zoology at the University of Massachusetts and was an evolutionist with an international reputation in embryology. He apparently did not appreciate a scientific alternative to evolution, but he declared to me very clearly that evolution was not applicable in the field of embryology. It was obvious to him that evolution actually had hurt embryological disciplines, because many fine scientists had wasted their time trying to fit data from their studies into some illusionary evolutionary scheme.

After graduation, I accepted a position as instructor in biology at The King's College in New York, and four years later took a leave of absence to complete a doctorate at Rutgers University. My advisor there was Dr. Alan Boyden, department chair of zoology, and the world's leader in serology. Using blood serum proteins, the professors and students in that department at Rutgers were classifying plants and animals. Another name for this field of research is biochemical taxonomy. In the implementation of a chemical approach to taxonomy (classification and naming) the Rutgers group were the pioneers.

Professor Boyden inclined to accept evolution, but actually he was very disillusioned about the value of evolution in his own field of research. He would call evolutionists "ancestor worshippers and people with a backward look." He showed considerable concern in teaching his students not to think macroevolution in their studies involving systematics (system used for taxonomy) of plants and animals, and he even published a book against popular evolution positions.[3] I did research and wrote a dissertation on the biochemical taxonomy of turtles, completing the doctorate in 1962. Then I returned to The King's College, where I was chairman of the Department of Biology most of the time until my retirement in 1994.

My research, especially on turtles over nearly 40 years, has increased my admiration of God as Creator. Along with thousands of other scientists, I do not believe that evolution was the method that God used in creating various types of life.[4] For example, there is no clear evidence that turtles ever evolved from anything else. However, there have been changes among the turtles. Actually, a purpose of my own research has been to understand better how turtles have diversified.[5]

The doctrine of evolution is popular, but I estimate that in the United States there are probably more than 25,000 scientists who reject the evolutionary doctrine that all living organisms are related. There are other thousands around the world who share similar feelings. Many who do not support evolution but rather prefer a creation position are Christians, but there also are Jews, Muslims, and those of other faiths (including atheism) who are anti-evolutionists and who have a variety of views regarding how living things appeared on the earth and developed their present features on this planet.

Also, as a Christian, I accept the historicity of the Bible, this being supported by much external empirical evidence, and I have found no reasons from science to reject the Bible. Of course, there are some figures of speech, such as "the rivers clap their hands" (Ps. 98:8), or when Christ called Herod "a fox" (Luke 13:32). But it has been my custom for more than 40 years, a custom which is consistent with that of conservative Christian biblical scholars, to take an inductive-historical approach to the Bible. This means that to construct our theology we start with accepting the Bible as literally and historically true, and we compare one passage with others to obtain a consensus on their meanings.

The Bible clearly does not answer every question we can concoct, but it is certainly clear on the fundamentals as found in the Apostles' and other basic creeds. For instance, it does not clearly explain whether there is physical life outside the earth. The Bible in 1 Corinthians 13:12 tells us that we know only in part while we are in this life; so it is possible to live with some questions here on this earth, but someday in heaven we will know. In order to grow in better understanding our God's revelation in the Bible, I have been reading completely through both the Old and New Testaments at least once a year for about 40 years.

There is much objective factual evidence (for example, from archaeology) for accepting the Bible as God's revealed truth. But also it is very important to realize that the Scriptures deal realistically with the nature of humans. The Bible says that we all have sinned (Rom. 3:23) and need to experience the salvation made possible when Christ died for us (Rom. 5:8). We can experience biblical truths for ourselves, for example, when we realize that our attitudes to issues in life have noticeably changed following our acceptance of Christ as Savior (2 Cor. 5:17). I recall some time after my salvation experience reading the verse in Romans 8:16 that God's spirit testifies with our spirit that we are God's children; and it was exhilarating for me to realize that I had already experienced this glorious truth.

In our scientific studies we learn a lot about nature, which is God's creation. Also, God reveals himself in history and our consciences, but most importantly in His inspired Word, the Bible. For a full and fruitful life, no matter what our occupation is, I believe we must live in accord with this book.

Endnotes
1 Wayne Frair and Percival Davis, *A Case for Creation* (Lewisville,TX: School of Tomorrow, 1983).
2 W. Frair and G.L. Woodside, "Effects of 8-azaguanine on Early Chick Embryos Grown in Vitro," *Growth*, 1956, 20:9–18.
3 Alan Boyden, *Perspectives in Zoology* (New York: Pergamon Press, 1973).
4 Frair and Davis, *A Case for Creation.*
5 W. Frair, "Original Kinds and Turtle Phylogeny," *Creation Research Society Quarterly*, 1991, 28(1):21–24. Also see K.P.Wise, "Practical Baraminology," *Creation Ex Nihilo Technical Journal*, 1992, 6(2):122–137 and D.A.Robinson, "A Mitochondrial DNA Analysis of the Testudine Apobaramin," *Creation Research Society Quarterly*, 1997, 33(4):262–272.

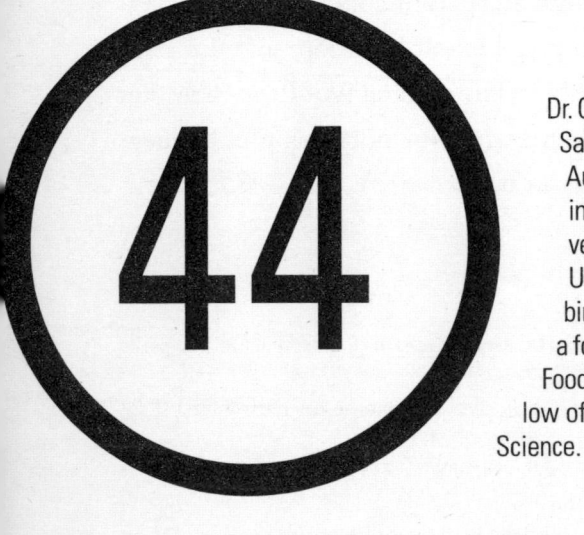

sid cole

Physical Chemistry

Dr. Cole is a research associate at the Sanitarium Health Food Company in Australia. He holds a B.S. and M.S. in chemistry from Melbourne University and a Ph.D. from Newcastle University for studies of ligand binding by metalloporphyrins. He is a former director of the Australasian Food Research Laboratories and a fellow of the Australian Institute of Food Science.

I am a practicing scientist with a very healthy respect for the power of the scientific method of investigation and validation of the data we observe and the hypotheses and theories that we develop. It is sometimes frustrating to realize that our theories of the origin of life cannot be tested by scientific methodology. We just cannot carry out the experiments necessary. We have to look outside of science for a basis on which to build our belief.

What we believe about creation depends mostly on what we believe about God. If a person does not believe in God, development of life over a long period of time is the only alternative. For one who believes in a God who is interested in us, creation over a period of six days, as set out by Moses in Genesis 1, is a viable alternative.

There is much data which does not fit well. I struggle to interpret some of the dating information into my understanding of creation. On the other hand, I am overwhelmed by the chemical complexity of living things and the fragility of the life process. The possibility of the conditions for life occurring because of a random coming together of the right molecules at the right time under the right conditions seems so remote as to be impossible even in huge time spans. The more detailed our understanding becomes, the more remote is the possibility that life as we know it could have originated by a chance meeting of molecules.

To sum it all up, I believe in a six-day creation for four basic reasons:

I have a firm belief in a personal God who revealed himself in the Bible. This revelation, while containing much which is obviously symbolic, is best understood in a literal sense unless there is strong evidence to do otherwise. The Bible presents a six-day creation cycle as the origin of life on this earth.

This belief in a personal God is consistent in my experience of life and gives reasonability to much of what I see around me. Much of this does not lend itself to validation by the scientific method because it is outside the realm with which science is able to deal.

My belief in a six-day creation cycle, while encountering some information which is difficult to fit in, does not present any practical difficulty to the application of science to the areas which I investigate or with which I am familiar.

A belief in the origin of life based on chance encounter of the necessary molecules under the conditions necessary for their survival and multiplication requires an acceptance of a huge degree of improbability. This is difficult when one considers the amazing complexity and vulnerability of the process of living organisms.

don b. deyoung

Physics

Dr. DeYoung is chairman of physical science at Grace College, Indiana. He holds a B.S. in physics from Michigan Technological University, an M.S. in physics from Michigan Technical University, and a Ph.D. in physics from Iowa State University. He has published technical papers in the *Journal of Chemical Physics* and the *Creation Research Society Quarterly*. Dr. DeYoung is the author of eight books on Bible-science topics.

During my early years of physics training, I was not a six-day creationist. The literal view simply was not known to me. My professors and textbooks described in great detail the big bang origin of the universe and also our animal ancestry. Then one day a scientist colleague challenged me to consider the possibility of a recent, supernatual creation. I have been considering this exciting idea with great interest ever since.

My scientific belief in creation is largely based on two thermodynamic laws of nature. In fact these are the two most basic laws in the entire science realm. The first law states that energy is conserved or constant at all times. Energy, in whichever of its many forms, absolutely can be neither created nor destroyed. This rule ensures a dependable and predictable universe, whether for stars or for human life. Energy conservation likely was established at the completion of the creation week. At this time the Creator ceased the input of energy into the physical universe from His infinite reserves. This fundamental energy law cannot be disobeyed like a man-made law. Only the Creator has the power to lay His laws aside, for example with miracles.

The second basic law of nature also involves energy. It describes unavoidable losses in any process whatsoever which involves the transfer of energy. The energy does not disappear, but some always becomes unavailable, often as unusable heat. Stated in another way, everything deteriorates, breaks down, and becomes less ordered with time. Ultimately, death itself is a consequence of the second law of thermodynamics. This law is directly related to the Curse which was placed upon nature at the fall of mankind in Eden.

Energy conservation implies that the universe did not start up by itself. Energy decay further implies that this universe cannot last forever. Secular science has no satisfactory explanation for such laws of nature. These principles simply transcend natural science. Their origin is supernatural, which by definition does not require a long time to develop. The addition of long ages of time is an unnecessary and confusing complication. Instead, these laws are entirely consistent with the biblical, six-day creation.

george s. hawke

Meteorology

Dr. Hawke is a senior environmental consultant with an electricity supply company in Sydney, Australia. He holds a B.S. with first class honors in physics from the University of Sydney, and a Ph.D. in air pollution meteorology from Macquarie University. Over the past 22 years, Dr. Hawke has worked as an environmental scientist and environmental consultant for a state government regulatory authority and the electrical power industry. He is also a certified environmental auditor with the Quality Society of Australasia.

Introduction

There are two main views about the origin of the universe and the origin of life: those based on *naturalism* and those based on an *intelligent Creator.* As these events occurred long ago and are not subject to direct observation or experimental tests, both of these perspectives are mainly philosophical beliefs based on certain assumptions about the physical world.

This fact is ignored or distorted in most modern treatments of the topic of origins. For example, the March 1998 issue of *National Geographic* included an article titled "The Rise of Life on Earth." The editor of the magazine wrote concerning this article on the origin of life: "Science is the study of testable, observable phenomena," and religious faith is "an unshakeable belief in the unseen." This "straw man argument" diverts the discussion away from the issues of science and logic to the separate topic of *science* versus *religious faith*. It also ignores the fact that there are no obvious "testable, observable phenomena" on the origin of life. Furthermore, the language used in the article demonstrates that naturalism also relies on faith in the unseen.

The naturalistic view of origins is that everything that exists can be explained by physical and chemical processes alone. This differs from the view that matter, energy, physical and chemical processes, and life were established by a Creator as revealed in the Holy Bible.

Seaching for Truth

An environmental auditor relies on two main factors: objective evidence and agreed standards. The outcome of each part of an audit depends on comparing the observable evidence against the relevant standard. Of course, environmental standards change in time and space across the world. Similarly, any explanation of origins should be consistent with the body of "observable evidence" and any relevant "standards." This is complicated by the fact that the evidence is viewed today, a long time after the beginning of the universe and life. Also, in a changing world, it is not immediately obvious which standards are relevant. The Bible is the only reliable and consistent source of truth; it is like a fixed frame of reference. Other authorities, such as science and logic, are not sufficient, as they may change in time and space; they are like a changing frame of reference.

The laws of physics and chemistry are examples of the relative standards of science, which change with time as knowledge develops. They were developed under present conditions and assume that the universe already exists. Two of these fundamental laws are that life always comes from earlier life and that mass/energy is conserved. Applying them to the origin of life assumes that all these conditions were true at that time. To say, then, that naturalism explains the origin of life is "circular reasoning," as the outcome is largely determined by the assumptions made. Although these laws may describe the present world, it would be a gross assumption to extrapolate them back to the unobserved initial conditions. Yet this is done frequently by those with a naturalistic viewpoint, without acknowledgement of the uncertainties involved and the limitations of the scientific method.

The assumptions of both naturalism and biblical creation and the principles of the scientific method are stated clearly in W. Gitt's *Did God Use Evolution?*[1]

The Bible is a source of "absolute" truth that has stood the test of time much longer than any other document or philosophy. Of course, as in the case of any literature, it requires interpretation as to what is historical and what is metaphorical or symbolic. Besides obvious literary techniques, the most reliable method is to use the whole message of the Bible to interpret any particular passage. Otherwise, an interpretation may not be consistent with the rest of the Bible.

The Bible contains three clear tests for determining whether a belief, teaching, or philosophy is true or false. To be true it must pass each of the three tests:

The Jesus test: This test states: "Every spirit that acknowledges that Jesus Christ has come in the flesh is from God, but every spirit that does not acknowledge Jesus is not from God. This is the spirit of the Antichrist. . . . This is how we recognize the Spirit of truth and the spirit of falsehood" (1 John. 4:2–6). The question to be answered in this test is: *What does it say about Jesus Christ?* The Bible teaches that Christ was unique: divine and human, sinless, eternal, and the Creator. It is false to deny that Christ was the divine Son of God. Beliefs that fail this test usually claim that Christ was, at best, a great teacher or a prophet. They may even encourage the view that Christ and other events in the Bible are mythical.

The gospel test: The Bible warns about those promoting a different gospel, "If anybody is preaching to you a gospel other than what you accepted, let him be eternally condemned!" (Gal. 1:9). The question to be answered in this test is: *What is its gospel?* In other words: What is the core belief or hope? The Bible says that the root cause of all our problems is that everyone has sinned and fallen short of God's requirements — resulting in death. The only means of rescue is salvation by faith in Christ. "Different gospels" are those that differ from this. They either add to it or take away from it. There is a warning against adding to or taking away from the words of the Bible (Rev. 22:18–19). Broader aspects of the gospel include the original creation and the ultimate restoration of all things (Rev. 4:11; 21:1–22:6). We need to be careful when applying this test because a "different gospel" may deceive by using words similar to the true gospel but give them different meanings.

The fruit test: Jesus Christ warned, "Watch out for false prophets. They come to you in sheep's clothing, but inwardly they are ferocious wolves. By their fruit you will recognize them" (Matt. 7:15–20). The question to be answered in this test is: *What kind of fruit is evident?* In other words, what type of attitudes and behavior does it encourage? Is the divine nature or the sinful nature most evident? The former is characterized by the fruit of the Spirit: love, joy, peace, patience, kindness, goodness, faithfulness, gentleness, and self-control. The sinful nature may involve idolatry, sexual immorality, selfish ambition, pride, hostility, quarrelling, and outbursts of anger (Gal. 5:19–23).

These tests will now be used to assess the naturalistic view of origins.

Testing Naturalism

The Jesus test: As naturalism means that nature is all there is, it is associated with atheism. For example, the American Association of Biology Teachers states:

> The diversity of life on earth is the outcome of evolution: an unsupervised, impersonal, unpredictable and natural process of temporal descent with genetic modification that is affected by natural selection, chance, historical contingencies and changing environments.

This view of origins has no need for a Creator or the divine, and so is consistent with a belief that Jesus Christ was only a human being and not divine. Naturalism clearly fails the Jesus test.

The gospel test: As naturalism assumes there is no God, it accepts no absolute standards of "right" and "wrong," and rejects the existence of "sin" in the sense of falling short of God's standard. Therefore, it teaches that there is no need of a savior. Its gospel is that nature has made itself and the Genesis account of origins is not true. A biblical consequence of this is that if there was no paradise at the beginning as described in Genesis, then there can be no hope for a future paradise. In fact, naturalism rejects all the basic biblical truths, such as creation, the beginning of evil, the need for salvation, and the ultimate destiny of human beings. So, naturalism fails the gospel test.

The fruit test: Naturalism supports and is associated with materialism, humanism (man is self-sufficient, capable of solving all his difficulties), and pantheism ("nature" replaces God). Its acceptance leads to less value on human life (practices such as abortion and euthanasia are more acceptable). Other examples are racism, less value on family life (marriage is less important; divorce is more acceptable), less value on morals (truth is now relative, not absolute), a "might is right" attitude that supports the strong, but not the weak (survival of the fittest, a competitive world, compassion involves saving "weak genes").

As these are opposite to the values of the Bible, naturalism fails the fruit test. It is clear from this that the viewpoint of naturalism fails all three biblical tests for determining what is true. Therefore, it is false and is not consistent with the overall message of the Bible.

Due to the influence of the above philosophies, claims are often made in the name of "science" that go far beyond the available evidence, and some aspects of modern science have become increasingly tenuous and speculative. In fact the everyday use of the word "science" has changed from dealing with things that are observable and testable to meaning "naturalism" and so includes conjecture and dubious hypotheses.

Although we live in a "cause-and-effect" universe, ultimate causes, such as origins, are outside the realm of reliable science. Science can only reliably deal with the present world; it cannot reliably deal with the past (such as origins) or the future (such as ultimate destinies), as it cannot directly observe these. I believe all scientists should be wary of their assumptions, as these can largely determine their findings. They should also be wary of extrapolations outside the range of observation. The further the extrapolation, the less reliable the prediction. Changes in the assumptions will change the prediction. This applies in particular to boundary conditions, such as those involving initial conditions (or origins). Therefore, scientists can only speculate, imagine, and guess about the origin of life.

Endnotes
1 Werner Gitt, *Did God Use Evolution?* (Bielefeld, Germany: CLV Christliche Literatur-Verbreitung e.V., 1993).

kurt p. wise

Geology

Dr. Wise is director of origins research at Bryan College, Dayton, Tennessee. He holds a B.A. with honors in geophysical sciences from the University of Chicago and an M.A. and Ph.D. in geology from Harvard University. He studied under Professor Stephen Jay Gould. Dr. Wise has written a wide range of articles on origins issues. He is a member of the Geological Society of America.

Eighth grade found me extremely interested in all fields of science. For over a year, while others considered being firemen and astronauts, I was dreaming of getting a Ph.D. from Harvard University and teaching at a big university. I knew this to be an unattainable dream, for I knew it was a dream, but . . . well, it was still a dream. That year, the last in the series of nine years in our small country school, was terminated by the big science fair. The words struck fear in all, for not only was it important for our marks and necessary for our escape from the elementary sentence for crimes unknown, but it was also a sort of initiation to allow admittance into the big city high school the next year. The 1,200 students of the high school dwarfed the combined populations of three towns I lived closer to than that high school. Just the thought of such hoards of people scared us silly. In any case, the science fair was anticipated years in advance and I started work on mine nearly a year ahead of the fair itself.

I decided to do my science fair project on evolution. I poured myself into its study. I memorized the geologic column. My father and I constructed a set of wooden steps representing geologic time where the run of each step represented the relative length of each period. I bought models and collected fossils. I constructed clay representations of fossils I did not have and sketched out continental/ocean configurations for each period. I completed the colossal project before the day of the fair. Since that day was set aside for last minute corrections and setup, I had nothing to do. So, while the bustle of other students whirred about us, I admitted to my friend Carl (who had joined me in the project in lieu of his own) that I had a problem. When he asked what the problem was I told him that I could not reconcile what I had learned in the project with the claims of the Bible. When Carl asked for clarification, I took out a Bible and read Genesis 1 aloud to him.

At the end, and after I had explained that the millions of years of evolution did not seem to comport well with the six days of creation, Carl agreed that it did seem like a real problem. As I struggled with this, I hit upon what I thought was an ingenious (and original!) solution to the problem. I said to Carl, "What if the days were millions of years long?" After discussing this for some time, Carl seemed to be satisfied. I was not — at least not completely.

What nagged me was that even if the days were long periods of time, the order was still out of whack. After all, science said the sun came before the earth — or at least at the same time — and the Bible said that the earth came three days before the sun. Whereas science said that the sea creatures came before plants and the land creatures came before flying creatures, the Bible indicated that plants preceded sea creatures and flying creatures preceded land creatures. On the other hand, making the days millions of years long seemed to take away *most* of the conflict. I thus determined to shelve these problems in the back recesses of my mind.

It didn't work. Over the next couple of years, the conflict of order nagged me. No matter how I tried, I could not keep the matter out of mind. Finally, one day in my sophomore year of high school, when I thought I could stand it no longer, I determined to resolve the issue. After lights were out, under my covers with flashlight in hand I took a newly purchased Bible and a pair of scissors and set to work. Beginning at Genesis 1:1, I determined to cut out every verse in the Bible which would have to be taken out to believe in evolution. Wanting this to be as fair as possible, and giving the benefit of the doubt to evolution, I determined to read all the verses on both sides of a page and cut out every *other* verse, being careful not to cut the margin of the page, but to poke the page in the midst of the verse and cut the verse out around that.

In this fashion, night after night, for weeks and months, I set about the task of systematically going through the entire Bible from cover to cover. Although the end of the matter seemed obvious pretty early on, I persevered. I continued for two reasons. First, I am obsessive compulsive. Second, I dreaded the impending end. As much as my life was wrapped up in nature at age eight and in science in eighth grade, it was even more wrapped up in science and nature at this point in my life. All that I loved to do was involved with some aspect of science. At the same time, evolution was part of that science and many times was taught as an indispensable part of science. That is exactly what I thought — that science couldn't be without evolution. For me to reject evolution would be for me to reject all of science and to reject everything I loved and dreamed of doing.

The day came when I took the scissors to the very last verse — nearly the very last verse of the Bible. It was Revelation 22:19: "If any man shall take away from the words of the book of this prophecy, God shall take away his part out of the book of life, and out of the holy city, and from the things which are written in this book." It was with trembling hands that I cut out this verse, I can assure you! With the task complete, I was now forced to make the decision I had dreaded for so long.

With the cover of the Bible taken off, I attempted to physically lift the Bible from the bed between two fingers. Yet, try as I might, and even with the benefit of intact margins throughout the pages of Scripture, I found it impossible to pick up the Bible without it being rent in two. I had to make a decision between evolution and Scripture. Either the Scripture was true and evolution was wrong or evolution was true and I must toss out the Bible. However, at that moment I thought back to seven or so years before when a Bible was pushed to a position in front of me and I had come to know Jesus Christ. I had in those years come to know Him. I had become familiar with His love and His concern for me. He had become a real friend to me. He was the reason I was even alive both physically and spiritually. I could not reject Him. Yet, I had come to know Him through His Word. I could not reject that either. It was there that night that I accepted the Word of God and rejected all that would ever counter it, including evolution. With that, in great sorrow, I tossed into the fire all my dreams and hopes in science.

Beginning only a couple of weeks later, however, God began to show me that the rejection of evolution does not necessarily involve the rejection of all of science. In fact, I have come to learn that science owes its very existence and rationale to the claims of Scripture. On the other hand, I have also learned that evolution is not the only claim of modern science which must be rejected if Scripture is assumed to be true. It is my understanding, for example, that the claim of an old earth denies the veracity of the first 11 chapters of Genesis (e.g., the order of creation, the distinctness of created kinds, the absence of pre-Fall carnivory, the lack of higher animal death before the Fall, the creation of Adam and Eve, the "very good" status of the creation at the end of the creation week, the great longevities of the patriarchs, the global nature of the Noahic flood, the dispersion of people away from the Tower of Babel). This in turn challenges the integrity of any concept built upon these chapters. Yet, it is my understanding that every doctrine of Christianity stands upon the foundation laid in the first few chapters of Genesis (e.g., God is truth, God is a God of mercy and love, Scripture is true, all natural and moral evil on the earth can be traced back to man's fall, Christ's return is global, heaven is a perfect place with no sin or death or corruption of any sort). Thus, an earth that is millions of years old seems to challenge all the doctrines I hold dear.

Although there are scientific reasons for accepting a young earth, I am a young-age creationist because that is my understanding of the Scripture. As I shared with my professors years ago when I was in college, if all the evidence in the universe turned against creationism, I would be the first to admit it, but I would still be a creationist because that is what the Word of God seems to indicate. Here I must stand.

j.h. john peet

Chemistry

48

Dr. Peet is travelling secretary for the Biblical Creation Society in the United Kingdom. He holds a B.S. with honors in chemistry and an M.S. in chemistry from the University of Nottingham, and a Ph.D. in photochemistry from Wolverhampton Polytechnic. Dr. Peet, who is a fellow of the Royal Society of Chemistry, has served in higher education for 22 years with 2 years service as international development manager for science education projects. He is the author of two textbooks and a number of research papers in chemistry and science education. He is also the author of the book *In the Beginning God Created . . .*[1] and serves as the editor of the journal *Origins*.

One subject creationists are often asked about is the nature of the *days* in Genesis 1. I am convinced both biblically and scientifically that the creation record in Genesis 1 is historical and should be treated as straightforward fact. It is often argued we "know" that the creation days were longer than the present 24-hour days. Such bold claims need justification and the purpose of this article is to explore them. I believe it can be demonstrated that this is an assumption which is invalidated by Scripture and unnecessary in science.

What Does the Bible Claim?

As a Christian who is concerned to be subject to the Bible, I naturally want to follow the Bible rather than any man-made ideas, however clever and interesting they may be. So, let's go back to the Bible. We read in Genesis 1 of a series of days in which God created the heavens and the earth. In each case, the days are enumerated (first, second, third, etc.) and are delineated by "the evening and the morning." Whenever the Hebrew word for day, *yôm*, is used in the Bible (359 times) with the ordinal (first, etc.), it clearly means a normal day. In addition, there is an alternative word in Hebrew, *olam*, used elsewhere in the Bible to indicate a long period of time.

I believe that any unbiased reader would interpret the passage as meaning real, or natural, days. We understand a day to be 24 hours. Though there may have been some variation in this period of time during history, that would not be significant in understanding this wording. The period of time called a day is the time of rotation of the earth about its axis. To my knowledge, most Hebrew scholars who have examined the subject admit that this is the clear intention of the writer; that is, to convey the idea of creation being completed in six periods of 24 hours.[2] To avoid any misunderstanding, I am not saying that God took 24 hours to complete each stage of creation. The acts of creation may well have been instantaneous, but each group of activity described is limited to this discrete period of time. There is an interesting consequence of this. The terms day, month, and year have clear astronomical meanings, but where does the concept of the week come from?[3] It is only derived from the Genesis account of creation *and* is defined by "six days of activity and one of rest." This is reiterated in the fourth commandment (Exod. 20:11).

Our doctrine of Scripture is on trial. Do we believe in its

perspicuity, that is, that the Scriptures are clear in what they say and understandable to the ordinary reader? What are our principles of interpretation? These must be established first and then applied to our reading of, in this case, the creation account. It does seem that for many we can hold traditional evangelical principles of interpretation lightly when we are embarrassed by the ideas of modern academics. We do not seem to be so concerned about the embarrassment of abandoning these ideas when they are out of fashion or by the embarrassment of querying God's word.

What Did God Mean?

Many who would agree with my response to the first question would go on to say, "Ah, yes, but God. . . ." The gist of their comments would be that the passage cannot be interpreted in a literal sense. That is, this was a convenient way of communicating the idea, be it by parable, vision, or something else. But, does this approach hold water? Many claim that Genesis 1 (and through to chapter 11) is not written as a historical narrative, but in some other form. Varied claims have been made: poetry, metaphor, myth, parable, story, analogy,[4] allegory, drama, and so on. With so many suggestions, it clearly does not conform to any one of these well-known Hebrew or Near Eastern literary forms. As Professor Gerhard F. Hasel put it, "The obvious consensus is that there is no consensus on the literary genre of Genesis 1." So, it would seem that these are all cases of special pleading in order not to face the obvious fact that it is written as, and reads as, a straight historical narrative.

For whatever reason, the non-historical approach implies that God could not explain the real facts to man in a way that is intelligible to him. Surely this cannot be a serious suggestion! If I can describe the concept of creation over a long period of time to a child (and I could!), then God, the perfect communicator, would have no problem. So, why should God use this misleading imagery?

But the question goes deeper. It hits at the very heart of our belief in God's integrity. It is more than us being mistaken about the meaning of Genesis 1. Turn over to Exodus 20:8–11, the command concerning the Sabbath. Why was the nation of Israel to keep the Sabbath? Because God arbitrarily chose one day in seven? Here is cause and effect. The Sabbath law is directly based on His creation activity. The Jews were to work six days and rest on the Sabbath because God used that pattern in His creation work. But, it goes deeper. God is stating that *this is what He did*. Is His testimony true or untrue? If it is not true, then He breaks His own commandment, "Do not lie." Where, then, would be His integrity? He has broken His own moral law. (See also Exod. 31:17.) So, we conclude that the issue is concerned with our doctrine of God with respect to His integrity. Further, it affects our view of His omnipotence. At the end of the debate, we are left with the question of His ability to do the work of creation in a miraculous way. Genesis 1 and 2 are not about natural processes of science (biology, chemistry, physics, cosmology, etc.) but are about miracle. Further, the Bible tells us (Gen. 2:2–3) that His creation work is finished and completed. We cannot see God creating now. We are living within and under His providence.

Why Do We Want Any Other Meaning?

I presume it is not because we think God cannot create the universe in six days. Then again, it is not because the biblical text requires some other meaning. The answer to this question usually involves some statement such as "Because modern science demands it." Of course, *science* does not require anything. It is a body of observable facts and a process of research. From that, *scientists* develop interpretations and theories to explain the observations. A Geiger counter will give a reading, but it is the scientist who interprets it and explains what the reading implies.

The basic argument is that scientists have shown through the geological column that the earth is very old[5] and so the great ages demonstrated through dating the rocks in the column must be equivalent to the days of Genesis 1. The geological column is the theoretical correlation of the different rock formations around the world. Though it does not occur anywhere in this complete form, geologists can relate different strata in the different regions to give what they interpret as the earth's history. It incorporates many fossil remains and the strata are given ages of tens and hundreds of millions of years. So, it is argued, this time span has to be found in Genesis.[6] This is the fundamental error in the day/age theory. The geological column has *nothing* to do with Genesis 1. An alternative interpretation of the geological column can be found elsewhere, but for the purposes of this study it is sufficient to emphasize the non-equivalence of the creation account and the geological column. Once this perceived link is broken, there is no reason to distort Scripture and the apparent meaning of the days in Genesis 1.

This non-equivalence is demonstrated by comparing the two systems. Genesis 1 is about the creation of what is good, indeed very good (Gen. 1:31). It is about beauty and order. It is about that which gives our God pleasure (Rev. 4:11). It is about harmony. The rocks and their fossils speak of death, destruction, agony, and conflict.[7] Whatever the geological column has to say about age, it has no relation to Genesis 1 and creation. If millions of years have to be found, they are not to be located within the creation week of Genesis 1 and so there is no need to make the days mean anything other than normal days.

If we want to turn to scientific evidence which supports the normal day time frame, we can find it in such biological aspects as *symbiosis*, the mutual dependence of one species on another. One cannot survive without the other for extended periods of time. This observation is made throughout the biological world. You *might* propose their parallel evolution, but that is clearly not what Scripture describes. I believe that if you wish to accept the biblical revelation on special creation, you must accept the consequence of the need for a short time span between the creative acts.

The concept of a six-day creation is obviously anti-evolutionary. Evolution requires a long time, though I would dispute whether any amount of time could be sufficient for such a scenario. Six-day creation also requires design. There is no time for chance processes. The fauna and flora had to be fit for the environment in which they were placed. Consequently, too, there had to be built into the living organisms the potential for future variation. This is consistent with the observations from genetics.

Conclusion

If we are to take the Bible account seriously, then we must recognize that the days of Genesis 1 are normal days, i.e., the period of the rotation of the earth about its axis, defined by "the evening and the morning." I believe there is no scriptural reason for believing otherwise. There is no relevant scientific need for reinterpreting God's revelation. And, for the Christian, I believe the Scripture is definitive rather than the thoughts of scientists (or theologians).

Endnotes

1 J.H. John Peet, *In the Beginning God Created* . . . (London: Grace Publication Trust, 1994).

2 This is acknowledged by Professor James Barr in a letter to David C.C. Watson (April 23, 1984): "So far as I know, there is no professor of Hebrew or Old Testament . . . who does not believe that the writer(s) of Genesis 1–11 intended to convey to their readers the ideas that . . . creation took place in six days which were the same as the days of 24 hours we now experience." Quoted by Ken Ham, Andrew Snelling, and Carl Wieland in *The Answers Book* (Green Forest, AR: Master Books, Inc., 1991), p. 90.

3 The *day* is the period of rotation of the earth on its axis; the *month* is defined by the period of the moon's orbit around the earth. The *year* is described by the time of the earth's orbit around the sun.

4 Meredith G. Kline ("Space & Time in the Genesis Cosmogony" on the World Wide Web) recently argued from analogy (replication relationship) that the days were part of the heavenly register (And God said . . .) and the results in the lower, earthly register (and it was done). The allocation of the day to the upper register is arbitrary and the author fails to deal adequately, if at all, with the "evening and morning" framework.

5 It is not my purpose to discuss here the issue of the age of the earth. It does not affect the issue of the length of the "creation day." However, I believe that the Bible does imply that the age for the earth is measured in thousands of years rather than in thousands of millions of years.

6 I believe that the column can be understood in terms of biblical history. (See, for example, the material published by the *Biblical Creation Society*.)

7 In addition, the order of the creation acts does not correlate with the evolutionary mode. For example, the sun is created on the fourth day (not the first outcome), the fish are made on the fifth day (they were not an earlier form of earthly life), the birds are also created on the fifth day, before the reptiles.

The author acknowledges helpful comments made by members of the *Biblical Creation Society* committee in the preparation of this chapter.

werner gitt

Information Science

Dr. Gitt is director and professor at the German Federal Institute of Physics and Technology, Germany. He is the head of the Department of Information Technology. He holds a diploma in engineering from the Technical University of Hanover and a doctorate in engineering *summa cum laude* together with Borchers Medal from the Technical University of Aachen. Dr. Gitt has published numerous research papers covering the fields of information science, numerical mathematics, and control engineering. He is the author of the recent creation book *In the Beginning Was Information*.[1]

A while back, there was a panel discussion in Bremen, Germany, on creation/evolution. The invited participants were a geologist, a palaeontologist, a Catholic priest, a protestant minister, and myself as an information scientist. Before long, the moderator asked, "How long did creation take?" The palaeontologist and the geologist were quickly unanimous — millions of years. When the clergy were asked, both were very definite that, nowadays, theology had no problem with millions of years. Even billions of years could be effortlessly interpreted into the creation days. Finally the moderator asked me for my opinion. I answered as follows:

For me, as an information scientist, the key question is the source of information. Regarding the length of the creation days, there is only one information source, and that is the Bible. In the Bible, God tells us that He created everything in six days.

Since no one else could nominate a source for their opinion, this part of the discussion stopped dead in its tracks.

The question of the length of the creation days has aroused much passion. Adherents to theistic evolution try to interpret the creation account to allow for long time spans. There have been many attempts to arrive at "long creation days." Here are four examples.

1. The "day-age" theory: The expression "day" is interpreted as actually meaning a long period of time. "Ages," "periods," or "epochs" of time are referred to. Psalm 90:4 is frequently used for justification: "For a thousand years in thy sight are but as yesterday [i.e., one day] when it is past."

2. The "days-of-revelation" theory: The days of Genesis are not viewed as days of creation, but as days of revelation. This assumes that the various statements in this account were progressively revealed to the writer in six consecutive days. The motive is clearly to avoid the idea that creation actually took place within these 24-hour periods.

3. The "movie" theory: Originating with Hans Rohrbach, this concept tries to explain the creation account as if it were time-lapse cinematography of a process which "in reality" took a long period of time. He writes that "It is as if the prophet is seeing a film, in which the mighty process of creation, compressed using time-lapse photography, is screened in front of him. He sees move-

ment, a happening and becoming, hears God speaking; he observes the earth becoming clothed in the green of plant life, and sees everything graphically, like a modern 3-D widescreen film in sound and color."[2]

4. The "literary-days" theory: This maintains that the creation days are merely a literary device, in order to establish a thematic structure. According to this concept, the individual "creation days" are to be regarded like the chapters of a book.

The Length of the Days of Creation

There is a widespread opinion that the creation account is only concerned with communicating "the fact that God actually created." However, this it totally implausible in light of the numerous precise statements contained in Genesis. If God had only wanted to tell us that He was behind everything, then the first verse of Genesis would be enough. However, the many particulars in the account make it quite clear that God wants to give us much more information than that. In the account of creation we have not only conveyed to us matters relevant to faith and belief, but also a range of facts which have scientific significance. These facts are so foundational to a true understanding of this world that they immediately distinguish themselves from all other beliefs, from the cosmologies of ancient people and from the imaginings of today's natural philosophy.

The creation account of the Bible stands alone in its declarations. Here we find none of the ancient mythical imaginings of the world and its origin, but here rather we find the living God communicating reality, the truth about origins. The course of correct or false biblical exposition is firmly set, according to the expositor's convictions, on the first page of the Bible. Separating "faith" from "science" (widely practiced in the Western world), has frequently driven Christians into the ghetto of a contemplative inner piety, which fails to achieve any penetrating effect upon their surroundings, while science is driven into the wasteland of godless ideologies and philosophical systems.

As a result, it has been widely presupposed that biblical statements about the origin of the universe, life, and in particular mankind (as well as nations and languages) are not scientifically trustworthy. This has had grave consequences. Alexander Evertz bemoaned the rampant worldwide spiritual decline as follows:

> Belief in the Creator is now largely only a display piece in the glass case of dogmatics. It resembles the stuffed birds one sees perching on rods in a museum.[3]

We should be thankful for the details God has seen fit to reveal to us in Genesis, this brief glimpse at the origin of this world and life. Thus, we note that God created everything in six days. That they were really 24-hour days, that is solar days or calendar days, should be settled by way of several arguments.

The Day as a Unit of Time

In order to describe physical processes quantitatively, one needs a method of measuring and a corresponding unit. The Bible repeatedly uses technical parameters of measurement in describing the length, area, or volume of something. The units are generally taken from nature or daily life, e.g., the cubit represents the distance from elbow to fingertips. The span is the spread of the fingers of one hand. An acre is that area able to be plowed with a yoke of oxen in one day. One of the most important units is that of time. It is the first unit defined in the Bible. In Genesis 1:14 this takes place at the same time as the other purposes of the heavenly bodies are stated. Their function is as light bearers and to divide day from night. Also, to define the time-units "day," "year," and "seasons" and as signs pointing to particular happenings (e.g., Matt. 24:29 regarding the end times).

With the definition of day and year, mankind is given reproducible units. These enable us to quantify statements about the age of something, the distance by which two occurrences are separated in time, or the duration of a process. Thus the unit "day" is utilized to inform us of the duration of the work of creation: "For in six days the Lord made heaven and earth, the sea and all that in them is" (Exod. 20:11).

So we should trust God's Word, because "God is not a man, that he should lie" (Num. 23:19). If God really took billions of years in order to create everything, why does He then tell us it was only a matters of days?

The Meaning of the Word "Day" in the Bible

The word "day" occurs in the Bible 2, 182 times[4] and is used overwhelmingly in the literal sense. Just as in English, German, and many other languages, the word "day" (Hebrew *yom*) can have two meanings. The first is a time period of (roughly) 24 hours, which also includes the night. This is how calendar days are measured. The second meaning would be the daylight portion of a calendar day (e.g., Gen. 1:5, 8:22; Josh. 1:8). In the creation account, the words "day and night" (Gen. 1:5, 14–18) occur nine times in the sense of referring only to the light or dark portion of a normal 24-hour day.

In exceptional cases, which are always clearly identifiable by the context, "day" means not a physically or astronomically definable span of time, but specially designated occurrences such as "the day of the Lord," "the day of Judgment," and "the day of Salvation." In John 9:4, "I must work the works of Him that sent me, while it is day; the night cometh, when no man can work," the word "day" is immediately recognizable from the context as referring to a non-physical time span in which it is possible to work. In over 95 percent of cases, the word for day indicates 24 hours.

"Day" with a Numeral

The word "day," associated with a numeral, occurs in the Old Testament over 200 times. In all of these cases, a 24-hour day is indicated. At the end of the account concerning each of the six creation days, we read (Gen. 1:5, 8, 13, 19, 23, 31), "And there was evening, and there was morning — the first [to sixth] day." So here we always have the grammatical construction "numeral in connection with day."

"Evening and Morning"

The fact that each of the intervals of creation is bounded by "evening and morning" is a further indication that the creation days were ordinary 24-hour days. The word "evening" occurs 49 times and the word "morning" 187 times, always in the literal sense. If "day" were supposed to mean a long epoch of time, it would not be bounded by such precisely-named descriptions of times of day. The Old Testament consistently observes the same sequence of these times of day, i.e., evening followed by morning (e.g., Ps. 55:17; Dan. 8:14, 8:26). A new day starts with evening (sundown) and ends with the beginning of the evening on the following day. With this definition of a day, the sequential flow of these times of day is "evening-morning." Thus, we read literally (Elberf. translation): "And it became evening, and it became morning: first day."

Creation Days and God's Omnipotence

The works of creation demonstrate the omnipotence of God and His mighty power (Rom. 1:20), the outworking of which is not tied to long periods of time. Throughout the Bible there are countless instances of acts of creation, which take place without any passage of time. The creation miracles of Jesus in the New Testament (wine at the wedding in Cana, loaves and fishes at the feeding of the 5,000) took place instantly. Psalm 33:9 also testifies to the rapid nature of God's creative acts: "For He spake, and it was done; he commanded, and it stood fast." This is exactly the same impression conveyed by the creation account itself through the repeated use of the constructions: "And God said ... and it was so." "And God said ... and God saw" (that which had just been created).

If we were to here arbitrarily insert the oft-cited millions of years, we would rob God of the honor which is His due. The total testimony of the Bible, in all manner of ways, is that of instant results in response to the commands of God. Whatever the situation, this principle is valid — a command of the Lord is sufficient, and spontaneously the created Word is fulfilled: the blind immediately see, the dumb instantly speak, the lame take up their bed and walk, lepers become clean, and the dead rise without delay.

Mankind: Created on a Particular Day

The Bible emphatically testifies that man was not created over a long period of time, but on a very particular day: "In the day, that God created Adam, He made him in the likeness of God; male and female He created them, and He blessed them and gave them the name 'mankind,' in the day, that they were created" (Gen. 5:1–2; Elberf. translation).

Summary

The question about the duration of the creation days arises frequently. I believe it can be shown from a biblical and scientific viewpoint that one can have full confidence in the biblical account of a creation in six ordinary days.

Endnotes

1　Werner Gitt, *In the Beginning Was Information* (Bielefeld, Germany: Christliche Literatur-Vertreitung, 1997).

2　Hans Rohrbach, *Ein neuer Zugang zum Schöpfungsbericht (A New Approach to the Creation Account)* (Schritte, 1982), p. 5–10.

3　Alexander Evertz, *Martin Luther als Christ, als Mensch und als Deutscher (Martin Luther as a Christian, as a Person and as a German)* (Assendorf, 1982).

4　*Dake's Annotated Reference Bible* (Grand Rapids, MI: Zondervan Pub. House, 1961).

don batten

Agricultural Science

Dr. Batten is a research scientist for Answers in Genesis in Australia. He holds a B.Sc.Agr. with first-class honors from the University of Sydney and a Ph.D. in plant physiology from the University of Sydney. Dr. Batten worked for 18 years as a research scientist with the New South Wales Department of Agriculture, studying the floral biology, environmental adaptation, and breeding of sub-tropical tropical fruit tree species such as the lychee, custard apple, and mango.

I was sent to Sunday school as a child. I found "our" church terribly dry and boring, but a godly man taught me and laid some foundational biblical truths in my life. When I was still in primary school, a street preacher visited the little country town where I was growing up. I listened and came to understand the gravity of my sin and its eternal consequences and received God's free gift of salvation.

I went to Hurlstone Agricultural High School, a government boarding school. This school had a large, active Christian fellowship, through which I was encouraged to grow in my Christian walk. However, I was in the second-year intake of the new education system known as the "Wyndham Scheme." This involved a total overhaul of the education system, such that evolutionary ideas for the first time pervaded the syllabus, especially the science syllabus.

Troubled by this, I was attracted to read a book titled *Science Returns to God*. The author had ten earned degrees — five in theology and five in science. As a brash 15-year-old teenager, I thought this man might know even more than I did! In hindsight, his message, in essence, was, "Science is an infallible way of knowing about the past, so we must make the Bible fit what the scientists are saying." In other words, God used evolution over hundreds of millions of years of death, struggle for survival, "nature red in tooth and claw," as the means of creating everything.

Deep down inside I knew that this undermined the Word of God. But how could a man with so many degrees be wrong? I tried not to think about it. If a non-Christian challenged me about "science" and the Bible, I would trot out the clichés such as "The Bible is a book of religion, not science," "God could have used evolution," "The days could have been long periods of time," "With the Lord a day is as a thousand years," and so on. However, I basically tried not to think about it.

Two Boxes

I adopted the "two boxes" approach to the issue. In one box I had my Christian faith. It had a label on it which read, "Open at church and Bible studies, but keep closed at other times." In the other box were my school and then university studies. This box had another label on it: "Open at school/university, but never at church or Bible studies." I had compartmentalized my life into the sacred and secular, and the secular was becoming more and more dominant.

At this stage I knew no Christian who believed what the Bible said about creation (recent and in six days), the Fall, and the (global) Flood. The gap theory "solved" the problem for older Christians I talked to (they did not understand the problems, because they had not been taught evolution, and I could never see that the plain meaning of Genesis even hinted at any gap, let alone Lucifer's flood and other fanciful ideas, like pre-Adamite soulless humans). Others "just believed the Bible," not being able to give reasons (contrary to 1 Pet. 3:15). Most of the younger people thought much as I did ("God used evolution").

However, there must have been some Christians at university who believed the biblical account and were willing to challenge the evolutionary teaching being dished up. In a lecture one day, the professor of zoology said, "Some of you are worried about this evolution thing. Don't worry too much about it, I don't know whether I believe it myself." In hindsight, I think he was just trying to defuse the issue for a few "fundamentalists" who actually believed what the Bible said (unlike me). However, the words stuck in my mind (like nothing else he said!). *Did he use the word "believe"?* I reflected. *But this is science, science is not a matter of belief! Science is facts!* That's what I thought, in my naivety.

Adam and Eve: Standing on a Pile of Bones Miles Deep?

That thought jolted me into being more open-minded about the evolutionary paradigm. The two boxes started to get opened at the same time. I started to be challenged about the ways in which the evolutionary scenario contradicted the theology of the Bible — for example, the teaching about the character of God and redemption could not be divorced from the historicity of the Bible's account of creation and the Fall. Evolution, if it were true, was a totally incompatible belief about the history of the world. I mean, how could a loving, holy, just, omniscient, omnipotent Creator-God use such a cruel, destructive means of creating everything? He described the creation, after He finished creating everything, including mankind, as *very good* (Gen. 1:31). Could the creation be described as *very good* if Adam and Eve were standing on a pile of bones miles deep? That's what "God used evolution" and the gap theory both entailed.

Genesis and the Gospel

And then there were the implications for the meaning and reason for Jesus' death and resurrection. If I got a chance to talk to someone about my faith, I would avoid the Old Testament (OT), and try to direct the discussion onto the historical evidence for the resurrection of Jesus. I almost wished the OT was not part of the Bible! But Jesus had confirmed the veracity of the OT Scriptures. He also cited Abraham with approval: "If they do not listen to Moses and the Prophets, they will not be convinced even if someone rises from the dead" (Luke 16:31; compare John 5:46–47).

The reason for Jesus' death and resurrection rests upon the historicity of what happened back in Genesis — that the rebellion of Adam and Eve brought the curse of death and suffering upon the world. Each of us has sinned, so we all deserve God's wrath (Rom. 5:12). Jesus took that curse of death upon himself on the cross so that we who trust God for salvation will be free from death for all eternity (Rom. 5:12–19; 1 Cor. 15:21–22). If evolution were true, death and suffering were always here; they were not the result of sin. So what meaning has Jesus' death?

When I was trying to believe in evolution, without thinking about it much, I tried to explain the curse on Adam as *spiritual* death. Why? Because, if evolution were true, death was already here when Adam sinned. But the curse was fundamentally physical death ("to dust you shall return" Gen. 3:19) — that's why Jesus died bodily on the cross, as we remember at the communion table (1 Cor. 11:23–26).

And that's why he rose bodily from the dead, conquering sin and death. So we who are in Christ look forward to a bodily resurrection (1 Cor. 15).

Futhermore, the OT contains the Law, which the New Testament calls the *schoolmaster to bring us to Christ* (Gal. 3:24). How can people respond to the *Savior*, Jesus Christ, unless they know they need to be *saved*? And how can they know they need to be saved unless they know that they have rebelled against their Creator in not keeping His standards of righteousness, that they are lost, that they deserve the condemnation of God, and will suffer His wrath at Judgment? The Law helps us to see that we are indeed lost without God's provision of salvation in Christ Jesus.

Christianity — a Package Deal

So, I started to see that the Christian life is a "package deal." Evolution is, in essence, a whole other way of thinking which is designed to exclude God (remember that the fundamental axiom of evolution is that mutations are random, purposeless). "Theistic evolution" is an oxymoron. If it is evolution, then God has nothing to do with it. If it is God, then it is not evolution!

I realized that I could not pick and choose what I found convenient to believe. If the Bible is the inspired Word of the One who was there in the beginning, who never makes mistakes and never lies, then it should be the ultimate authority. It should not be "reinterpreted" to fit the speculations of fallible men who were not there in the beginning and certainly make mistakes. This would make man the ultimate authority, not God. The Bible tells us that since people have turned their backs on God, they have become corrupted in their thinking (Rom. 1:21). So it's not very sensible to overturn the Word of God because of "scholars" who contradict it.

Jesus called us to "Love the Lord your God with all your heart and with all your soul and with all your mind" (Matt. 22:37). I had been excluding a large slab of my life from God's sovereignty — my learning at university.

Putting Things to the Test

I had been like a sponge, soaking up all I was taught without checking it out. Now I started to put things to the test. Did it really stack up? Were there myriads of transitional fossils showing the transformation of one animal (or plant, or microbe) into another — as Darwin predicted? No, there was just a handful of disputable ones. Did the fossils show a gradual transformation of one kind into another? No, the fossils showed stasis (i.e., no directional change, remaining basically the same). Many creatures which are known as fossils supposedly hundreds of millions of years old — such as starfish, jellyfish, snails — are still here today. How can that be if evolution can so easily change one kind into another?

Spontaneous Generation?

In the evolutionary scenario, life arose spontaneously from simple chemicals. But this is impossible with what is now known of the mind-boggling complexity of the simplest of living things — even the simplest conceivable self-reproducing cell. There are so many problems with this idea, which has become even more untenable since I was a student at university. Chirality is a huge problem — the "handedness" of amino acids and sugars, for example. Physical chemistry can produce amino acids under the right conditions, but they are wrong for life to form because they are mixtures of left- and right-hand forms, not the pure ones needed in living things. Only enzymes produce the pure amino acids and sugars necessary for life, but enzyme manufacture requires a living cell. Life is based on life.

Then there is the insurmountable problem of getting even one functional enzyme by random processes, even if you could get all the ingredients assembled together. Let us consider just one enzyme comprised of a typical 300 amino acids. Even if we are generous to the materialist and assume that only 150 amino acids have to be specified for the function of the enzyme, the probability of getting a functional sequence is less than 1 in 10^{195}. We cannot imagine such an improbability. There are possibly 10^{80} atoms in the universe. If we made every atom in our universe another universe just like ours, and every one of those atoms were an experiment for every millisecond of the presumed evolutionary age of our universe, this would amount to 10^{181} experiments — still a long way short of even the remotest chance of getting one functional enzyme. That's just one enzyme. This simplest living cell must have at least several hundred enzymes/proteins.

I vividly remember, in Biochemistry II, a series of lectures on the lactosidase operon (a group of genes all coding for enzymes involved in the metabolism of lactose) in *E. coli*. This had just been elucidated (the details of how the enzymes do their jobs are still being fleshed out, over 20 years later). The intricate control mechanism which switched on the enzymes only if lactose was available, and regulated the amount of enzyme manufactured, was truly marvellous. The lecturer was obviously enjoying teaching us about such freshly discovered wonders. At the end of the series, in a question/discussion time, someone asked, "How could such an integrated control system evolve by random mutations and natural selection?" To my surprise, the lecturer simply answered, "It couldn't."

Since then, many other highly integrated biochemical machines and mechanisms have been discovered, machines which will not function if any single part is missing. This means that they cannot be built up by small changes accumulating over time because the small changes would not be functional for the organism, so natural selection could not act upon them. Only the complete apparatus works, so it must all be present for it to confer any advantage on the organism and thus be accessible to natural selection. Such biochemical machines include the rotary flagellum, used for propulsion in bacteria, and the blood-clotting system in vertebrates. These design features are examples of "irreducible complexity."[1]

About this time, Dr. Duane Gish, from the Institute for Creation Research in the USA, made a timely visit to the University of Sydney, his meeting sponsored by the Evangelical Union. His presentation really consolidated things for me. Interestingly, it was the philosophy students who wanted to debate the issue with Dr. Gish, not the science students. This reinforced for me that this whole issue is fundamentally a philosophical/religious issue. Karl Popper, the well-known philosopher of science, came to the conclusion that "Darwinism is not a testable scientific theory, but a metaphysical research program — a possible framework for testable scientific theories."[2]

Darwinism, from the beginning, has been essentially a materialistic, atheistic, framework for thinking. It's a world view, a paradigm. As Adam Sedgwick, Woodwardian Professor of Geology at Cambridge University, wrote, in 1861, of Darwin's *Origin of Species*, "From first to the last it is a dish of rank materialism cleverly cooked up. . . . And why is this done? For no other reason, I am sure, except to make us independent of a Creator."[3]

Sir Julian Huxley, atheist and first director general of UNESCO, said, "Darwin's real achievement was to remove the whole idea of God as the Creator of organisms from the sphere of rational discussion."[4]

Apparently no one at the conference celebrating the centennial of Darwin's publication of *Origin of Species* objected to Huxley's statement. More recently, William Provine, professor of biological sciences at Cornell University, said, "Let me summarize my views on what modern evolutionary biology tells us loud and clear. . . . There are no gods, no purposes, no goal-directed forces of any kind. There is no life after death. When I die, I am absolutely certain that I am going to be dead. That's the end for me. There is no ultimate foundation for ethics, no ultimate meaning to life, and no free will for humans, either."[5]

Theologians who think that they can draw circles around science and Christianity and say that "religion" has nothing to do with "science," and vice versa, had better do some hard work to convince the evolutionists!

Do Accidents Create Books of Information?

A typical microbe has the equivalent coded information on its genome of a book of about 500 printed pages. A human has about 1,000 such books of information coded on the DNA in each cell. Let's assume that the first cell did make itself. How then did it transform itself into all the living things on earth? Mutations and natural selection are supposed to be the heroes of the evolutionary plot, according to modern-day Darwinian prophets such as Richard Dawkins, who has been described as "the apostle of atheism."

Mutations arise when errors occur as the DNA is copied to pass on to offspring — nucleic acid base "letters" in the code are changed, lost, or added. These errors are supposed to generate all the new genetic information, and natural selection sorts out the improvements from the degenerative effects.

Do accidental copying mistakes add the complex genetic information needed to transform microbes into mollusks, mites, mangoes, magpies, and mankind? Do random changes to information ever increase the amount of meaningful information? When a typist hits the wrong key, does the "typo" ever add further meaning to the information being typed? Do random changes to a computer program ever increase the functionality of the program?

Intuitively, we would never expect random changes to generate additional functional information, but this is supposed to be the stuff of fantastic information-creation in the evolutionary paradigm.

But is intuition enough? There have been detailed studies of this problem published in recent years, which show that the generation of new functional complexity by accidents is so improbable that it would never happen, even in the evolutionists' billions of years.[6] Mutations cause loss of information, loss of functional complexity — not an increase, as evolution requires.

Sometimes loss of complexity/specificity can be advantageous — for example, the loss of wings in beetles descended from a species of flying beetles blown onto a windy island. In this situation, flying is a health hazard, as the flying beetles could be blown into the sea, so loss of wings can be an advantage. A mutation in one of the genes controlling wing formation could easily cause loss of wings. So such a mutation can be beneficial, but it is nevertheless a *loss* of information, not the increase that evolution requires.

Antibiotic resistance can arise through loss of genetic information. For example, *Staphylococcus* resistance to penicillin happened through the loss of control over the production of an enzyme which breaks down the penicillin. This results in the over-production of the enzyme, which is helpful in the presence of the antibiotic but a hopeless waste of resources normally.

Another mechanism for gaining antibiotic resistance is the acquisition of parcels of genes from other types of bacteria through conjugation, a mating process in bacteria.

However, there is no new complex functionality arising through any of these processes. All involve either loss of information or acquisition from something else, neither of which supports the belief in upwards progression through evolution.

Making a Profit by Going Broke Slowly

There are also huge problems with the rates of mutation necessary and the cost of getting rid of the predominant "bad" mutations (requiring "death of the unfit"). Also, for a good mutation to become fixed in a population, all those individuals which do not have the new trait must die. When these considerations are combined with the low rates of reproduction of many animals, it becomes clear that there has not been enough time (even with the evolutionists' time scale) for such animals to evolve. J.B.S. Haldane, one of the formulators of the modern "neo-Darwinian" theory, wrote about these problems many years ago. Motoo Kimura tried to solve it with the neutral mutation theory, but this does not help, because it does not get rid of the cost of substitution — at the time when a supposed neutral mutation becomes beneficial via a change in the environment, those not having the mutation must still die for it to become fixed in the population.[7]

Natural selection is a problem, also. It was originally proposed as a conservative mechanism for weeding out the misfits, the mistakes, which occur in a fallen world. Darwin tried to turn it into a creative force to make new things. But just as mutations destroy complex, coded genetic information, so natural selection also eliminates genetic information.

If a population of animals has individuals with various lengths of hair and the environment changes such that it gets extremely cold, the short-haired animals will die, with only the long-haired surviving. The population has adapted to cold conditions, but has lost the genetic information for short hair.

Loss of information occurs with both natural selection and artificial selection, or breeding. Plant breeders seek to use wild types in their breeding because our highly selected varieties are lacking genetic information present in their wild counterparts. As one involved in breeding plants such as lychees, custard apples, and guavas over the years, I was very much aware of that.

What about Similarities ("Homology")?

Doesn't homology show that we are related to the animals in a "great chain of being"? If one assumes that evolution must have occurred, because we are here, then one can argue that similarities are evidence for evolution.

However, maybe the similarities are there for a different reason. Maybe they exist because there is a common Creator who made everything. Furthermore, maybe the Creator made things with a pattern which is meant to tell us something — namely, that there is only one Creator-God. Romans 1:20 tells us that God's invisible attributes are clearly evident in what He has made, so that no one has any excuse for claiming lack of knowledge. If there were no similarities, and every organism was entirely unlike any other, we might logically conclude that there were many creators, many gods.

Interestingly, the patterns of similarity actually speak against the evolutionary explanation. For example, the marsupial mole and the placental mole, and the marsupial mouse and the placental mouse, look incredibly similar. But this cannot be due to evolutionary relatedness because, in the evolutionary scheme, the marsupial body plan and the placental body plan diverged before the moles and mice supposedly evolved. So an *ad hoc* "explanation" is offered for the similarities: they just happened to look alike because they evolved in similar environments — "convergent evolution."

A horse's leg is quite different from ours, but we are both classified as placental mammals. A frog's leg is much more like ours, but it is an amphibian, a long way removed from us. How come? Well, here is another *ad hoc* story: the horse's leg evolved/adapted to a different form specialized for running, etc.; the frog and human legs have not changed much from the prototype vertebrate leg — that's why they look so similar.

These scenarios are not science; they are "just so" stories. The need for the stories arises because evolutionists misinterpret the hierarchical classification system as an evolutionary pattern. The molecular biologist Dr. Michael Denton, as a non-creationist, spelled this out in his classic book *Evolution: Theory in Crisis.*[8]

So life did not arise by natural processes, nor could the grand diversity of life have arisen through non-intelligent natural processes (evolution). Living kinds were created by God, as the Bible says. Plants were created to reproduce after their kind (Gen. 1:11–12), as were other kinds of living things. We see variation, but it's limited. Dogs/wolves/jackals/coyotes — members of the wolf kind — will never turn into something basically different by any natural process, any more than breeding tomatoes will change them into beans. God created things with the ability to adapt, to vary within limits; otherwise they would not have been able to "fill the earth." Mutations and natural selection occur in our fallen world, but they do not create new basic kinds of organisms. Lately, some evolutionists are starting to realize this:

> We can go on examining natural variation at all lev-
> els . . . as well as hypothesizing about speciation events in

bed bugs, bears, and brachiopods until the planet reaches oblivion, but we still only end up with bed bugs, brachiopods, and bears. None of these body plans will transform into rotifers, roundworms, or rhynchocoels.[9]

Science *has* "returned to God" in a sense here, because this could be learned from reading Genesis chapter 1.

God created things to show that they were created, so that we would worship Him and not the creation.

Endnotes
1 Michael J. Behe, *Darwin's Black Box: The Challenge to Biochemical Evolution* (New York: The Free Press, 1996).
2 Karl Popper, *Unended Quest* (Glasgow: Fontana-Collins, 1976), p. 151.
3 A. Sedgwick, 1861, quoted from Ronald W. Clark, *The Survival of Charles Darwin* (New York: Random House, 1984), p. 139.
4 Keynote address, Darwin Centennial, 1959.
5 William B. Provine, *Origins Research,* 16(1/2), 1994, p. 9.
6 Lee Spetner, *Not by Chance* (Brooklyn, NY: Judaica Press, 1997). For information on concepts of information, see Werner Gitt, *In the Beginning Was Information* (Bielefeld, Germany: Christliche Literatur-Vertreitung, 1997).
7 See Walter James ReMine, *The Biotic Message* (St. Paul, MN: St. Paul Science, 1993, p. 208–253.
8 Michael Denton, *Evolution: Theory in Crisis* (London: Burnett Books, 1985).
9 G.L.G. Miklos. "Emergence of Organizational Complexities During Metazoan Evolution: Perspectives from Molecular Biology, Palaeontology and Neo-Darwinism," *Mem. Assoc. Australas. Palaeontols*, 15, 1993, p. 25.